Contributions to Management Science

D1827291

More information about this series at http://www.springer.com/series/1505

Ricardo Aguado • Almudena Eizaguirre
Editors

Virtuous Cycles in Humanistic Management

From the Classroom to the Corporation

 Springer

Editors
Ricardo Aguado
Deusto Business School
University of Deusto
Bilbao, Spain

Almudena Eizaguirre
Deusto Business School
University of Deusto
Bilbao, Spain

ISSN 1431-1941   ISSN 2197-716X   (electronic)
Contributions to Management Science
ISBN 978-3-030-29428-1   ISBN 978-3-030-29426-7   (eBook)
https://doi.org/10.1007/978-3-030-29426-7

This Springer imprint is published by the registered company Springer Nature Switzerland AG.
The registered company address is: Gewerbestrasse 11, 6330 Cham, Switzerland

The Necessity of a Paradigm Shift in Business Education: Humanistic Management as a Bridge to Link Social Needs with Corporate Purposes

The original idea of this research project has been developed by a group of researchers which form the HUME (Humanism in Management and Economics) research group, headquartered at the University of Deusto, Deusto Business School (Bilbao, Spain). The main purpose of HUME is to work in interaction with others in the creation of new knowledge in the field of management (management education, theory of the firm, people's management, monetization of social value created by firms, spirituality) and economics (sustainable development), closely linked with the protection and development of human dignity and social well-being. This book is one of the ways in which HUME tries to fulfill the aforementioned objective. Authors are scholars participating in the HUME research team, plus other international professors and practitioners from Europe, America, Australia, and Asia, which are also interested in the widespread of humanistic management in organizations around the world.

The aim of the book is to show the linkages between business and management education at graduate and undergraduate levels and the way corporations are managed. If, as contributors to this book, we are able to show paths to deliver a management education with humanistic foundations, it could be easier for corporations to include those humanistic principles in their strategic planning and daily operations. A second aim of the book is to include existing cases of this kind of management style, so that other practitioners could find examples and ways to implement humanistic management (HM) in their organizations. We hope that the work we present in these pages will be a source of inspiration for universities, professors, practitioners, and corporations.

Well before the economic and financial crisis that took place in 2008, many academics started to worry about the role of corporations regarding their whole set of stakeholders and society at large (Porter & Kramer, 2002). Traditionally, shareholders required all the attention from managers, and corporations based their actions in achieving profit maximization (Jensen & Meckling, 1976). In contrast, some academics and practitioners started to ask for a responsible behavior of corporations not only regarding shareholders but also the environment and society (Freeman & Ginena, 2015).

After the crisis of 2008, the necessity of incorporating corporations in achieving the well-being of society within the environmental limitations has grown in importance. Initiatives coming from the UN (such as PRME, the Global Compact, and the sustainable development goals), the academia (developing concepts such as shared value, CSR, sustainability, business ethics, education in values), and the corporations themselves highlight the role of corporations in making a positive contribution toward social well-being, the environmental protection, and the satisfaction of all stakeholders (including, but not only, shareholders) (Hiller, 2013).

In this regard, the long-standing tradition of humanism applied to the economic activity provides a comprehensive framework to link the purpose of corporations with the development of all persons that are engaged with them (Kimakowitz, Pirson, Spitzeck, Dierksmeier, & Amann, 2011). At the same time, humanism connects the satisfaction of stakeholders (employees, customers, shareholders, suppliers, public agencies) with the making of a positive contribution to social well-being in a sustainable way (Melé & Dierksmeier, 2012).

The core concepts that are in the base of humanism (human dignity, freedom, human integral development, cooperation) make possible this linkage between individual development and social well-being, between corporate social performance and sustainability (Melé & Schlag, 2015). In order to have a greater impact on the management of corporations and other social and economic organizations, it is important to introduce the basic concepts of humanistic management inside the undergraduate and graduate programs in business schools. In this way, current and future managers could develop leadership styles rooted in a kind of understanding of economic activity that is focus in serving stakeholders and social well-being in a sustainable way (Kassoy, Houlahan, & Gilbert, 2016; Keay, 2007; Naughton, 2015).

Following this idea, the book has three distinct parts that analyze the interaction between business education and management inside organizations. At the same, the book illustrates that humanistic management is a real possibility that is currently applied in many organizations which, at the same time, are competitive institutions and engaged in fostering human dignity among their stakeholders and society at large. According to some authors (Aguado, Alcaniz, & Retolaza, 2015), there are important interactions between academic education in the field of management (undergraduate and graduate levels), current management procedures in corporations, and demands about the role of firms in society coming from governments, international agencies (Global Compact, PRME, Sustainable Development Goals), and citizens (Hibbert & Cunliffe, 2015). In fact, leading corporations which are supportive of UN programs or activities in the field of sustainability are demanding management procedures that may facilitate them the alignment between financial and social goals (Retolaza, San-Jose, & Aguado, 2016). In order to provide this kind of knowledge in the field of management, universities are building new programs and methodologies both in the undergraduate and graduate levels, so that current managers and students could internalize this knowledge and put it in practice in the process of decision-making in institutions (Aguado, Alcaniz, Retolaza, & Albareda, 2016). This kind of interaction between higher education institutions, corporations, and society could create virtuous cycles that may facilitate the widespread of a kind of management based on humanistic principles, such as human dignity and social well-being (Lepeley, Kimakowitz, & Bardy, 2016; Stachowicz-Stanusch & Amann, 2018).

Each part of the book is understood as one of the cycles that, in interaction with the other two, can set in motion the whole paradigm shift in business education toward a humanistic management approach. The first part is devoted to humanistic education (including three chapters), the second part analyzes humanistic manage-ment (with three chapters), and, finally, we include four chapters that highlight humanistic management in practice. Each part symbolizes a new virtuous circle that is added to the previous one in order to foster the dissemination of humanistic management (HM) among corporations and social institutions. Each of these parts is presented below.

Humanistic Education

This first part begins with the chapter titled "How to Develop the Humanistic Dimension in Business and Management Higher Education" written by Almudena Eizaguirre, Leire Alcaniz and María García-Feijoo from the University of Deusto in Spain. The chapter highlights how societies today face very complex social, eco-nomic, political, or environmental challenges. In order to address these challenges, it is necessary to train new generations of graduates in management with a new conception of organizations. In this challenge, higher education plays a fundamental role. The chapter begins by clarifying what is meant by the development of the humanistic dimension of university graduates. The challenges and difficulties we may encounter in developing the humanistic dimension of graduates are described below. This chapter concludes that there are two complementary lines of action. On the one hand, it is important to educate for humanism and, at the same time, this cannot be achieved without educating in a humanistic way. In this sense, the authors have proposed three approaches to educate in a humanistic way: questioning stu-dents' beliefs and values about themselves, the world around them, or the business world, incorporating a theoretical basis around humanistic management in the curriculum, and/or inviting students to experience the humanistic dimension and connect with reality. The main idea defended throughout the text is that it is not enough to incorporate some concepts into the existing curriculum but that it should be addressed transversally throughout the entire curriculum.

The second chapter has been written by Ernestina Giudici, Angela Dettori, Federica Caboni from the University of Cagliari (Italy). Under the title "Challenges of Humanistic Management Education in the Digital Era." This chapter aims to reflect on the challenges of humanistic management education in the digital age, based on an analysis of existing literature. Specifically, the authors explore the issue, shedding light on new perspectives; and highlighting to what extent, and in what way, universities in general, and business schools in particular, are modifying their curricula so that they are more social and less rational. On the other hand, the chapter aims to expose the new role that teachers have to play in giving digital students the essential humanistic training that will enable them to run businesses in the third millennium. Are they instilling in their students the values and skills necessary to be "humanistic managers"? What kind of activities, methods, and strategies are they adopting in their courses to create a more prosperous collaboration dedicated to the implementation of a more appropriate and focused management education?

We end the first part of this book with the chapter titled "Developing Ethical Commitment Competence in Higher Education: Comparing Stakeholder, Disciplinary and Regional Perspectives" signed by Pablo Beneitone (University of Deusto, Spain), Maria Yarosh (University of Deusto, Spain), Margarete Schermutzki (Aachen University, Germany) and Elke Kitzelmann (Universität Innsbruck, Austria). The chapter is based on the analysis of the surveys carried out in the framework of several Tuning projects that have taken place in recent years. The first Tuning project started in Europe in 2000 and involved 100 universities in reflecting on the different ways in which a competency-based approach could be the basis for building a common higher education area. The Tuning methodology combines a series of already established steps, the first of which is to carry out a survey of the different stakeholders of the university environment: graduates, teachers, students, and employers. Currently, 34 projects have been carried out with the collaboration of more than 600 academics from 118 countries around the world. These projects have been supported and financed mainly by the European Commission, which has invested more than 22 million euros in their implementation, and have had the support of national governments and universities. The aim of this third chapter of the work is to explore what Tuning's quantitative data can reveal about what different actors in different regions think about the competence of the ethical commitment. The authors have drawn a complete picture of what Tuning data can tell us in terms of stakeholders, disciplinary and regional perspectives on the importance and development of the ethical commitment competence, with a particular focus on respondents in business, business administration, economics, and management programs. One of the main conclusions of the results is that the data available from Tuning indicate that the ethical commitment is presented as a very important competence for a graduate of any higher education program in any country. All stakeholders—academics, students, graduates, and employers—unanimously share this view. The Tuning data available today also indicates that there are no significant differences between stakeholder groups or regions. They invite us to test these hypotheses in future research, with new data and possibly with additional data collection instruments.

Humanistic Management

The second part of the book is focused on the implementation of humanistic management to corporations.

This part begins with the chapter titled "Integral Human Development Through Servant Leadership and Psychological Androgyny" written by Alejandro Amillano,

Josune Baniandrés and Leire Gartzia from the University of Deusto in Spain. The aim of the chapter is to introduce a critical psychological perspective centered on two specific antecedents of individual orientations for the common good in organizations: psychological androgyny and service leadership. The authors point out that the promotion of a common good orientation in organizations depends on these two interconnected orientations. They maintain that androgyny is a necessary psychological variable for a common good orientation; and service leadership is a specific behavioral perspective through which a common good approach can be implemented and have real impact on organizations. The approach of this chapter bridges these literatures, which have emerged and evolved in relatively separate dynamics, and provides support for an integrative approach of human development that takes into account how these two key dimensions are inherently associated with the development of common good in organizations. Underscoring the relevance of androgyny for psychological orientations toward the common good and presenting servant leadership as a useful set of leadership behaviors through which such orientations can be materialized clears the way for new connections between literature on integral human development and these more social and psychological dimensions of organizational behavior.

The second chapter of this part entitled "Utilitarian Ethics in the Praxis of Companies: Challenges of Imposition and Duplicity" by Andrzej Sarnacki from the Jesuit University Ignatianum in Kraków (Poland). The chapter describes how organizations often adopt a short-sighted vision, even defending certain corporate practices that have an undesirable effect in the long term. The leadership style is key if we want to achieve companies that seek a balanced relationship with all stakeholders and that the relationship is mutually positive. The author reminds us that in the long term an employee has a more precious value than an immediate benefit, but on many occasions, it seems that we forget this statement in organizations. Only through the exercise of trust can a manager empower the people in the organization to adapt to the complexity of the market. The company that advocates not only the optimization of results but also transparency and work ethics will ultimately achieve better results and a healthy organizational environment, where people can develop personally and professionally.

To finish this second part of the work, we include the chapter titled "From Utility to Dignity: Humanism in Human Resource Management" written by Greg Latemore, Peter Steane, and Robin Kramar from Notre Dame University Australia (Sydney, Australia). The chapter critiques the resource-centered assumptions within HRM studies and presents an alternative approach toward the conceptualization of the employee. Reimagining the employee as person is proposed, employing the distinction made by the French philosopher, Jacques Maritain (1882–1973) between the individual as "lower self" and the person as "higher self." An understanding of person as a subject not object is envisaged, and that dignity, growth, self-determination, and the pursuit of the common good are regarded as key elements within a person-centered conceptualization. The chapter's contribution is to propose an integral humanism which respects the whole person of the employee, who is not just a valuable resource but a valued person within a community of valued persons.

Humanistic Management in Practice

This part begins with the chapter titled "Managing for Good Work: Principles and Practices of Humanistic Management Based on Catholic Social Thought" written by Benito Teehankee and Yolanda Sevilla from the De la Salle University (Manila, Philippines). Authors in this chapter combine humanistic principles based on Catholic social thought with the actual management of a medium-sized corporation in the Philippines. The interest of this chapter is twofold. On one hand, authors show that it is compatible to introduce values and principles that are common in both the catholic and humanistic traditions with the management of medium-sized company that has to struggle in the market to compete and survive. Solidarity, subsidiarity, dignity, the common good, and a true interest in the development of each person are common ground in these two traditions. At the same time, the need to keep a high level of competitiveness in an emerging economy asks for a clever management able to align humanistic principles with economic sustainability. After a brief theoretical introduction, the chapter deepens in the practical implications of the aforementioned challenges.

The second chapter of this third part comes through Robin Roslender (University of Aalborg, Lissa Monk (University of Dundee School of Business), and Nicola Murray (University of Aalborg) and is entitled "Promoting Greater Levels of Employee Health and Wellbeing in the UK: How much Worse Do the Problems Have to Get?" The chapter deals with the fundamental role played by employees in the contemporary process of creating, delivering, and capturing value. It is a reality that absences from the workplace due to health and welfare problems reduce employee contributions, and increase costs to organizations. Despite claims to the contrary, there is evidence that the UK continues to have a persistent problem of health and well-being at work, the important dimensions of which remain relatively invisible. Although many employers have introduced a range of responses to these problems, it can be recognized that these actions are accommodative in nature and are not intended to address the structural issues at stake. The chapter begins with documentation of the problem of sick leave in the UK. After this, the wider implications of this sickness absence problem are considered. Below is an indication of how some employers have attempted to respond to the continuing challenges of health and well-being at work, while evidence is also gathered from a recent empirical study that corroborates the largely ephemeral nature of these interventions. The chapter argues for the need to design more ambitious initiatives as part of a new business narrative.

The third chapter is titled "Humanistic Management in the Corporation: From Self-Interest to Dignity and Well-being" and the authorship corresponds to Ricardo Aguado and José Luis Retolaza (University of Deusto, Spain). In this chapter, authors explore how to introduce inside the different processes of decision-making in corporations the main characteristics of humanistic management. In short, authors analyze the anthropological model that underlies the shareholder model (based on short-term profit maximization) and propose a complementary one that is able to take into account the interests of all stakeholders of the corporation and, at the same time, aligns social interests with the aims of the corporation. Furthermore, authors explore the possibility of not only maintaining but also enhancing human dignity through economic activity performed at the level of the corporation.

We finish this part and the complete work, with the chapter signed by Iñigo Calvo-Sotomayor and Massimo Cermelli (University of Deusto, Spain) and titled "Civil Economy and Population Aging: A Prospective Framework for a Global Phenomenon." In this chapter, the authors base their study in the principles of the civil economy. Although civil economy has its own trajectory and experiences, both humanistic management and civil society share a number of characteristics (Bruni & Zamagni, 2004). Among them, the main one is the centrality of the person regarding economic activity. According to both traditions, corporations are at the service of the entire society, have to make a positive contribution to all stakeholders of the company, and should operate taking into account the long term, not only the short term. In this chapter, authors analyze the economic impact of the process of population aging, which will affect economic actors in many parts of the world (Japan, China, European Union, and many others). Instead of focusing in alarming situations, authors propose a new lens to analyze the process of population aging, acknowledge the positive points of the process, and present civil economy as a way to understand better this process, and manage it in order to convert it into a pleasant economic experience at both micro- and macroeconomic levels.

To conclude, we can only hope that the reading of this book will contribute to some extent to the complex world of management, in which a humanist view is so important today. We also hope that the readers of this work will be more aware of the important task that we, managers and academics, share: building humanistic management inside organizations. We have no doubt that if we all take up the challenge in a collaborative way (academics, entrepreneurs, employers, graduates, employees, policy makers, and society in general) of introducing humanistic management inside organizations, both current society and future generations will be very grateful to us.

Deusto Business School   Ricardo Aguado
University of Deusto, Bilbao, Spain   Almudena Eizaguirre

References

Aguado, R., Alcaniz, L., & Retolaza, J. L. (2015). A new role for the firm incorporating sustainability and human dignity. Conceptualization and measurement. *Human Systems Management, 34*(1), 43–56.

Aguado, R., Alcaniz, L., Retolaza, J. L., & Albareda, L. (2016). Jesuit business education model: In search of a new role for the firm based on sustainability and dignity. *Journal of Technology Management & Innovation, 11*(1), 12–18.

Bruni, L., & Zamagni, S. (2004). The economy of communion: Inspirations and achievements. *Finance & The Common Good/Bien Comun, 20*, 91–97.

Freeman, R. E., & Ginena, K. (2015). Rethinking the purpose of the corporation: Challenges from stakeholder theory and "the corporate objective revisited". *Organization Science, 15*(3), 364–369. Theory. Notizie di Politeia, 117, 9–18.

Hibbert, P., & Cunliffe, A. (2015). Responsible management: Engaging moral reflexive practice through threshold concepts. *Journal of Business Ethics, 127*(1), 177–188.

Hiller, J. S. (2013). The benefit corporation and corporate social responsibility. *Journal of Business Ethics,* 118(2), 287-301.

Jensen, M. C., & Meckling, W. H. (1976). Theory of the firm: Managerial behavior agency cost, and ownership structure. *Journal of Financial Economics,* 3, 305–360.

Kimakowitz, E. V., Pirson, M., Spitzeck, H., Dierksmeier, C., & Amann, W. (Eds.). (2011). *Humanistic management in practice.* New York: Palgrave Macmillan.

Kassoy, A., Houlahan, B., & Gilbert, J. C. (2016). *Impact governance and management: Fulfilling the promise of capitalism to achieve a shared and durable prosperity.* Center for Effective Public Management at Brookings. Washington, DC: The Brooking Institution.

Keay, A. (2007). Tackling the issue of the corporate objective: An analysis of the United Kingdom's enlightened shareholder value approach. *Sydney Law Review, 29,* 577.

Lepeley, M.-T., Kimakowitz, E. V., & Bardy, R. (2016). *Human centered management in executive education. Global imperatives, innovation, and new directions.* London: Palgrave – Macmillan. ISBN: 978-1-137-55540-3.

Melé, D., & Schlag, M. (Eds.). (2015). *Humanism in economics and business. Perspectives of the catholic social tradition.* New York: Springer.

Melé, D., & Dierksmeier, C. (Eds.). (2012). *Human development in business: Values and humanistic management in the encyclical caritas in veritate.* London: Palgrave Macmillan.

Naughton, M. (2015). Thinking institutionally about business: Seeing its nature as a community of persons and its purpose as the common good. In: Melé, D. & Schlag, M. (Eds.), *Humanism in economics and business. Perspectives of the Catholic social tradition* (pp. 179–199). New York: Springer.

Porter, M. E., & Kramer, M. R. (2002). The competitive advantage of corporate philanthropy. *Harvard Business Review, 80*(12), 56–68.

Retolaza, J. L., San-Jose, L., & Aguado, R. (2016). The role of shape holders as a link between a firm and non-stakeholders: The pursuit of an economy for the common good based on stakeholder theory. In: Crowter, D. & Seifi, S. (Eds.), *Corporate responsibility and stakeholding.* Bingley: Emerald Group. ISBN: 978-1-78635-626-0.

Stachowicz-Stanusch, A., & Amann, W. (2018). *Fostering sustainability by management education.* Charlotte, NC: IAP.

Contents

Editors and Contributors

About the Editors

Ricardo Aguado is Associate Professor at Deusto Business School—University of Deusto (Bilbao, Spain) and head of the Economics Department. He is the Senior Investigator of the research group Humanism in Management and Economics (HUME), recognized and funded by the University of Deusto. In this group, he has developed a line of research exploring the relationships between economic growth, sustainability (social, economic, and environmental), human dignity, and social well-being, both at the macroeconomic level and at the company level.

He is also the representative of Deusto Business School in the PRME program of the United Nations and coordinates the network of Jesuit universities in Spain (UNIJES) in the field of Catholic Social Thought. Prof. Aguado holds a PhD in Applied Economics from the University of the Basque Country and has taught graduate, postgraduate, and doctoral courses at various universities in the USA, Latin America, and Europe.

Almudena Eizaguirre holds a PhD in Advanced Management from the University of Deusto. She is currently Professor at Deusto Business School, where she teaches both different BA courses at the Faculty of Economics and Business Administration (in the subjects business, principles of marketing, operative marketing, and services marketing) and different postgraduate university syllabuses.

She is the Strategy Vice Dean at the Faculty and also the Director of the Innovation Unit at the University of Deusto.

She forms part of the HUME research team (Humanism in Management and Economics), has co-managed various PhD theses, and has taken part in different research projects that have received external funding. Her areas of research interest are higher education, competences-based learning in higher education, developing sustainable competencies in higher education, and humanistic management.

Contributors

Ricardo Aguado University of Deusto, Deusto Business School, Bilbao, Spain

Leire Alcaniz Deusto Business School, University of Deusto, Bilbao, Spain

Alejandro Amillano School of Psychology and Education, University of Deusto, Bilbao, Spain

Josune Baniandrés Deusto Business School, University of Deusto, Bilbao, Spain

Pablo Beneitone University of Deusto, Deusto International Tuning Academy, Bilbao, Spain

Federica Caboni University of Cagliari, Cagliari, Italy

Iñigo Calvo-Sotomayor Deusto Business School, University of Deusto, Bilbao, Spain

Massimo Cermelli Deusto Business School, University of Deusto, Bilbao, Spain

Angela Dettori University of Cagliari, Cagliari, Italy

Almudena Eizaguirre Deusto Business School, University of Deusto, Bilbao, Spain

María García-Feijoo Deusto Business School, University of Deusto, Bilbao, Spain

Leire Gartzia Deusto Business School, University of Deusto, Bilbao, Spain

Ernestina Giudici University of Cagliari, Cagliari, Italy

Elke Kitzelmann University of Innsbruck, Innsbruck, Austria

Robin Kramar The University of Notre Dame Australia, Sydney, Australia

Greg Latemore The University of Notre Dame Australia, Sydney, Australia

Lissa Monk School of Business, University of Dundee, Dundee, Scotland, United Kingdom

Nicola Murray School of Business, University of Dundee, Dundee, Scotland, United Kingdom

José Luis Retolaza University of Deusto, Deusto Business School, Bilbao, Spain

Robin Roslender Department of Business and Management, Aalborg University, Aalborg, Denmark

Andrzej Sarnacki Jesuit University Ignatianum in Krakow, Krakow, Poland

Margarete Schermutzki Higher Education and Tuning Expert, Berlin, Germany

Yolanda Sevilla The Leather Collection, Inc., Las Piñas, Philippines

Peter Steane The University of Notre Dame Australia, Sydney, Australia

Benito Teehankee Ramon V. del Rosario College of Business, Business for Human Development Network – Center for Business Research and Development, De La Salle University, Manila, Philippines

Maria Yarosh University of Deusto, Deusto International Tuning Academy, Bilbao, Spain

Part I
Humanistic Education

How to Develop the Humanistic Dimension in Business and Management Higher Education?

Almudena Eizaguirre, Leire Alcaniz, and María García-Feijoo

1 Introduction

Societies face complex social, economic, political, or environmental challenges. Some examples are the scarcity of natural resources, growth of waste generation, increasing social and economic inequalities, violent conflicts in different regions of the planet, etc. Although their effects are heterogeneous, in many cases those problems have an economic background. Society's main economic model is based on selfishness, prioritizing the maximization of the economic value over dignity and the intrinsic value of the human being (Ghoshal, 2005; Giacalone & Wargo, 2009; Helbing, 2013).

This concern exceeds citizens, governments, and countries and is part of the international agenda. The United Nations Security Council, based on the United Nations World Conference on Sustainable Development, started the process to define the so-called 2030 Agenda (as a continuation of the Sustainable Development Goals, SDG, which guided the work of the United Nations from 2000 until 2015). This agenda is focused on people and their human rights, in particular, on the eradication of poverty and sustainable development in its social, economic, and environmental dimensions. Table 1 shows the SDG that were adopted by the governments at the United Nations in 2015. They will guide global development until year 2030.

These objectives and goals, established from economic, social, and environmental dimensions, address new challenges related to inequality, gender equality, peace, security, or productive capacity. In the same way, they are formulated to achieve effective, responsible, and inclusive institutions, fostering dignity and integral human development within organizations and institutions.

A. Eizaguirre (✉) · L. Alcaniz · M. García-Feijoo
Deusto Business School, University of Deusto, Bilbao, Spain
e-mail: almudena.eizaguirre@deusto.es; leire.alcaniz@deusto.es; maria.garciafeijoo@deusto.es

© Springer Nature Switzerland AG 2020   3
R. Aguado, A. Eizaguirre (eds.), *Virtuous Cycles in Humanistic Management*,
Contributions to Management Science,
https://doi.org/10.1007/978-3-030-29426-7_1

Table 1 Agenda 2030. The Sustainable Development Goals to transform our world (www.un.org, retrieved on July 2018)

The 17 sustainable development goals (SDGs) to transform our world
GOAL 1: No Poverty
GOAL 2: Zero Hunger
GOAL 3: Good Health and Well-being
GOAL 4: Quality Education
GOAL 5: Gender Equality
GOAL 6: Clean Water and Sanitation
GOAL 7: Affordable and Clean Energy
GOAL 8: Decent Work and Economic Growth
GOAL 9: Industry, Innovation and Infrastructure
GOAL 10: Reduced Inequality
GOAL 11: Sustainable Cities and Communities
GOAL 12: Responsible Consumption and Production
GOAL 13: Climate Action
GOAL 14: Life Below Water
GOAL 15: Life on Land
GOAL 16: Peace and Justice Strong Institutions
GOAL 17: Partnerships to achieve the Goal

The objective of this chapter, within the part of the book focused on education, is to propose some strategies and techniques to develop a humanistic approach within business schools. Considering that business schools train future main actors of the political, economic, and institutional decisions, it is important to train them considering the challenges they will face and from a holistic perspective. It is not enough if they are good technicians or if they master key contents of strategy, finance, economics, or marketing, but they should also develop a series of values that guide their way of approaching the reality and their way of acting. The SDGs may be an adequate guide for the efforts to be made in the education of graduates of business schools.

In this chapter, after this brief introduction, we start by clarifying what the development of the humanistic dimension of university graduates means, and more specifically in management education (Sect. 2). Next, we describe the challenges and difficulties that we can find to develop this humanistic dimension (Sect. 3). Section 4 introduces a series of strategies, methods, and activities for the development of the humanistic dimension: questioning of paradigms by teachers and students, development of new faculty capacities, addition of new contents, experimentation of volunteering programs, mentoring, use of real study cases in the classroom, etc. Finally we collect the main conclusions of this work (Sect. 5).

2 Development of the Humanistic Dimension in Business and Management Higher Education

As already stated in the introduction, one of the origins of the problems faced by society is the conception of human beings. Why do we form communities, create companies, have political systems, etc. if this does not lead us to a greater development of the human being globally?

In the following lines, we develop our proposal, in coherence with the humanistic management approach, considering the education of graduates in business and management as the base to incorporate this approach in organizations.

2.1 Humanistic Management

Incorporating the humanistic management principles into the company means making a paradigm shift and moving from conceiving the human being as *homo economicus* to considering him/her as a social being, with a moral orientation, free and with dignity (*homo socialis*). According to shareholder theory, the economistic person (*homo economicus*) is considered totally selfish and is only interested in maximizing his/her immediate utility (Dierksmeier, 2011).

On the other hand, under the humanistic management conception, individuals use their freedom to carry out social interactions in the long term, considering the rest of the parties as aims in themselves and not as means (Pirson & Lawrence, 2010). This model assumes that people are intrinsically motivated to improve and acquire virtues that make them grow as human beings (Melé, 2003). Therefore, humanistic management understands that human behavior can be improved, through education and learning, and attributes inalienable rights to all people, regardless of their ethnicity, nationality, social status, or gender. Human beings guide their actions by universally applicable ethical principles, look for long-term relationships, search for self-actualization, and want to serve humanity through their actions. In short, the first ones (*homo economicus*) want to acquire and defend themselves; the second ones (*homo socialis*) want also to generate links and understand (Helbing, 2013).

Based on this new conception of the individual, management in the company should change, moving from the neoclassical paradigm (based on shareholders' profit maximization) to the humanistic management approach. The bases of the latter can be summarized in four points. First, there is a change in the way of understanding work, with less rigid structures and better suited to people and their organization. Second, the way of understanding the company varies from a nexus of contracts to being a community of people who cooperate with each other for a common purpose. Third, the role of the individual in society and the company changes, from being a resource to having a participatory role and greater commitment. And, fourth, the company's aim will change, from maximizing the value for the shareholder to having a value-based purpose in the society (Melé, 2009, 2016).

Fig. 1 Two pillars in education for humanism in business and management studies (Developed by authors)

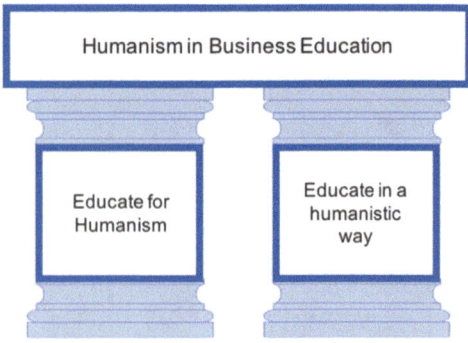

2.2 Humanistic Management in Higher Education

When talking about humanistic management, promoting a change of perception of the individual and of the business is important, in such a way that managers serve the objectives of society and not vice versa (Dierksmeier, 2011). In that sense, it is relevant to highlight the role played by education. Firstly, we must consider how to educate for humanism, and, secondly, we must bear in mind that this cannot be achieved without educating in a humanistic way (Fig. 1).

2.2.1 Educate for Humanism: Awareness and Theory

Educating in order to develop a humanistic management means trying to break with the neoclassical paradigm, changing the underlying theory taught in business schools and questioning the assumptions of the prevailing model. A new academic framework that includes moral issues in the relationship between business and society and where the student is asked about the narrow vision about the world and the economy that exists today and about how to achieve a more decent society (McDonald, 2000). This supposes, therefore, to debate on the very same purpose of the company.

But it is not only about changing the way of seeing the company but also the way of seeing the individual, understanding that the human being works to increase his potential, to flourish (McDonald, 2011). This change will even expand the way in which students-individuals will see themselves and their capacity to act when managing. Their possibility of renouncing to self-interest in order to achieve a greater good, to be honest, authentic and committed (Holland, 2011) and, thus, ensuring that their careers have a real meaning and to preserve the good name of the profession (Giacalone & Wargo, 2009).

The change of the economic paradigm and the paradigm about the individual will have an effect on the technical knowledge taught. However, in order to educate humanistic managers, besides the technique, it is necessary to develop skills and abilities to be a more humane, free, moral, and cooperative manager. While the maximization of value for the shareholder is easier to measure, and causes to be educated according to the technique, the assessment of humanistic management is not so simple. It requires a moral understanding of the discipline (Dierksmeier, 2011) and education in values (Elkanova & Chedzhemova, 2013; Giacalone & Wargo, 2009), but also other soft skills such as critical self-reflection, judgment, and proactivity (Pirson, 2011). The theory of the free market is based on the fact that leaving the markets to operate freely will maximize the results and the welfare. If this is so, human being does not develop his full potential and does not believe in his power to change and self-actualize. However, "responsibility for creating a decent and fair society is held firmly in our own hands but not in the dynamics of market society... In such a faithful order, the market takes away our intention to live our lives with a proactively positive purpose" (McDonald, 2011, p. 133).

2.2.2 Educate in a Humanistic Way: Coherence and Role Models

So far we have commented that theories, knowledge, and skills should be developed to promote humanistic management in students, but as important as those is to educate in a humanistic way. The heritage and heroes of the university as well as the way of acting of the educational institution in general, and of the professors in particular, act as moral amplifiers (Hanson et al., 2017). They are an example for the students, empowering them to act at least morally or making them feel pressured not to act unethically (Zhu, Avolio, Riggio, & Sosik, 2011).

It is necessary to have coherence between the values promoted by the institution and those perceived by the students in order to achieve a change in their way of thinking and their actions. Messy teachers, who do not keep their word or do not care about their students, or an institution with corrupt people on its board, who participated in some (managerial, financial, or in his private life) scandal, will not inculcate humanistic values although they speak of them. It is necessary to have consistency between acts and words to have legitimacy and promote ethical behavior among peers or followers (Paterson & Huang, 2018). Since people learn more from the example they see, than from the words they hear, the students learn more from teachers' performances than from their speeches and words (Hanson et al., 2017; Lunenberg, Korthagen, & Swennen, 2007).

3 Difficulties and Challenges to Develop the Humanistic Dimension in Business and Management Higher Education

Developing the humanistic dimension in business schools, in the two areas previously mentioned, is currently a considerable challenge. Many of them are institutions of great tradition and size, which generate an inevitable inertia that is difficult to

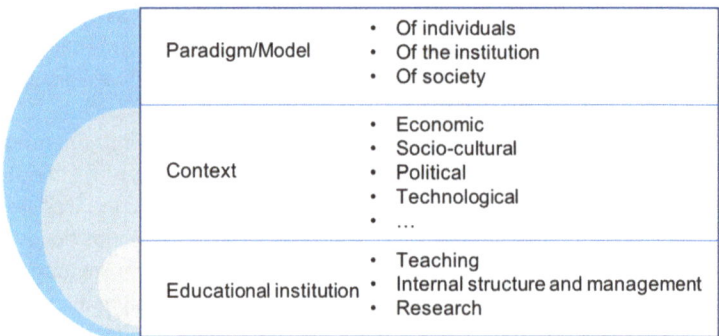

Paradigm/Model	• Of individuals • Of the institution • Of society
Context	• Economic • Socio-cultural • Political • Technological • …
Educational institution	• Teaching • Internal structure and management • Research

Fig. 2 Difficulties faced by educational institutions when developing their students' humanistic dimension (Developed by authors)

counteract (Ghoshal, 2005; McDonald, 2011; Pfeffer & Fong, 2002). As Hanson et al. (2017) point out, there is great concern that educational organizations and their members are moving away from their responsibility for the moral and ethical development of students.

In this section, we will present the main difficulties and challenges faced by educational institutions in incorporating the humanistic dimension in the broadest sense of the term. As shown in Fig. 2, we will move from the most external and global level to the internal level of the institution itself.

The first challenge, derived directly from the very definition of humanistic management that we defend here, is the difficulty of **being aware of the paradigm in which organizations are functioning**. The paradigm from which each person, institution, or society operates is unconscious and subtle. It is the result of one's history, formal and informal education received in different spheres, previous experiences, past actions, etc. As a previous step toward a change of the economic and social paradigm, these frameworks in which students, teachers, and managers move must be made conscious. As in other areas, in the context of business higher education, many people move in an utilitarian paradigm, seeking the maximum profit (why do students study management?), which may conflict with values such as respect, harmony, wisdom, sustainability, or justice, linked to humanistic concepts (Giacalone & Wargo, 2009; McDonald, 2000; Rowe, 2007). Therefore, a first challenge in higher education institutions is to highlight the values and assumptions from which teachers teach, students learn, and managers decide, as well as the assumptions underlying our teaching in economics, business, and management.

Giacalone and Wargo (2009, p. 150) point out four basic assumptions of the dominant economic theory (shareholder theory): "(1) the behavioral assumption of radical self-interest of individuals; (2) that morals, other than obeying the law and corporate policy, have no place in corporate management; (3) that profit maximization is the only proper goal of managers and (4) that humans are imperfect and thus we must create organizations that prevent bad people from doing harm as much as enabling good people to do good." Precisely for this reason, and quoting Ghoshal

(2005, p. 87), "if we are to have an influence in building a better world for the future, adapting the pessimistic, deterministic theories will not get us there. If we really wish to reinstitute ethical or moral concerns in the practice of management, we have to first reinstate them in our mainstream theory."

A second set of difficulties refers to **the economic, socio-cultural, political, etc. context in which universities are immersed**. Universities and business schools are in an environment where their resources are scarce (Nejati, Shahbudin, & Amran, 2011), which means that they sometimes have to rely on funding from business groups whose interests are not neutral (Godfrey, Illes, & Berry, 2005; Jain, 2009). This is an environment in which hard skills are overvalued, to the detriment of certain soft skills, which are important for the business world, such as communication, interpersonal relations, cross-cultural sensitivity, global perspective, and ethical standards (Jain, 2009). Universities have put technical skills first, relegating the professional skills and the spiritual formation of their students (Cortés, 2014). Finally, it is an environment in which the demands of external bodies (international accreditation bodies, national and international quality agencies, rankings, etc.) dictate what business schools must be and achieve, leaving little room for innovation and for the specific and differentiating characteristics of each institution (Godfrey et al., 2005; Khurana, cited in Holland, 2011).

In a third group of challenges, we find those difficulties related to the **internal environment of the educational institution** itself (Nejati et al., 2011), which are linked to the fundamental activities and duties of universities.

Regarding **research**, several authors refer to the lack of connection between research carried out in business and management schools and management practice in the real business world (Jain, 2009; Pfeffer & Fong, 2002), as well as the difficulty of moving away from mainstream research (due to the high demands placed on the faculty to develop their curriculum based on research).

When focusing on **teaching**, there are difficulties related to both the contents and the teaching-learning methodologies. Humanistic contents are not usually incorporated into the business and management curriculum, and when they are, they appear decontextualized and as additional material, and not as essential content of the degrees. A Net Impact (2011) study showed that 77% of undergraduate students in 2009 felt that universities should place more emphasis on training socially and environmentally responsible individuals (37% of them thought that companies worked to improve society; and 90% thought they could do good through business). On the other hand, knowledge is fragmented (Cortese, 2003), and this does not allow approaching the problems and concerns of business and society globally.

As for methodologies, they do not favor students' contact with the real world, and therefore do not expose them to the heterogeneity and diversity of cultures, conditions, and realities that would facilitate the questioning of their principles and a deeper reflection on themselves and the society in which they live (McDonald, 2011; Rowe, 2007). It is an education, as described by Cortese (2003), that does not interact with the community in which it is located. In addition, many of the methodologies used do not favor a proactive and autonomous role for the student, thus increasing the aforementioned problems. In the words of Mintzberg (quoted in

Holland, 2011, p. 102), "we can corrupt not only by the content we leave people with (...) we can corrupt as well by the procedure and the framework and the structures of our programmes."

In relation to the **structure and internal organization** of the schools, attention must be rise on the selection policies, promotion schemes, retribution systems, governance, etc. that prioritize certain activities and attitudes of the teaching staff that hinder both training for humanism and training in a humanistic way (Hanson et al., 2017). We are referring to a greater focus on research than on teaching and attention to students (Jain, 2009), an increase in individualism as opposed to collegiality, lack of coherence in certain behaviors, lack of independence of schools and their members, lack of teacher training in ethics, values, responsibility and morals, etc. As Ghoshal (2005, p. 87) notes, "all the way from the structure of PhD training to the requirements for publishing in top journals, from the criteria of faculty recruitment to the processes for granting tenure, the institutional structures within and around business schools are rigidly built around the dominant model."

In this context of difficulties and challenges, we frame the following section on what we can do in business and management higher education institutions to further develop the humanistic dimension of our graduates.

4   What Can Be Done in Higher Education in Business and Management to Develop the Humanistic Dimension?

Following the scheme showed in previous sections, we will firstly address some strategies to respond to the challenge of educating for humanistic management, and, secondly, we will expose some ideas to educate in a humanistic way.

The first section (4.1) contributes to working on the challenges related to the change of paradigm, and it is more focused on teaching. In contrast, the second section (4.2) addresses the challenges linked to the context and the institution itself, and it is therefore centered in the two other areas of the academic activity: research and management.

4.1   Proposals to Educate Students for Humanistic Management

The challenge of educating in humanistic management principles invites universities to implement three different types of approaches, according to their nature (see Fig. 3). On the one hand, there is that set of actions to move students from the economist paradigm to the humanistic paradigm, encouraging them to review their own map of beliefs, the world around them and the business world (Nejati et al., 2011). Secondly, it is necessary that both students and faculty incorporate the

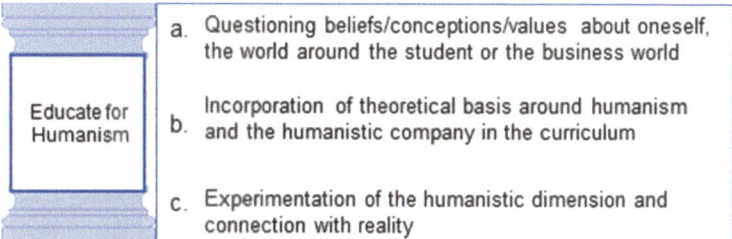

Fig. 3 Three approaches for the development of the humanistic dimension of the graduates (Developed by authors)

theoretical foundations of humanistic management, which allows right discernment and decision-making centered in the human being (the person). Thirdly, it is essential to generate opportunities for students to experiment the humanistic dimension and to be connected with the real world. In this regard, nonformal education is crucial (Caza & Brower, 2015). Some issues related to these three approaches are described below.

4.1.1 Questioning Beliefs/Conceptions/Values About Oneself, the World Around the Student or the Business World

As it has already been mentioned, there are two competing paradigms that are the "economism" (shareholder theory) and the "humanism" approaches (Pirson & Lawrence, 2010). These two paradigms involve a series of conceptions about companies and organizations in general: about strategy (from maximizing profit to the conviction that there are multiple objectives, and that harmony and balance among them must be sought); about governance ("agency theory" versus "stewardship theory"); about structure (very hierarchical structures, based on authority, versus flatter structures); about leadership (transactional versus transformational); and about culture (individual or community-oriented). Dierksmeier (2011) urges us to look at the human being not as the unreal *homo economicus* but as the real, socially and culturally integrated and morally oriented human being. He points out that businesses should serve the goals of humanity and not vice versa (Dierksmeier, 2011). For McDonald (2011), humanistic education is based on the belief that one can, and should, work toward the realization of the potential that confers dignity: good judgment, wisdom, self-control, empathy, love, and justice, to name but a few. This freedom brings with it more mature responsibilities, and it is a crucial development for business schools' graduates.

If dominant approach in management theory indicates that the individual is selfish and opportunistic, managers will adapt their behaviors and treat them that way (Giacalone & Wargo, 2009). That is why it is important to challenge these beliefs, since theories in the social sciences are often self-fulfilling (Ghoshal, 2005). It is not possible to force the student to act ethically, but it is possible to teach him/her to recognize the implications (not only economic) of his/her decisions (Giacalone & Thompson, 2006).

How to reverse these beliefs? First of all, generating self-awareness (Wolf, 2018). McDonald (2000) proposes some steps that change these consolidated beliefs: (1) reaffirming faith in human potential, (2) helping to discover a human intent for economy, and (3) learning to take into consideration moral feelings. In each step, he suggests essays, film clips, and debates to raise awareness of the consequences of some paradigms against others. Nejati et al. (2011), in a similar sense, suggest the regular organization of workshops and talks, the distribution of information leaflets, pamphlets, etc. or even rewarding those on campus who contribute to the implementation of the humanistic dimension. Moreover, Wolf (2018) proposes two specific methodologies to use in the classroom to develop ethical maturity and the questioning of paradigms: group discussions and realistic case scenarios (Wolf, 2018).

But it is not just about using different techniques and methodologies. Humanistic pedagogy should move us to a different domain, where the authority to discern the truth moves from the control of the teacher to the collective hands of the students (McDonald, 2011). This is a challenge because it means believing in students and their potential to show a mature behavior in class. From this author's point of view, traditional pedagogy is based on filling students' heads with information. But PowerPoint presentations and numbers are of little relevance in their lives and experience. Teachers tend to focus on providing answers to questions of little interest to students. Instead, they should focus, first, on building good questions and then on encouraging students to find meaningful answers for themselves in open discussions and deep reflections, following guiding principles that include critical reflection, reflective thinking, connective thinking, or collaborative leadership (Euler & Seufert, 2011).

4.1.2 Incorporation of Theoretical Basis Around Humanistic Management in the Curriculum

In order to understand correctly the anthropology of the humanistic management approach, several authors point out the importance of incorporating both specific content related to ethics and values and humanities disciplines (literature, critical studies, and philosophy) in the curriculum (Euler & Seufert, 2011; Godfrey et al., 2005; Hanson et al., 2017).

Melé (2016) enunciates seven basic propositions of humanistic management that the graduate must know and master: (1) integrity, (2) integral knowledge, (3) human dignity, (4) development, (5) the common good, (6) transcendence, and (7) co-responsibility-sustainability. In addition, the student will have to distinguish how humanistic management differs in a particular conception of the individual and his or her work, a notion of society and the role that the person plays within it and in interaction with others and with nature, a concrete vision of business (as a community that cooperates and not as a sum of people), and the purpose of business within society.

Cortese (2003) proposes incorporating content related to the environmental and sustainability aspects and curriculum development connected with the improvement of the local community. Elkanova and Chedzhemova (2013), as well, propose to introduce into the educational process a wide range of compulsory and optional courses of a socio-cultural and interdisciplinary integrating nature. The introduction of these courses would generate advantages such as the promotion of a comprehensive system of knowledge of the human being, society, and nature to build a better understanding of the world in the ontological sense; the creation of conditions for self-development, self-perfection, and self-realization of students; the inclusion of a humanitarian component to respond to the contemporary demands of the development of society, science, culture, and the individual; the promotion of interest and respect for the cultures of the peoples of our planet; the development of a sense of personal responsibility for the direct or indirect consequences of professional and civic activities; the development of a capacity to understand the profound interdependence and inter-conditionality of the lives of all people in the world, the values and meaning of human life, the unique nature of personality, one's rights and freedoms; among other elements (Elkanova & Chedzhemova, 2013).

However, it is not only a question of adding content but also of including it transversally in every subject, since "as long as all the other courses continue as they are, a single, stand-alone course on corporate social responsibility will not change the situation in any way" (Ghoshal, 2005, p. 88).

Teaching should be focused not only to make students aware of unethical situations that arise but also to analyze them and take action. The first thing to do is to teach the student to realize that he/she is facing an unethical situation. The second is to train him so that he can analyze a specific case and decide how to act. To this end, models of reasoning and analysis (deontology, utilitarianism, etc.) are important. Finally, situations in which the student can practice creating and expressing action plans should be encouraged. One scheme to be followed could be asking them: what would you do? what information and allies do you need? what would you say? to whom? in what order? what would they say to you and what would you respond to them? (Gentile, 2011).

It should be noted here that formal and informal learning must be combined to develop the skills identified (Barth, Godemann, Rieckmann, & Stoltenberg, 2007). This informal learning not only happens in the students' free time but also within the institution, but in a way that is not explicit or directed by the curriculum, such as when talks, workshops, excursions, or relationships with teachers and other students are held.

4.1.3   Experimentation of the Humanistic Dimension and Connection with Reality

Management is not a science but an art, and it is crucial to practice to truly consider that the person has incorporated the necessary knowledge, skills, and instruments (Melé, 2016). Managers need to motivate people to acquire virtues and try to discover and promote beliefs and values within the organizational culture that fosters human virtue to its fullest extent (Melé, 2003, p. 85).

Theory and practice must therefore be united, and in no case can they be watertight compartments (Ghoshal, 2005; Pfeffer & Fong, 2002). The literature's proposals are related to multidisciplinarity and the clinical or action component (Pfeffer & Fong, 2002), the generation of opportunities to put moral thinking into action (Hanson et al., 2017), the incorporation of transformative experiences (Lotz-Sisitka, Wals, Kronlid, & McGarry, 2015), or the transfer of responsibility for the learning process to the student (Pfeffer & Fong, 2002).

Many authors defend the **service-learning methodology** in higher education as a way of bringing closer students to real situations, which also allows them to develop their specific degree competences (an example of this methodology is to invite students to make strategic plans, to carry out accounting or to design a digital marketing plan for a specific non-profit institution) (Bringle & Hatcher, 1999; Eyler & Giles, 1999; Godfrey & Grasso, 2000; Kenworthy-U'Ren & Peterson, 2005). However, it is necessary to design correctly this practice, since sometimes service-learning does not provide the expected results, the specific project does not provide worthwhile work to students or exceeds the competences of the students, or even because students are not committed with the project or do not have the basic competences to tackle the project (Godfrey, 1999). In fact, four elements should be provided, in order to achieve a proper functioning of this methodology: reality, reflection, reciprocity, and responsibility. In addition, professors who wish to apply this methodology should take into account four factors: centrality, commitment, community engagement, and continuous improvement (Godfrey et al., 2005).

Other strategies to bring students closer to business reality include the creation of **laboratories** that promote social entrepreneurship (Bloom & Pirson, 2011), **student mentoring** (Hanson et al., 2017), **volunteer programs** to learn about different socioeconomic realities, the introduction of real practical **cases** in the classroom, the invitation to the classroom of **professionals, conferences and workshops, etc.** always with the ultimate aim of promoting students reflection on the consequences of the decisions and activities of institutions and organizations.

On the other hand, it is important to bring the student to reality, but also **to incorporate what students already know about reality into the classroom**, so that content can be shared, refined, and improved (McDonald, 2015). Without this, students will perceive that their ideas are not important and will therefore believe that these ideas have no consequences. Moreover, they will not get involved, they will learn more slowly, and they will be passive, substituting their ideas for those of others.

Finally, we would like to conclude that the **extracurricular sphere** is a privileged space to experience business reality (Caza & Brower, 2015; Tough, 1982), since it connects students with new perspectives and makes them develop new skills.

4.2 Proposals to Educate Students in a Humanistic Way

As we commented in previous sections, it is necessary to seek coherence between what is taught to students and university management processes. The most relevant

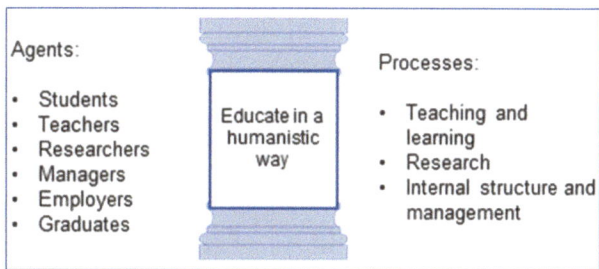

Fig. 4 Processes and agents to consider when developing the humanistic dimension in business higher education (Developed by authors)

agents in university life (students, faculty, management team, and administrative and service staff) should incorporate humanistic concepts in the three dimensions of the university: teaching, research, and management. The previous section placed special emphasis on teaching, and now the proposal is completed with some relevant ideas both in research and in the management of the institution itself, so that there is coherence between the dimension to be developed in the students and how they work in the institution.

We must be aware that there are four key groups to manage if we want graduates to develop the humanistic dimension: the teaching staff, the students themselves, and the people who work in the educational institution, both the management team and the administrative and service staff.

Teachers are a powerful part of the development process, and an important catalyst for reform efforts toward greater humanistic student development (McDonald, 2000). It is very important to contribute to an environment in which educators take the time to develop close relationships of caring and professional support for students (Hanson et al., 2017).

Developing the humanistic dimension of an educational institution also has implications for the internal structure and management of the educational institution (Fig. 4). Some of the considerations that managers should take into account are listed below:

- Regarding the internal structure and organization:

  - To change the role of school boards to one of co-responsibility, support, and challenge rather than detachment and control (Ghoshal, 2005)
  - To have a flexible organization that makes viable the growth of interdisciplinary research (Cortés, 2014)
  - To develop good governance practices that promote a strategic vision and allow for sound decision-making and good resource management (Cortés, 2014)
  - To establish codes of ethics: the establishment of reporting lines and an extracurricular approach and social participation (Hanson et al., 2017)
  - To be aware of the role of external accreditation (e.g., AACSB) in establishing certain criteria and indicators, as they call for one policy or another (Giacalone & Thompson, 2006)

- Regarding teacher management policies:

  - To recruit and promote teachers in a humanistic way, and bearing in mind that they must be able to display humanistic values (Ghoshal, 2005)
  - To design an incentive system that is detached from mere student satisfaction and linked to the ability to develop graduates who transform the world (Godfrey et al., 2005)
  - To encourage collaborative work among teachers and do not separate them by functional areas (Jain, 2009)

- Regarding the student management policies and processes:

  - To rethink student selection processes by evaluating them in a comprehensive manner (Giacalone & Wargo, 2009)
  - To involve students actively in the university community, because participation in its structures and functions generates ethical understanding and enhances ethical outcomes (Hanson et al., 2017)

Finally, if we seek to implement humanistic management principles in business schools' research: (a) research questions need to be real and connected to practice and to the great problems of humanity (Jain, 2009; Pfeffer & Fong, 2002); (b) research teams have to be interdisciplinary and inter-university (Cortés, 2014); and (c) research questions and publication spaces should be plural (Ghoshal, 2005).

As a summary of this fourth section, Table 2 contains the key issues discussed above.

5 Conclusions

We are in a world in constant change and with increasingly complex and global challenges. For this reason, we need management teams that take into consideration not only the economic profit but also their own well-being, others' well-being, and society as a whole. This is the challenge that literature refers to as humanistic management and the approach we have advocated in these pages.

Our first conclusion is that in order to generate this change in the conception of organizations, higher education plays a fundamental role. That is to say, it is not enough to intervene in organizations, but rather to begin with the education of managers and leaders. From our point of view, the education of future leaders makes a more lasting and sustainable change than intervening only through legislation.

A second conclusion, following the literature review, is the relevance of insisting on two complementary courses of action. On the one hand, it is important to educate for humanism, and, at the same time, this cannot be achieved without educating in a humanistic way.

Table 2 Key elements to develop the humanistic dimension in business and management higher education (Developed by authors)

Key elements to develop the humanistic dimension in business and management higher education		
Teaching	Research	Internal structure and management
• Question beliefs, conceptions and values about oneself, the world around the student or the business world • Incorporation of theoretical basis around humanistic management in the curriculum • Experimentation of the humanistic dimension and connection with the reality (service-learning, internships, volunteering, etc.)	• Solve real questions, connected to practice and to the great problems of humanity • Promotion of interdisciplinary and inter-university research teams • Promote plural research questions and publications spaces	• More flexible organizations • Good governance practices • Faculty incentive systems that reward what is taught and not student satisfaction • Appropriate teacher recruitment and promotion systems • Change the role of boards of directors • Encourage collaborative work • Rethink student selection processes • Ensure that students are active participants in the university community • Develop codes of ethics and set "red lines" for management

To educate for humanistic management, we have proposed three approaches: to question students beliefs and values about themselves, the world around them or the business world, to incorporate theoretical basis around humanistic management in the curriculum, and/or to invite students to experiment the humanistic dimension and to be connected with reality. Moreover, it is not enough to incorporate these concepts on an ad hoc basis, but it must be addressed in a transversal way throughout the curriculum.

In order to educate in a humanistic way, the faculty and the institution have a great responsibility. We must encourage professors to incorporate a more humanistic perspective of the world. In this sense, our proposal is that this approach should involve all the university activities: not only teaching, but also research, internal organization, people management processes, etc. Coherence and role modeling (what teachers communicate with their behavior, what the institution encourages with its mission, etc.) are relevant sources for students learning processes as well.

Educating for humanistic management and in a humanistic way makes students better trained as professionals and citizens. Students, faculty, and higher education institutions would share the same purpose: to develop students in a holistic and integrative way so they become professionals who will act in the organizations to transform the world.

References

Barth, M., Godemann, J., Rieckmann, M., & Stoltenberg, U. (2007). Developing key competencies for sustainable development in higher education. *International Journal of Sustainability in Higher Education, 8*(4), 416–430.

Bloom, G., & Pirson, M. (2011). Unleashing a rising generation of leading social change agents: An emerging university pedagogy. In W. Amann, M. Pirson, C. Dierksmeier, E. Von Kimakowitz, & H. Spitzeck (Eds.), *Business schools under fire. Humanistic management education as the way forward* (pp. 246–256). Houndmills: Palgrave Macmillan.

Bringle, R. G., & Hatcher, J. A. (1999). Reflection in service learning: Making meaning of experience. *Educational Horizons, 77*, 179–185.

Caza, A., & Brower, H. H. (2015). Mentioning the unmentioned: An interactive interview about the informal management curriculum. *Academy of Management Learning & Education, 14*(1), 96–110.

Cortés, F. (2014). Fundamentos filosóficos de una propuesta de reforma de la educación superior. *Co-herencia, 10*(20), 215–233. Medellín, Colombia (ISSN 1794-5887).

Cortese, A. D. (2003). The critical role of higher education in creating a sustainable future. *Planning for Higher Education, 31*(3), 15–22.

Dierksmeier, C. (2011). Reorienting management education: From Homo oeconomicus to human dignity. In W. Amann, M. Pirson, C. Dierksmeier, E. Von Kimakowitz, & H. Spitzeck (Eds.), *Business schools under fire. Humanistic management education as the way forward* (pp. 19–40). Houndmills: Palgrave Macmillan.

Elkanova, T. M., & Chedzhemova, N. M. (2013). Humanization and humanitarization of education: The essence, principles, aims. *World Applied Sciences Journal, 22*(5), 697–702. https://doi.org/10.5829/idosi.wasj.2013.22.05.13175

Euler, D., & Seufert, S. (2011). "Reflective executives" – A realistic goal for modern management education. In W. Amann, M. Pirson, C. Dierksmeier, E. Von Kimakowitz, & H. Spitzeck (Eds.), *Business schools under fire. Humanistic management education as the way forward* (pp. 212–226). Houndmills: Palgrave Macmillan.

Eyler, J., & Giles, D. E., Jr. (1999). *Where's the learning in service-learning?* San Francisco, CA: Jossey-Bass Higher and Adult Education Series, Jossey-Bass.

Gentile, M. C. (2011). Giving voice to values – A pedagogy for values-driven leadership. In W. Amann, M. Pirson, C. Dierksmeier, E. Von Kimakowitz, & H. Spitzeck (Eds.), *Business schools under fire. Humanistic management education as the way forward* (pp. 227–237). Houndmills: Palgrave Macmillan.

Ghoshal, S. (2005). Bad management theories are destroying good management practices. *Academy of Management Learning & Education, 4*(1), 75–91. https://doi.org/10.5465/AMLE.2005.16132558

Giacalone, R. A., & Thompson, K. R. (2006). Business ethics and social responsibility education: Shifting the worldview. *Academy of Management Learning & Education, 5*(3), 266–277.

Giacalone, R. A., & Wargo, D. T. (2009). The roots of the global financial crisis are in our business schools. *Journal of Business Ethics Education, 6*, 147–168. https://doi.org/10.5840/jbee200969

Godfrey, P. C. (1999). Service-learning and management education: A call to action. *Journal of Management Inquiry, 8*(4), 363–378.

Godfrey, P. C., & Grasso, E. T. (Eds.). (2000). *Working for the common good: Concepts and models for service-learning in management.* Sterling, VA: Stylus Publishing, LLC.

Godfrey, P. C., Illes, L. M., & Berry, G. R. (2005). Creating breadth in business education through service-learning. *Academy of Management Learning & Education, 4*, 309–323.

Hanson, W. R., Moore, J. R., Bachleda, C., Canterbury, A., Franco, C., Marion, A., & Schreiber, C. (2017). Theory of moral development of business students: Case studies in Brazil, North America, and Morocco. *Academy of Management Learning & Education, 16*(3), 393–414.

Helbing, D. (2013). Economics 2.0: The natural step towards a self-regulating, participatory market society. *Evolutionary and Institutional Economics Review, 10*(1), 3–41.

Holland, K. (2011). Insights from the W. Edwards Deming memorial conference. In W. Amann, M. Pirson, C. Dierksmeier, E. Von Kimakowitz, & H. Spitzeck (Eds.), *Business schools under fire. Humanistic management education as the way forward* (pp. 95–103). Houndmills: Palgrave Macmillan.

Jain, S. C. (2009). Enhancing international business education through restructuring business schools. *Journal of Teaching in International Business, 20,* 4–34. https://doi.org/10.1080/08975930802671216

Kenworthy-U'Ren, A. L., & Peterson, T. O. (2005). Service-learning and management education: Introducing the "WE CARE" approach. *Academy of Management Learning & Education, 4*(3), 272–277.

Lotz-Sisitka, H., Wals, A. E., Kronlid, D., & McGarry, D. (2015). Transformative, transgressive social learning: Rethinking higher education pedagogy in times of systemic global dysfunction. *Current Opinion in Environmental Sustainability, 16,* 73–80.

Lunenberg, M., Korthagen, F., & Swennen, A. (2007). The teacher educator as a role model. *Teaching and Teacher Education, 23*(5), 586–601.

McDonald, R. A. (2000). Reframing management education: A humanist context for teaching in business and society. *Interchange, 31*(4), 385–401.

McDonald, R. (2011). What are the principles of a humanistic education? In W. Amann, M. Pirson, C. Dierksmeier, E. Von Kimakowitz, & H. Spitzeck (Eds.), *Business schools under fire. Humanistic management education as the way forward* (pp. 130–146). Houndmills: Palgrave Macmillan.

McDonald, R. (2015). Leveraging change by learning to work with the wisdom in the room: Educating for responsibility as a collaborative learning model. *Journal of Business Ethics, 131* (3), 511–518. https://doi.org/10.1007/s10551-014-2477-0

Melé, D. (2003). The challenge of humanistic management. *Journal of Business Ethics, 44*(1), 77–88.

Melé, D. (2009). Current trends in humanism and business. In H. Spitzeck, M. Pirson, W. Amann, S. Khan, & E. Von Kimakowitz (Eds.), *Humanism in business* (pp. 123–141). Cambridge: Cambridge University Press.

Melé, D. (2016). Understanding humanistic management. *Humanistic Management Journal, 1,* 33–55. https://doi.org/10.1007/s41463-016-0011-5

Nejati, M., Shahbudin, A. S. M., & Amran, A. (2011, October). Barriers to achieving a sustainable university in the perspective of academicians. In *The 9th AAM International Conference 2011* (pp. 14–16).

Net Impact. (2011). Undergraduate perspectives: The business of changing the world. In W. Amann, M. Pirson, C. Dierksmeier, E. Von Kimakowitz, & H. Spitzeck (Eds.), *Business schools under fire. Humanistic management education as the way forward* (pp. 65–73). Houndmills: Palgrave Macmillan.

Paterson, T. A., & Huang, L. (2018). Am I expected to be ethical? A role-definition perspective of ethical leadership and unethical behavior. *Journal of Management, 45*(7), 2837–2860. https://doi.org/10.1177/0149206318771166

Pfeffer, J., & Fong, C. T. (2002). The end of business schools? Less success than meets the eye. *Academy of Management Learning & Education, 1*(1), 78–95.

Pirson, M. (2011). What is business organizing for? The role of business in society over time. In W. Amann, M. Pirson, C. Dierksmeier, E. Von Kimakowitz, & H. Spitzeck (Eds.), *Business schools under fire. Humanistic management education as the way forward* (pp. 41–51). Houndmills: Palgrave Macmillan.

Pirson, M. A., & Lawrence, P. R. (2010). Humanism in business – Towards a paradigm shift? *Journal of Business Ethics, 93*(4), 553–565.

Rowe, D. (2007). Education for a sustainable future. *Science, 317*(5836), 323–324.

Tough, A. (1982). *Intentional changes*. Chicago: Follet.

Wolf, R. (2018). Self-awareness: A way to promote ethical management. In Information Resources Management Association (Ed.), *Business education and ethics: Concepts, methodologies, tools, and applications* (pp. 860–871). Hershey: IGI Global. https://doi.org/10.4018/978-1-5225-3153-1.ch045

Zhu, W., Avolio, B. J., Riggio, R. E., & Sosik, J. J. (2011). The effects of authentic transformational leadership on follower and group ethics. *The Leadership Quarterly, 22*(5), 801–817.

Challenges of Humanistic Management Education in the Digital Era

Ernestina Giudici, Angela Dettori, and Federica Caboni

1 Introduction

In recent decades, scandals such as the failure of Enron, the financial crisis of 2008 (Melé, 2008), and immense, numerous environmental damages have contributed in creating a world where nothing is like it ever was before. Following these dramatic events, numerous discussions such as that by Setò-Pamies and Papaoikonomou (2016, p. 254) have been triggered on the need for a more ethical business culture and how this change could and should directly involve the educational system.

In this regard, Swanson (2004, p. 57) suggested that, "While strengthening ethics education will not cure all ills; it is a necessary ingredient in repairing the tarnishing of the social contract between business and society."

Numerous questions have emerged to address this concern. In spite of the abovementioned warning from Swanson, we cannot avoid asking ourselves if a portion (no matter how big or small), of responsibility must be charged to the business schools and their teachers.

The financial crisis, in particular, has created a perception that there is a serious ethics and values problem among managers, in addition to significant economic-financial problems (Minkes & Minkes, 2008). The awareness that corporate crimes are attributable to individual liabilities for misconduct and growing corruption (Lair, 2015) is becoming increasingly widespread. In such a situation, business schools are subject to careful analysis by civil society because they are considered unable to prepare "good" managers (Holland, 2009).

The main criticisms of business schools are that the training they provide is primarily oriented toward increasing profits and shareholder returns without behavioral limits (Denning, 2013); yet the economic and social reality of this millennium is

E. Giudici (✉) · A. Dettori · F. Caboni
University of Cagliari, Cagliari, Italy
e-mail: giudici@unica.it; angela.dettori@unica.it; federica.caboni@unica.it

© Springer Nature Switzerland AG 2020
R. Aguado, A. Eizaguirre (eds.), *Virtuous Cycles in Humanistic Management*,
Contributions to Management Science,
https://doi.org/10.1007/978-3-030-29426-7_2

characterized by complexity, uncertainty, and high dynamism. These are character-istics that cannot be properly exhibited solely by applying knowledge based on paradigms inspired by rationality and the econometric models of planning and control.

Complexity has been defined as "the number of items or elements that must be dealt with simultaneously by an organization" (Scott, 1992, p. 230). Attention to complexity can be traced back to the years following the Second World War, with fundamental contributions from various scholars (Burns & Stalker, 1966; Emery & Trist, 1965; Lawrence & Lorsch, 1967), and considerations in numerous modern-day works (Chandler, 2014; Child & Rodrigues, 2011; Faulconbridge & Muzio, 2015; Reus, Ranft, Lamont, & Adams, 2009). As reality is complex, uncertain, and dynamic, it is essential to transfer skills to students and future managers that will enable them to facilitate flexibility and creativity and acquire behavioral awareness based on ethics, social responsibility, and sustainability, or, rather, to be humanistic managers.

The transition from mainly technical competences to skills based on intangible resources such as knowledge, constitute a peculiarity of this historical era, which is also known as the knowledge economy. An important implication is that "actively instructing or guiding students" is indispensable, and learning "how to learn" and "cooperate with others" is inevitable (Kuang & Sung-Lin, 2016, p. 1698).

In relation to the changes taking place scholars such as Pirson and Turnbull (2011) are becoming increasingly convinced that without a humanistic culture, it is not possible to face the economic challenges of the contemporary society.

Therefore, these issues require a significant commitment from society as a whole, and from business schools and teachers. In relation to these imperative requirements, have business schools significantly changed their curricula? Have teachers altered their teaching methods to consider both the available technologies and the fact that their students are digital natives? It is clearly evident that the educational system faces a challenge whose boundaries are not easily identifiable: on one side, there is the adoption of an orientation capable of considering ethical values, social responsibility, and sustainability, while on the other hand, there are increasing digital technologies, which cannot be ignored, and are "familiar" to the younger generations.

Today's students are born digital. In fact, as children, many learned the letters of the alphabet, numbers, and the basics of music through television entertainment lessons. Videos of the inhabitants of Sesame Street (Kermit the Frog, Bert and Ernie, Cookie Monster, etc.) are easily memorable, as they were based on a rigorous pedagogical curriculum by the Carnegie Corporation and the Ford Foundation. This entertainment "was designed as a preschool educational program tailored specifically for TV" (Kaplan & Haenlein, 2016, p. 442).

There have been many occasions for change in higher education throughout history. However, this historical period is different from others in that these changes are occurring rapidly, in less than one generation. This rapid change has resulted in the emergence of a great challenge for business schools and teachers.

The two aforementioned factors—social values and digital technologies—appear, at first glance, as two irreconcilable worlds. Paradoxically, correct use of technologies can favor the development of ethical, socially responsible, and sustainability-oriented behaviors. For example, the use of social media in training can provide the skills necessary for understanding the value of collaboration, an essential aspect for companies (and organizations in general) in this era of knowledge.

The aim of this chapter is twofold: (1) to establish whether universities, and specifically business schools, are modifying their curricula to be more social and less rationale-oriented and (2) to point out the new role that teachers must play to give digital students the essential humanistic education for properly managing firms in the third millennium.

After this introduction, the attention will shift to the two questions. More specifically, the next section will focus on understanding how business schools are responding to the need for greater attention to ethics, social responsibility, and sustainability. The following points are devoted to considering these questions: Are teachers aware of the need to change their teaching methods with regard to changing socioeconomic needs? Are they also aware of the specific learning methods of "digitally native" students? What teaching methods are the most relevant to satisfy these needs? Finally, some concluding observations will be presented.

2   Are Business School Curricula Becoming More Humanistic-Oriented?

Alsop (2006) argued that "universities have a critical role to play in preparing leaders to create an ethical and socially responsible climate in the world's business enterprises" (p. 12). Business schools, and especially finance and economics professors, have taught students that markets are efficient because people are rational decision-makers and that decisions must primarily focus on profits based on a cost-benefit analysis. Much research has shown that teaching basically financial aspects results in future managers who are inclined to adopt decisions that are less social, less cooperative, and less ethical than those who have received a training that is not centered on profit maximization (Gino & Mogilner, 2014; Kouchaki, Smith-Crowe, Brief, & Sousa, 2013; Palazzo, Krings, & Hoffrage, 2012; Vohs, Mead, & Goode, 2006). In other words, student social values are misguided if their training is focused on the economy and business instead of emphasizing social aspects (Dasgupta & Menon, 2011; Gentile, 2002; Huhn, 2014; Kenrick & Griskevicius, 2013; Liberman, Samuels, & Ross, 2004).

The loss of validity of the rational actor's model has also been highlighted by studies in behavioral psychology, cognitive science, and various other fields that have shown that decision-making behavior is far from rational (Gilovich, Griffin, & Kahneman, 2002; Kahneman, 2011). In addition, it is worth noting that behavioral finance courses have been introduced slowly in business schools (Baker & Ricciardi, 2014), as well as behavioral economics courses (Camerer, Loewenstein, & Rabin,

2004). Furthermore, the growing awareness of corporate influence on the global environment has made corporate social responsibility (CSR) a problem that can no longer be ignored (Wilburn, 2008).

In a study of European business school curricula (Wymer & Rundle-Thiele, 2017), 51% of undergraduate programs and 35% of graduate programs offered an optional CSR module. The real problem was not in the percentages detected but in the fact that most of the CSR courses were electives rather than the required courses. However, this is considered partially positive since it is *better to have elective courses than no courses*. In reality, these courses are not within the educational policy of the business school but fall within the exclusive sensitivity of the individual teacher.

According to Wymer and Rundle-Thiele (2017), the importance of the inclusion of CSR is expressed by the following concept: "Corporate social responsibility is a concept whereby organizations consider the interests of society by taking responsibility for the impact of their activities on customers, suppliers, employees, shareholders, communities and other stakeholders, as well as the environment" (p. 21). This means that while the importance of corporate growth and profitability has been recognized, it is also necessary for each corporation to pursue social goals, such as environmental protection, justice, and social equity, together with economic development (Wilson, 2003).

The Institute for Sustainability Education (2015) emphasized that business students should learn to be both citizens and managers who can contribute to the creation of healthy and sustainable communities. From the Wymer and Rundle-Thiele research, which was reported in a special issue of the Journal of Business Ethics about business schools on every continent, specific themes clearly emerged: "Undergraduate business curricula are not effectively responding to societal needs to have more socially responsible managers," and "In a period in which sustainability has become such an important societal issue, only about one-third of our universities offered a sustainability-related course" (Wymer & Rundle-Thiele, 2017, p. 128). Moreover, from the aforementioned research, it clearly emerges that few universities encourage students to attend courses on globalization from a prosocial perspective, keeping unchanged the managers' education as profit maximizers, loyal especially to shareholders.

The inclusion of courses about social responsibility, ethics, and sustainability is made even more problematic due to the absence of consensus on the meaning and conceptual domain of the concepts. This reduces their validity and makes what is taught questionable.

In the presence of this lack of adjustment of universities and business schools, there is growing concern that business students do not possess the skills required to manage the problems of this millennium, including those of environmental degradation generated by industrialization (Waddock, 2007). Abandoning the neoclassical economic models is essential in order to shift to suitable models for educating socially responsible managers capable of utilizing a humanistic perspective instead of merely focusing on profit (Ghoshal, 2005; Waddock, 2007). Profit is a means, not the main purpose.

Moreover, structural changes alone would not be sufficient because they do not ensure a shift in people's attitudes and mentality. This means that it is not sufficient to introduce ethics or sustainability courses without the full involvement of the teachers and, most importantly, the students. The real challenge is creating enough emotion and passion for understanding that a company's activity must be seen as a problem of respect for human beings and that company results come from understanding the interdependences inside and outside the company.

Dobson (2007) argued that the educational system is the most suitable place to promote sustainability, as it can give students a broad vision of the existing problems and contribute to a more relevant social change. In this regard, the United Nations (2007, p. 3) made an interesting and incisive statement: "Any meaningful and lasting change in the conduct of corporations toward sustainability must involve the institutions that most directly act as drivers of business behavior, especially academia. Academic institutions help shape the attitudes and behavior of business leaders through business education, research, management development programs, training, and other pervasive, but less tangible, activities, such as the spread and advocacy of new values and ideas. Through these means, academic institutions have the potential to generate a wave of positive change, thereby helping to ensure a world where both enterprises and societies can flourish."

Since universities are considered, the main providers of training (education suppliers), modifying the curricula to offer students the knowledge and skills to interact with the changes taking place is fundamental. Therefore, integrating ethical principles, social responsibility, and sustainability into the curricula would provide students with knowledge and skills to interact with the new business paradigm and broaden their "moral imagination" (Fougère, Solitander, & Young, 2014).

This means that universities (and business schools) must get rid of the technicalities that characterize their curricula and insert content to train future managers capable of acting in a responsible economy.

As Hailey (1998, p. 40) argued, "University programs should not only focus on developing operational skills and interpersonal competencies, but, by exploring core values, ethical considerations and issues of wider environmental and geo-political concern would also place a strong emphasis on critical analysis of the changing environment." The aforementioned suggestion to include courses in business school curricula, and more generally, at every university level that train more "humanistic-oriented" students (Amann, Pirson, Dierksmeier, Kimakowitz, & Spitzeck, 2011), has not always been addressed considering that ethics, social responsibility, and sustainability are three strongly interrelated, yet distinct areas. This means that omitting disciplines related to all three areas of knowledge leads to incomplete training: missing one of the pillars means creating managers attentive only to the needs of the economic sector but not to the needs of the society as a whole.

It is difficult to move toward a cultural change oriented to new values and attitudes. Although universities alone, without the involvement of other institutions operating in the society, play an important role in the movement toward cultural change, they cannot be considered a panacea that will resolve all ethical dilemmas.

Comparing the inclusion of ethics, social responsibility, and sustainability in universities in different global contexts is not easy due to the differences in terminology adopted. A lack of clear distinction tends to be the most prominent between CSR courses and business ethics courses (Rossouw, 2011). Sometimes, the inclusion of business ethics courses in the curricula stems from government reforms aimed at fighting corruption.

In his final essay in the special issue of the Journal of Business Ethics that focused on the Global Survey of Business Ethics as a field of training, teaching, and research Rossouw (2011, p. 93) presented a list of the research topics that were most often addressed during the years taken into consideration, 2010–2011 (Table 3, Rossouw, 2011, p. 99), underlining the quantitative growth of researches concerning ethics, social responsibility, and sustainability issues.

Table 1 shows the same research themes, highlighting the trend in each of the research topics from 2010 to 2017. The survey was carried out using the Web of Science database by using research themes as keywords and limiting the keywords to those that were present in article titles.

Analyzing the data exposed in Table 1, it emerged that topics like CSR, sustainability, and corruption increased relevantly. It is important to understand that the growing attention to "humanistic oriented" research themes does not mean a consequent greater humanistic orientation of the business schools' curricula. The aforementioned increase in attention is, however, significant because it highlights a growing awareness of the centrality of humanistic values for the management of an increasingly complex world.

Moreover, even if there is no cause/effect relationship between research topics and didactic contents, it is realistic to assume that the attention to humanistic themes in research also influences the didactic proposals for students' training.

It should not be forgotten, as highlighted in the research by Wymer and Rundle-Thiele (2017), the sensitivity of teachers plays a non-secondary role in the

Table 1 Trend of research themes from 2010 to 2017

Themes	Year 2010	Year 2017
Governance of ethics	3	33
Management of ethics	16	19
CSR	240	562
Corporate stakeholder relations	1	1
Sustainability	1431	3310
Economic ethics	18	14
Business and social justice	3	2
Business and human rights	3	33
Theories of ethics	1 (2009)	1 (2016)
Corruption	215	680
Ethics and business performance	1 (2009)	2
Ethical dilemmas and decision-making	5	3 (2016)

Source: Data processed by the authors

introduction of humanistic management topics. It is an essential process in order to achieve the goal of training more humanistic citizens and managers.

Because of the essential role played by teachers, it is important to carefully consider the tools and teaching methods used. Current students are digital natives, which imply that teaching tools and methods cannot ignore this peculiarity to be able to promote effective interactions with the students. In the next point, this aspect is taken into consideration.

3 Teachers' Challenges

This point is devoted to highlighting the teachers' essential role in the training of future "humanistic" managers. The need to consider the fact that modern-day students are familiar with digital devices makes this task even more difficult. This is why it is essential for teachers to innovate their teaching and to modify teaching methods in line with the characteristics of their students. This, however, does not mean that previous methods must be completely eliminated, but they must certainly be remodeled (e.g., storytelling becoming digital storytelling).

Teaching in the third millennium is a multi-layered, multi-faceted job. This is not easy because it is impossible to rely on routine when working with inquisitive people (Melé, 2003). With reference to the new didactic perspectives suitable for students of the third millennium, it should be noted that the teacher's role cannot be ignored. Teachers need to radically modify their way of interacting with the students. They have to transform themselves from "knowledge communicators" to "learning stimulators." Teachers need to identify the best ways to interact with students in order to generate what Morin (1986) termed as "knowledge of knowledge," which refers to being aware that the frontier of knowledge does not exist, and that every new cell of knowledge stimulates the search for further knowledge in an endless process.

For this reason, it is essential to change an orientation—or, more correctly, the paradigm—in order to abandon the concept of rationality as a connotation of *homo economicus* and to gain awareness of the indispensability of a humanistic orientation, which is capable of enhancing and developing the dynamic, flexible, and inexhaustible skills and abilities of human beings to create economic and social well-being based on the values of ethics, social responsibility, and sustainability. Management can be considered "humanistic" when "its outlook emphasizes common human needs and is oriented to the development of human virtue" (Melé, 2003, p. 77).

The essential role of teachers in inspiring humanistic orientation in students has also been supported by the fact that "we are not born Human, we *become* Human" (Erasmus). Furthermore, each human being becomes humanistic oriented, thanks to education, the acquisition of knowledge, and the development of the capacity to properly practice the right to liberty and distinguish good from evil.

In the digital age, the teacher must "relocate" his relationship with the class and reshape his relationships with the students, who must be more involved and become "actors" and not "passive receivers" of knowledge. Students have to learn to "think outside the box" (Leigh, Bassendowski, & Petrucka, 2013).

The need for students to be the main "actors" of the training process is not easy to satisfy. Furthermore, the traditional lesson model is still prevalent all over the world (Saavedra & Opfer, 2012). This predominant approach generates limited student involvement and can lead to apathy, distractions, and other negative behaviors in students. In short, it is an unsuitable and ineffective model for creating the knowledge and skills that students need in the third millennium (Scott, 2015).

In the last 20 years, students' learning behaviors have changed dramatically. The ways through which students seek, gather, and process information have been transformed from analog to digital modes (Eyring & Christensen, 2011). A UNESCO publication (Scott, 2015) emphasized that "Project and problem-based learning are ideal instructional models for meeting the objectives of twenty-first century education, because they employ the *4Cs Principle*—critical thinking, communication, collaboration and creativity—alongside 'teaching for transfer' and learning structured in real-world contexts" (p. 5).

Above all, transforming the teacher–student relationship means acquiring a new relational dimension that significantly affects the students' propensity to learn. As such, the dynamics of this relationship will affect the formation of a future manager capable of enhancing interpersonal relationships and being more sensitive to social and cultural values. This means learning to consider human beings operating in companies as essential to the operations. In fact, adopting a new perspective in relationships with students ensures a greater understanding of the fact that companies are "communities of human beings that work together" (Giudici, 2016). The main implication is that the effects of the paradigm of rationality (*homo economicus*) on behaviors and actions can be significantly reduced. Therefore, the awareness of the essential and exclusive role played by human beings as custodians of knowledge and ethical, social, and sustainability values is increased. To reduce harmful behaviors for businesses and the economy, managers need to shift from appliers of technicalities to facilitators of relationships among human beings at different levels of the firm.

The need for managers to be more flexible and "social"—capable of creating positive relationships both inside and outside the company—has clearly emerged. So far, the answer to this problem, which is usually ineffective, has been mainly based on strengthening interventions with the aim of influencing different levels of operational flexibility.

To perceive the goal to have "flexible humanistic managers" requires the understanding of how to interact with students, and potential future managers.

If the course content, adopted teaching methods, and the subsequent evaluations are primarily based on skills and business techniques, it will be difficult for these students to change their behavior in their future work and to place relationships and the value of human beings first. This means that teachers must adopt new approaches and, more precisely, teach a "sense of community." It is not sufficient to speak about a "community" referring to a firm as a group of people that work together, but rather it is essential to explain the value of a "sense of belonging." Sharing knowledge, experiences, difficulties, good results, and others, gives a unique and inimitable value to each firm that through this approach, can reach success.

Due to the familiarity young people have with technology and the need for technology to be used increasingly in the training process, the role of teachers will be significantly modified. "Their roles will be extended as mentors, mediators and guides, facilitators, learning coordinators, assessors, and designers and compilers of learning tools" (Scott, 2015, p. 16).

Learning will become more individualized to satisfy the needs and interests of each student. It will constitute not only formal but also informal learning opportunities, encourage real-world experiences, and stimulate collaboration among students. Technology will support personalized learning processes, and the contribution of information and communications technology will enable more learner-centered approaches (Scott, 2015, p. 16).

4   Teaching Tools for Third Millennium Students

There are various teaching tools that can help teachers in the difficult task of training humanistic managers based on an awareness of the need to interact with digital native students and not disregarding the use of digital technologies. While it is not possible to consider all the educational tools that can be used, or to analyze those that are indicated here in depth, the objective of this section is to provide "food for thought" (Giudici, Varriale, Floris, & Dessì, 2011, p. 148). This is in order to stimulate teachers to be attentive to new teaching techniques and be creative in the use of traditional ones. After a brief mention of traditional methods and related tools, we choose to analyze the technological tools because they are effective, simple to use (i.e., suitable also for teachers not familiar with digital), and are not very expensive.

Among the traditional methods are case studies, which can be made more engaging by urging students to directly contact companies to learn about their activities and their problems (Bayona & Castañeda, 2017). Similarly, the use of storytelling can be "modernized" by transforming it to "digital storytelling," that is, "The practice that combining narrative with digital content, including images, sound and video, to create a short movie, typically with a strong emotional component" (Robin, 2018).

Less traditional, but increasingly widespread, is the use of full-length films, videos, music, theater, and cartoons. These teaching tools often complement other teaching methods, and all these tools stimulate students to be active participants and to experience emotional content that can "promote knowledge application, critical reflection, and moral imagination" (Giudici et al., 2011, p. 153). With specific reference to theater, Aristotle believed that theater emphasized "doing" rather than memorizing. This renewed attention has been devoted to several tools based on the "experiential learning approach," a new way to refer to "learn by doing" (van den Bemt, Doornbos, Meijering, Plegt, & Theunissen, 2018).

Current technologies can help teachers to create virtual environments, simulations, etc. that are useful for involving the student and developing critical thinking. The tools are many, ranging from a simple Multimedia Interactive Whiteboard (MIW) to e-books, virtual classes, cloud computing, and the use of social media.

The MIW is an electronic board that is a powerful tool because it catalyzes and guides the student's attention. It is a "window to the world" that makes learning more effective.

E-books, which are widely used at an individual level, have only recently entered the university classroom. The e-book is considered "a 'radical innovation' in the classroom, because of its widespread impact on traditional printed textbooks, its positive motivation for students, and its complementary role in the digital platform of a classroom and the university" (Martinez-Estrada & Conaway, 2012, pp. 125–126).

Computer networks represent the potential to realize collaborative learning and foster communication between students, between students and their teachers, and among teachers. Evolution of computer networks is referred to as CLOUD computing, which is a set of technologies and ways of using IT services that allow the use and delivery of software, as well as the storage and processing of large amounts of data via the Internet. Some cloud technologies are widely used without awareness, such as, geolocation features.

In the same sphere of communication that uses technologies, virtual classes have been positioned to link teachers and students in the same class. In these classes, it is possible to implement advanced learning methods, create an interactive context with research and collaboration initiatives on the web, and organize individual and/or group activities. For the adoption of this methodology, it is essential for the teacher to play an active role and possess appropriate technological knowledge.

Social media, without a doubt, are the most recent technologies used for educational purposes. Social media refers to not only Facebook, Twitter, and YouTube but also to the instant messaging service WhatsApp, among others. Their integration in teaching ranges from the possibilities offered by Facebook to exchange messages outside the classroom, to establishing groups to discuss and deepen the topics covered in the classroom. Similarly, Twitter allows immediate feedback and preservation of topics through a keyword. YouTube, on the other hand, is a tool that stimulates creativity by allowing one to use videos prepared by the teacher, as well as publish videos prepared by the students. It should be emphasized that the social media do not replace teaching activities but rather constitute a valid integration. Furthermore, they require commitment, continuity, time, content production, and information exchange—in other words, one cannot improvise.

The pursuit of individualized training (also suggested by the UNESCO study, Scott, 2015) to generate both basic knowledge and tools to learn by doing is important for the realization of continuous formation of students and future managers. Due to the growing numbers of students, individualized training seems almost impossible (Brinton et al., 2015). An answer to this problem comes from the possibility of using chat bots in education (Winkler & Soellner, 2018). Chat bots are computer programs used to manage textual or voice conversations of human interactions (Rouse, 2018). As Winkler and Soellner (2018) underlined, "Chat bots comprise all kinds of software enabling humans to make a conversation with a computer. This includes talk bots, chatter bots, conversational agents, artificial conversational entities and even virtual assistants such as Amazon's Alexa or Google's Home" (pp. 5–6).

Among the various chat bots that technology is making increasingly interactive are artificially intelligent chat bots. These tools allow the user to have an experience that is similar to real human-to-human interaction. Artificially intelligent chat bots can be one way or two way: the one-way chat bots use machine learning techniques to understand what the interlocutor is saying (Dutta, 2017), while the two-way chat bots "use on top of the artificial intelligence to feed the information back to the user" (Winkler & Soellner, 2018, p. 20). No two-way artificially intelligent chat bots are used in education.

The OECD (2014) has highlighted the fact that the use of chat bots in management education plays an important role in the development of various managerial skills that are crucial for future managers such as decision-making, giving and receiving feedback, and generating technological awareness.

It should be emphasized that the use of chat bots in training can generate a positive impact on learning and student satisfaction. Some studies have highlighted the success in the use of chat bots in training (Dutta, 2017; Huang, Lee, Kwon, & Kim, 2017).

Although the chat bots possess an intrinsic validity, they still present some weaknesses. The individual differences among the students influence the quality of interactions between them. In addition, chat bots present a shorter conversation length and a lesser vocabulary wealth compared to a human-to-human conversation. Nevertheless, despite the limits that chat bots possess, they are expected to only increase in use in education in the future.

In conclusion, it can be noted that both traditionally reformulated and modern technologies used in education have a couple of elements in common: increasing active participation among students and encouraging cooperation through activities. This constitutes the essential training base for students and future managers to learn to appreciate the abilities of each person, including the value of working together and the potential that is derived from such social behaviors. In this way, the formative process loses its technical characteristics and replaces them with humanistic ones. In other words, students acquire the basics to be humanistic managers through becoming proponents of ethical behavior and advocates of social responsibility and sustainability.

5   Conclusion

The purpose of this chapter was to highlight the behavior of business schools in adopting curricula with courses about ethics, social responsibility, and sustainability. In addition, it proposed a challenge for teachers to better interact with their students and identify potential teaching methods that are best suited for third-millennium students, i.e., future managers.

It is clear from the literature that the road to modifying curricula and adopting more suitable teaching techniques for better interaction with students is still long. Business schools are gradually introducing courses in ethics, social responsibility, and sustainability, but in most cases, these are voluntary courses and not structured in the curricula.

The growing attention of scholars to research on ethics, social responsibility, and sustainability, as highlighted in this chapter, can be considered as a first step toward addressing the challenge of introducing structured courses on ethics, social responsibility, and sustainability in a growing number of business schools.

We are aware that sometimes the topics of research do not become the teaching subjects; this does not mean that there is a growing awareness of the need not to neglect the indispensable attention to human subjects and their values, rather than using sterile techniques.

Closely related to the previous one and equally important, is the challenge of adopting teaching methods that use modern digital technologies. The difficulty emerges clearly when one considers that unfortunately, traditional lessons are still very present.

Furthermore, if the challenge of adopting suitable methods to interact effectively with students is important, teachers who have already adopted nontraditional teaching methods face another challenge in disseminating to other teachers the knowledge and the adoption of teaching methods that are most appropriate to interact with today's digital students.

Overcoming the challenges that have been so far referred to constitutes an important responsibility for business schools and their teachers, since their ability to form humanistic managers depends largely on the winning or losing configuration of the economy of the future.

References

Alsop, R. (2006). Business ethics education in business schools: A commentary. *Journal of Management Education, 30*(1), 11–14.

Amann W, Pirson M, Dierksmeier C, Von Kimakowitz E, Spitzeck H (2011) Business schools under fire: Humanistic management education as the way forward. Basingstoke: Palgrave Macmillan.

Baker, H. K., & Ricciardi, V. (2014). *Investor behavior*. New York: Wiley.

Bayona, J. A., & Castañeda, D. I. (2017). Influence of personality and motivation on case method. *The International Journal of Management Education, 15*, 409–428.

Brinton, C. G., Rill, R., Ha, S., Chiang, M., Smith, R., & Ju, W. (2015). Individualization for education at scale: MIIC design and preliminary evaluation. *IEEE Transactions on Learning Technologies, 8*(1), 136–148.

Burns, T., & Stalker, G. M. (1966). *The management of innovation*. London: Tavistock Publications.

Camerer, C., Loewenstein, G., & Rabin, M. (2004). *Advances in behavioral economics*. New York: Russell Sage Foundation.

Chandler, D. (2014). Organizational susceptibility to institutional complexity: Critical events driving the adoption and implementation of the ethics and compliance officer position. *Organization Science, 25*, 1722–1743.

Child, J., & Rodrigues, S. B. (2011). How organizations engage with external complexity: A political action perspective. *Organization Studies, 32*, 803–824.

Dasgupta, U., & Menon, A. (2011). Trust and trustworthiness among economics majors. *Economic Bulletin, 31*(4), 2799–2815.

Denning, S. (2013). How modern economics is built on the world's dumbest idea. *Forbes.* Available from http://www.forbes.com/sites/stevedenning/2013/07/22/how-modern-econom ics-is-built-on-the-worlds-dumbest-idea/

Dobson, A. (2007). Environmental citizenship: Towards sustainable development. *Sustainable Development, 15*(5), 276–285.

Dutta, D. (2017). *Developing an intelligent Chat-bot Tool to assist high school students for learning general knowledge subjects.* Atlanta: Georgia Institute of Technology.

Emery, F. E., & Trist, E. L. (1965). The causal texture of organizational environments. *Human Relations, 18*, 21–32.

Eyring, H., & Christensen, C. (2011). Changing the DNA of higher education. In *The innovative university: Changing the DNA of higher education from the inside out.* New York: Wiley.

Faulconbridge, J., & Muzio, D. (2015). Global professional service firms and the challenge of institutional complexity: "Field relocation" as a response strategy. *Journal of Management Studies, 53*, 89–124.

Fougère, M., Solitander, N., & Young, S. (2014). Exploring and exposing values in management education: Problematising final vocabularies in order to enhance moral imagination. *Journal of Business Ethics, 120*(2), 175–187.

Gentile, M. C. (2002). *What do we teach when we teach social impact management?* New York: Aspen Institute.

Ghoshal, S. (2005). Bad management theories are destroying good management practices. *Academy of Management Learning & Education, 4*(1), 75–91.

Gilovich, T., Griffin, D., & Kahneman, D. (2002). *Heuristics and biases.* New York: Cambridge University Press.

Gino, F., & Mogilner, C. (2014). Time, money & morality. *Psychological Science, 25*(2), 414–421.

Giudici, E. (2016). *Lecture notes for the management course.* University of Cagliari.

Giudici, E., Varriale, L., Floris, M., & Dessì, S. (2011). Teaching business students to be passionate about ethical sustainable development. In C. Wankel & A. Stachowicz-Stanusch (Eds.), *Management education for integrity: Ethically educating tomorrow's business leaders.* Charlotte, NC: IAP-Information Age Publishing.

Hailey, J. (1998). Management education for sustainable development. *Sustainable Development, 6*(1), 40–48.

Holland, K. (2009, March 15). Is it time to retrain B-schools? *New York Times, 158*(54615), BU2.

Huang, J. X., Lee, K. S., Kwon, O. W., & Kim, Y. K. (2017). *A chatbot for a dialogue-based second language learning system.* CALL in a climate of change: Adapting to turbulent global conditions: 151.

Huhn, M. (2014). You reap what you sow: How MBA programs undermine ethics. *Journal of Business Ethics, 121*(4), 527–541.

Kahneman, D. (2011). *Thinking: Fast and slow.* New York: Farrar, Straus & Giroux.

Kaplan, A. M., & Haenlein, M. (2016). Higher education and the digital revolution: About MOOCs, SPOCs, social media, and the Cookie Monster. *Business Horizons, 59*(4), 441–450.

Kenrick, D., & Griskevicius, V. (2013). *The rational animal.* New York: Basic Books.

Kouchaki, M., Smith-Crowe, K., Brief, A., & Sousa, C. (2013). Seeing green: Mere exposure to money triggers a business decision frame and unethical outcomes. *Organizational Behavior & Decision Processes, 121*(1), 53–61.

Kuang, S. L., & Sung-Lin, H. (2016). Effects of digital teaching on the thinking styles and the transfer of learning of the students in department of interior design. *Eurasia Journal of Mathematics, Science & Technology Education, 12*(6), 1697–1706.

Lair, D. (2015). Normative and descriptive approaches to organizational ethics post-crisis: A review essay. *Organization, 22*(1), 139–149.

Lawrence, P., & Lorsch, J. (1967). *Organization and environment*. Cambridge, MA: Harvard University Press.

Leigh, S., Bassendowski, S. L., & Petrucka, P. (2013). Are 20th-century methods of teaching applicable in the 21st century? *British Journal of Educational Technology, 44*(4), 665–667. https://doi.org/10.1111/bjet.12032

Liberman, V., Samuels, S. M., & Ross, L. (2004). The name of the game: Predicting power of reputation versus situational labels in deterring prisoner's dilemma game moves. *Personality and Social Psychology Bulletin, 30*(9), 1175–1185.

Martinez-Estrada, P. D., & Conaway, R. N. (2012). E-books: The next step in educational innovation. *Business Communication Quarterly, 75*(2), 125–135. https://doi.org/10.1177/1080569911432628

Melé, D. (2003). The challenge of humanistic management. *Journal of Business Ethics, 44*, 77–78.

Melé, D. (2008). Integrating ethics into management. *Journal of Business Ethics, 78*(3), 291–297.

Minkes, J., & Minkes, L. (2008). *Corporate and white collar crime*. London: Sage.

Morin, E. (1986). *La Méthode 3 La connaissance de la connaissance*. Paris: Edition de Seuil.

OECD. (2014). *OECD competency framework*. http://www.oecd.org/careers/oecdcorecompetencies.htm

Palazzo, G., Krings, F., & Hoffrage, U. (2012). Ethical blindness. *Journal of Business Ethics, 109*(3), 323–338.

Pirson, M., & Turnbull, S. (2011). Toward a more humanistic governance model: Network governance structures. *Journal of Business Ethics, 99*(1), 101–114.

Reus, T., Ranft, A. L., Lamont, B. T., & Adams, G. L. (2009). An interpretive systems view of knowledge investments. *Academy of Management Review, 34*, 382–400.

Robin, B. R. (2018). *The educational uses of digital storytelling*. University of Houston, College of Education. http://digitalstorytelling.coe.uh.edu/archive

Rossouw, G. J. (2011). A global comparative analysis of the global survey of business ethics. *Journal of Business Ethics, 104*, 93–101. https://doi.org/10.1007/s10551-012-1257-y

Rouse, M. (2018). *What is chatbot?* http://searchcrm.techtarget.com/definition/chatbot

Saavedra, A., & Opfer, V. (2012). Teaching and learning 21st century skills: Lessons from the learning sciences. *A Global Cities Education Network Report*. New York: Asia Society. http://asiasociety.org/files/rand-0512report.pdf

Scott, W. R. (1992). *Organizations: Rational, natural and open systems*. Englewood Cliffs, NJ: Prentice-Hall.

Scott, C. L. (2015). *What kind of pedagogies for 21st century?* UNESCO.

Setò-Pamies, D., & Papaoikonomou, E. (2016). A multi-level perspective for the integration of ethics, corporate social responsibility and sustainability (ECSRS) in management education. *Journal of Business Ethics, 136*, 523–538. https://doi.org/10.1007/s10551-014-2535-7

Swanson, D. L. (2004). The buck stops here: Why universities must reclaim business ethics education. *Journal of Academic Ethics, 2*(1), 43–61.

United Nations Global Compact. (2007). *Principles for responsible management education*. Retrieved September 25, 2007, from https://www.unprme.org/resource-docs/PRMEBrochure2018.pdf

van den Bemt, V., Doornbos, J., Meijering, L., Plegt, M., & Theunissen, N. (2018). Teaching ethics when working with geocoded data: A novel experiential learning approach. *Journal of Geography in Higher Education, 42*(2), 293–310. https://doi.org/10.1080/03098265.2018.1436534

Vohs, K., Mead, K., & Goode, M. (2006). The psychological consequences of money. *Science, 314*, 1154–1156.

Waddock, S. (2007). Leadership integrity in a fractured knowledge world. *Academy of Management Learning & Education, 6*(4), 543–557.

Wilburn, K. (2008). A model for partnering with not-for-profits to develop socially responsible businesses in a global environment. *Journal of Business Ethics, 85*, 111–120.

Wilson, M. (2003). Corporate sustainability: What is it and where does it come from. *Ivey Business Journal, 67*(6), 1–5.

Winkler, R., & Soellner, M. (2018). *Unleashing the potential of chatbots in education: A state-of-the-art analysis*. Paper accepted and presented at the Academy of Management Annual Meeting, Chicago, IL.

Wymer, W., & Rundle-Thiele, S. R. (2017). Inclusion of ethics, social responsibility, and sustainability in business school curricula: A benchmark study. *International Review Public Nonprofit Mark, 14*, 19–34. https://doi.org/10.1007/s12208-016-0153-z

Developing Ethical Commitment Competence: Comparing Stakeholder, Disciplinary, and Regional Perspectives

Pablo Beneitone, Maria Yarosh, Margarete Schermutzki, and Elke Kitzelmann

1 Introduction

This chapter is based on the analysis of surveys conducted within the framework of Tuning project, a global initiative, which has been running worldwide for the last 18 years. The aim is to explore what the Tuning quantitative data can reveal about what different stakeholders in different regions think about the Ethical Commitment competence. Due to the same format of consultations in most of the Tuning projects, Tuning can be seen as a goldmine-producing comparable data from more than 118 countries in different continents, across a variety of disciplines and target groups.

Tuning projects have demonstrated that Ethical Commitment is one of the global competences—competences considered key for all higher education (HE) programs across the world, regardless of the area of specialization or geographical region (Beneitone & Bartolomé, 2014). Ethics is key if human dignity is to be at the core of management (Melé, 2016) and when cross-cultural differences are to be treated both appropriately and successfully (Dierksmeier, 2016), which makes ethics central for understanding how humanistic management can be adopted across cultural differences and operationalizing the theory of humanistic management to make it work in management practice in concrete business environments. From the point of view of educational programs and desired graduate profiles—which is the focus of the Tuning projects—Ethical Commitment Competence could be, in turn, (one of) the

P. Beneitone (✉) · M. Yarosh
University of Deusto, Deusto International Tuning Academy, Bilbao, Spain
e-mail: pablo.beneitone@deusto.es; mariayarosh@deusto.es

M. Schermutzki
Higher Education and Tuning Expert, Berlin, Germany

E. Kitzelmann
University of Innsbruck, Innsbruck, Austria
e-mail: iww@uibk.ac.at

© Springer Nature Switzerland AG 2020
R. Aguado, A. Eizaguirre (eds.), *Virtuous Cycles in Humanistic Management*,
Contributions to Management Science,
https://doi.org/10.1007/978-3-030-29426-7_3

Table 1 General overview of the Tuning projects mentioned in this chapter

Project	Geographical scope	Year of data collection
Tuning Latin America	Argentine, Bolivia, Brazil, Chile, Colombia, Costa Rica, Cuba, Ecuador, El Salvador, Guatemala, Hoduras, Mexico, Nicaragua, Panama, Paraguay, Peru, Uruguay and Venezuela	2005
Tuning Europe	Austria, Belgium, Bulgaria, Denmark, Estonia, France, Germany, Greece, Hungary, Iceland, Ireland, Italy, Latvia, Lithuania, Malta, Norway, Poland, Portugal, Romania, Slovakia, Slovenia, Spain, Sweden, The Netherlands, United Kingdom	2008
Tuning Russia	Russia	2011
Tuning China	China	2013
Tuning Africa	Algeria, Angola, Burkina Faso, Cabo Verde, Cameroun, Djibouti, Egypt, Eritrea, Ethiopia, Ghana, Ivory Coast, Kenya, Lesotho, Libya, Madagascar, Morocco, Mauritania, Nigeria, RDC, Rwanda, South Africa, South Sudan, Tanzania, Tunisia, Uganda	2015

Source: Tuning project materials

answer(s) educational institutions can opt for in order to respond to the new needs through systematic, justified, and targeted curriculum changes.

This chapter looks at the data on importance and achievement of Ethical Commitment Competence obtained in Latin America, Europe, Africa, and Asia, particularly in the Tuning projects where Business, Business Administration, Economics, or Management were one of the focus areas.[1] It does not cover the latest changes in the world. Therefore, a lot more research in the field is necessary to understand the role of this competence and the change of value through changing of political and economic situations (Table 1).

Obtained using the same type of instrument with exactly the same scales and variables, these data permit to gain certain insights into similarities, as well as peculiarities, in the views on Ethical Commitment as a generic competence held by major HE stakeholders (academics, students, graduates, and employers) in different parts of the world—regional perspectives, as well as by stakeholders from the sector of interest for the present publication—disciplinary perspectives.

With all the primary data collected within the Tuning projects, Tuning conceptual and methodological frameworks are outlined first. Next, methodological approach followed in the present chapter is presented. After this, two major sections focus on regional and disciplinary perspectives held by different stakeholder groups—academics, students, graduates, and employers—in relation to importance and perceived level of achievement of the Ethical Commitment Competence; and a third section comments on how these two types of perspectives complement each other.

---

[1] These were chosen in accordance with the general focus of the present publication.

The chapter closes with brief conclusions and some proposals for future research that can build on the Tuning data, deepening and broadening the currently available picture, as well as operationalizing it to enhance educational practice.

2 Tuning Projects as Data Collection Framework

During the past 30 years, higher education at global level has undergone considerable change, partly in response to a growing need for places, partly from increasing demands from employers for greater clarity with regard to what students have achieved, and partly as a consequence of trends in globalization and internationalization.

There is a recognition that in spite of their valuable differences, higher education systems faced common internal and external challenges related to the growth and diversification of higher education, the employability of graduates, the shortage of skills in key areas, the need to further encourage staff and student mobility, and, in the longer term, the desire to attract the best scholars from around the world in order to be leaders in different areas of research. The reforms required to cover all areas of higher education; this was true in Europe, and in many other contexts as well. The first Tuning project (2000) was developed as a structure based on working academics, in which they shared together in international but subject-based groups to deliberate how the Bologna reforms and aspirations could best be implemented. Tuning may have been initiated as a response to reform in one continent, but the methodology developed has since been used in many countries and continents where reform of higher education was being undertaken, where governments perceived useful a model of reform that encouraged participation from all levels of academics, which provided links with the world of work, and had authenticity in terms of the spirit of education in the country.

Some of the contexts of the different Tuning projects have been challenging in size (e.g., the continents of Europe, Latin America, and Africa); others have had challenges of complexity, tradition, lack of resource, and language—to mention only a few. In all cases, the richness of diversity has been a positive motivation for the work achieved. A spirit of sharing, listening to each other, respect for other ways of doing, and a willingness to understand, informed all Tuning projects large or small and is the underlying reason for their success.

The Tuning approach consists of a methodology to (re-)design, implement, and evaluate study programs and provides platforms for reference points at subject area level. These are relevant to make degrees comparable, transparent, and compatible. As mentioned above, this chapter builds on the empirical data derived from over 43,000 Tuning questionnaires, which can offer a number of insights on how the Ethical Commitment Competence is perceived by different stakeholders who (should) have a say in defining higher education programs in areas of interest for the present publication.

The primary data was collected in different Tuning projects as part of the consultation stage (described below), and, thus, Tuning methodology with its definitions of key concepts and instruments has formed the data collection conceptual and methodological framework. Conceptually, Tuning definitions of *competence, generic competences*, and *global competences* are of relevance here. So is the definition of *Ethical Commitment* Competence itself. From the point of view of the methodology, the first steps of the Tuning methodology for degree design and revision need to be briefly explained, with a particular focus on Tuning consultations and the Tuning consultation instruments.

2.1 Tuning Definitions of Concepts

In the Tuning experience, particularly in joint reflection on degree profiles, **competences** emerge as an important element which can guide the selection of what is appropriate from a wealth of possibilities. Several terms—capacity, attribute, ability, skill, and competence—are used in discussions about HE with an often interchangeable, and to some degree overlapping meaning. They all relate to the person and to what he/she is able to achieve and demonstrate; but they also have more specific meanings.

Different cultural contexts influence the understanding of *competence,* and this is especially important in relation to the extent to which *competence* is defined by cultural literacy involving group identities. In fact, there is such debate concerning the concept of competence that it is difficult to arrive at a definition capable of accommodating and reconciling all the different ways that the term is used (e.g., Delamare le Deist & Winterton, 2005). Therefore, it was considered important to have a shared understanding of the concept of competence in all the Tuning projects, which would be both concrete and broad enough not to alienate any project participants, all of whom come from different disciplinary and national/regional cultures.

As a result, in its definition of the concept of competences, Tuning has tried to follow an integrated approach, looking at capacities via a dynamic combination of attributes that together permit a competent performance. Competences and skills are interpreted as including knowing and understanding (theoretical knowledge of an academic field, the capacity to know and understand), knowing how to act (practical and operational application of knowledge to certain situations), and knowing how to be (values as an integral element of the way of perceiving and living with others and in a social context). Summing up, the definition of competence shared by all Tuning project participants is as follows: "Competences represent a dynamic combination of knowledge, understanding, skills and abilities" (González & Wagenaar, 2008: 17).

In the Tuning project, two different sets of competences have been focused on: firstly, those which could be relevant to any HE program and which are considered important by society at large. The Tuning term for them is that of **generic competences**. In a changing world where demands tend to be in constant reformulation, *generic competences* assume a greater importance. The second set, *subject-specific* *competences*, are those competences which are subject-area related. These are intimately related to the specific knowledge and practices of a field of study. They give identity and consistency to the particular degree program and permit graduates to join their selected professional community of practice.

Generic competences are equally important for ensuring graduates employability and gain even greater significance when graduates seek employment not hundred percent related to their academic specialization, either because they want to move into a new field of work or studies or because their chosen studies do not have a one-to-one correspondence in the labor market (an increasingly common situation, even in such "professional" fields as teacher education or medicine). Furthermore, generic competences are deemed to prepare graduates for their future role of global and responsible citizens.

While the concepts of *competence* and *generic competence* formed part of the Tuning methodology from the very start, the third concept of interest here—**global competences**—emerged later (Beneitone & Bartolomé, 2014) and has been created to distinguish some of the *generic competences* identified as key across different world regions. Thus, *global competences* are *generic competences* that are seen as relevant of all HE graduates, regardless not only of their chosen discipline, HE program, and area of specialization (true of all generic competences), but also regardless of the region where they are pursuing their HE degrees or can be expected to live and work after graduation (the distinctive feature of global competences). **Ethical Commitment** was identified by Beneitone and Bartolomé (2014) as 1 of 16 global competences.

Finally, it is also important to mention how *Ethical Commitment* Competence was defined in different Tuning projects. Table 2 comprises the exact wordings used in each Tuning project within the scope of the present chapter, and this already gives an idea that each project was free to emphasize different aspects of this competence, and it is the analyses carried out by Beneitone and Bartolomé (2014) that permitted to group all these different competences under the global label of *Ethical Commitment*.

To delineate the concept, project participants were invited to make use of institutional, disciplinary, regional, and/or international sources of their choice,

Table 2 Different phrasing of Ethical Commitment competence per Tuning project

Project	Competence formulation
Tuning Latin America	Ethical commitment
Tuning Europe	Ability to act on the basis of ethical reasoning
Tuning Russia	Ability to act on the basis of ethical reasoning
Tuning China	Ethical commitment and professional attitude
Tuning Africa	Ability to work professionally with respect to ethical values and commitment to Ubuntu

Source: Tuning project materials

and the outcomes of these reviews can be found in project publications.[2] At the same time, to ensure coherence and comparability, certain sources served as a starting point in Tuning project discussions. Namely, for the definition of many generic competences, Villa Sánchez and Poblete Ruiz' (2008) publication that appeared within the Tuning framework was used. The definition found there is as follows:

> Being positively inclined toward the moral good of oneself or of others (that is, toward everything that is good or tends toward the wholesomeness or realization of the individual) and perseverance in that moral goodness (Villa Sánchez & Poblete Ruiz, 2008: 226).

2.2   Tuning Methodology: Consultation and Its Instruments

Methodologically, Tuning proposes a sequence of well-defined steps that can be followed in order to design well-structured, socially relevant, learner-centered, comparable, compatible, and transparent HE programs (or redesign existing programs to ensure they meet these criteria). Of interest here are the first two steps: (1) agreeing among academics on the lists of competences relevant for degree profiles and (2) consulting these lists with different groups of stakeholders (academics, students, graduates, employers).

One of the first tasks in every Tuning project is **identification of generic competences** that should be developed in any program, and which are considered important by society in a particular context or region. Defining these competences is the responsibility of academics, in consultation with other stakeholders (employers, students, and graduates), and the process followed has been the same in all Tuning projects. The objective of the exercise is to place in the forefront of degree profiling the needs and the current priorities of a particular society.[3]

In 2000, Tuning Europe was the first project to define competences, later revised in 2008. Europe agreed a list of 31 generic competences. Tuning Latin America in 2005 defined 27 generic competences for any university degree in the region. The academics taking part in Tuning Russia agreed to have 30 generic competences, while in Tuning Africa 18 were defined, in both cases in 2011. In 2013 China defined a list of 33 generic competences. A comparison of these lists conducted recently by Beneitone and Bartolomé (2014) led to creation of the notion of *global competences*, as already mentioned above. To reiterate, each region/country proposed a different formulation, but the essence of the competence was essentially the same.

Once such lists are agreed among all academics who take part in a Tuning project (this involves a negotiation and consensus building among academics from different

---

[2]Awono Onana et al. (2014), Beneitone et al. (2007), Demchuk et al. (2013), González and Wagenaar (2003), Wagenaar, Gilpin, and Beneitone (2015).

[3]The same is done for subject-specific competences (these are agreed among academics participating in Tuning projects first, and consulted with a much wider group of academics, as well as with other stakeholders, next). However, this is beyond the scope of the present chapter and is not discussed here.

Table 3 General overview of the Tuning data used in this chapter

Project	Number of respondents				
	Academics	Employers	Students	Graduates	Total
Tuning Latin America	4558	1669	9162	7220	22,609
Tuning Europe	2041	879	2219	1948	7087
Tuning Russia	2220	1856	2479	2314	8869
Tuning China	307	482	474	485	1748
Tuning Africa	693	473	879	739	2784
Total of respondents:	9819	5359	15,213	13,206	43,579

Source: Tuning project materials

institutions, different subject areas, and often different countries), **Tuning consultations** are organized. Change and variety of contexts both require a constant check on social demands for degree profiles. This imperative underlines the need for consultation, and constant revision of information on adequacy. The language of competences could be considered more adequate for consultation and dialogue with groups not directly involved in academic life and can contribute to the necessary reflection for the development of new degrees and for permanent systems of updating existing ones.

The Tuning enquiries are addressed to students, academics, employers, and graduates, contacted by the academics participating in each Tuning project. The questionnaire consists of the list of generic competences identified in each region. For each competence, the respondents are asked to indicate (1) the **importance** of the competence, in his/her opinion, for work in their profession (*rating of importance*) and (2) the level of **achievement** of the competence that they estimate is reached as a result of taking their degree program (*rating of achievement*).[4] To indicate this, respondents are asked to use a scale of 1 (none) to 4 (strong). Finally, a third aspect is consulted with the respondents: the **ranking** of the five most important competences (*ranking of importance*). The competence that is ranked highest by a respondent in a survey is given five points; the second highest receives four points and so on, with one point allocated for the last in the selection. If the competence is not chosen as one of the five most important ones, its score in the ranking is zero.

Table 3 gives an overview of the 43,579 questionnaires with data on Ethical Commitment as a generic competence that were collected involving 70 countries around the world and that form the basis for the present exploration. How these data are built on in the present chapter is explained in the next section.

---

[4]The degree program on which academics consulted teach, which students consulted are close to graduating from, which graduates consulted finished recently, and from which employers consulted are known to recruit graduates.

3   Chapter Methodology

This chapter presents a descriptive analysis that brings together from different Tuning projects primary data related to the different stakeholders' perspectives on the Ethical Commitment Competence. More specifically, data from five major Tuning projects are included: Tuning Latin America, Tuning Europe, Tuning Russia, Tuning Africa, and Tuning China. The geographical scope permits to compare not only different regions but also different continents, although clearly not all major world regions are accounted for. Availability of comparable data was one major criterion for the selection of projects. The other criterion was whether subject are relevant for the current publication—Business, Business Administration, Economics, or Management—took part in the project. Both the criteria were met by the five projects, which determined the geographical scope of the present chapter.

The nature of the data available, in turn, and the possibilities for comparison the data comprise defined the approach. Namely, (1) all three variables—rating for importance and achievement and ranking for importance—could be compared across the regions; (2) views of the same four stakeholder groups—academics, students, graduates, and employers—could be compared across the regions; and (3) views of stakeholders representing the subject areas relevant for the current publication could be compared to those of all the stakeholders from the respective regions.

Section 4 is structured accordingly. First, regional pictures are presented and compared, using data from all stakeholder groups and all subject areas who participated in each of the five projects.[5] Second, perspectives of stakeholders directly representing subject areas of Business, Business Administration, Economics, and Management are focused on.[6] Third, the two analyses are compared, since it is always instrumental to see how views of representatives of a particular subject area compare to the general regional perspective.

Thus, methodologically speaking, it is the first time that Tuning data from different projects are brought together in an attempt to show how one global competence is seen in different regions by different stakeholder groups. Nonetheless, as any account based on descriptive analysis, this chapter will necessarily open many

---

[5]For Tuning Latin America: Architecture, Business Administration, Chemistry, Civil Engineering, Education, Geology, History, Law, Mathematics, Medicine, Nursing and Physics. For Tuning Europe: Business Administration, Chemistry, Educational Sciences, European Studies, History, Geology/Earth Sciences, Mathematics, Nursing, and Physics. For Tuning Russia: Ecology, Economics, Education, Environmental Engineering, ICT, Interpreting and Translation, Foreign Language Teaching, Law, Management, Social Work, Tourism. For Tuning Africa: Agricultural Sciences, Applied Geology, Civil Engineering, Economics, Higher Education Management, Mechanical Engineering, Medicine and Teacher Education. Tuning China: Business Administration, Civil Engineering, and Comparative Education.

[6]The differences in the names or scope of the subject areas reflect the priorities of higher education systems in each region, as well as the cultural-historical conventions (how higher education degrees in the area are conceptualized and referred to traditionally in each region).

more questions than it can provide answers to, which makes the *conclusion, limitations, and further research* section a non-negligent part of the chapter whole.

4 Ethical Commitment as a Generic Competence

4.1 Regional Perspectives

Table 4 shows a comparison between the five regions in relation to the importance and achievement given by the four stakeholders to Ethical Commitment. The gap between the level of importance and the level of achievement implies a complementary aspect to be considered in the comparative analysis.

In the area of "importance," it is significant that all the regions rated Ethical Commitment above 3, on a scale in which 3 is equivalent to Moderate and 4 to Strong. This means that this generic competence agreed by the participants in the different Tuning projects received backing and/or confirmation from those consulted. They considered that Ethical Commitment should really be included in the definition of a university degree in the different regions.

Table 4 Regional views on the importance and level of achievement, as well as the gap between importance and achievement of the Ethical Commitment as a generic competence

Region	Stakeholder/ respondent group	Importance		Achievement	Gap between importance and achievement
		Mean	Ranking		
Latin America	Academics	3.794	6/27	2.794	1.00
	Employers	3.763	4/27	3.006	0.76
	Students	3.688	7/27	3.093	0.60
	Graduates	3.726	7/27	3.134	0.59
Europe	Academics	3.137	17/31	2.398	0.74
	Employers	3.085	24/31	2.532	0.55
	Students	3.053	23/31	2.462	0.59
	Graduates	3.050	25/31	2.434	0.62
Russia	Academics	3.43	22/30	2.80	0.63
	Employers	3.35	24/30	2.91	0.44
	Students	3.26	20/30	2.99	0.27
	Graduates	3.27	28/30	2.95	0.32
Africa	Academics	3.26	5/18	2.48	0.78
	Employers	3.22	6/18	2.53	0.69
	Students	3.23	7/18	2.62	0.61
	Graduates	3.20	6/18	2.61	0.59
China	Academics	3.38	13/33	2.56	0.82
	Employers	3.34	15/33	2.78	0.56
	Students	3.36	20/33	2.82	0.54
	Graduates	3.39	21/33	2.82	0.57

Another important aspect of the rating of importance is the comparability of the results within each region. It is clear that the four groups consulted in the different regions rated Ethical Commitment with a high level of correlation. This means that there is a high degree of compatibility among the four groups with regard to the level of importance given.

The average in importance is clearly higher for the four groups in Latin America. Europe is the lowest region in terms of mean of importance of Ethical Commitment, while Africa, Russia, and China are in an intermediate position (Graph 1).

The use of a second variable (ranking of importance) in analyzing the data collected has made it possible to verify the consistency of the information gathered. If we examine the table above, we again see a high level of coincidence among the four groups as it was shown with regard to the importance. This means that there was a high degree of compatibility among the four groups with regard to the ranking given to Ethical Commitment, with slightly less compatibility in the case of Europe, Russia, and China, and a particularly high correlation in Latin America and Africa.

In terms of achievement, it is worthy of mention that Ethical Commitment is rated between 2 and 3 on a scale in which 2 is equivalent to Weak and 3 to Moderate. Only students, graduates, and employers in Latin America rated its achievement over 3.

Lower scores were given for the level of achievement, indicating a good level of criticism and demand among those surveyed. The mean for *achievement* is normally lower than the mean for *importance*. But of course, the gap between both means is relevant as it shows how far both means are. It is quite relevant to compare the gap between regions and stakeholders. If we analyze the table in terms of the mean of importance, the order that is followed is more linked to the regions (this implies that the four stakeholders are grouped in relation to the region of belonging). When the

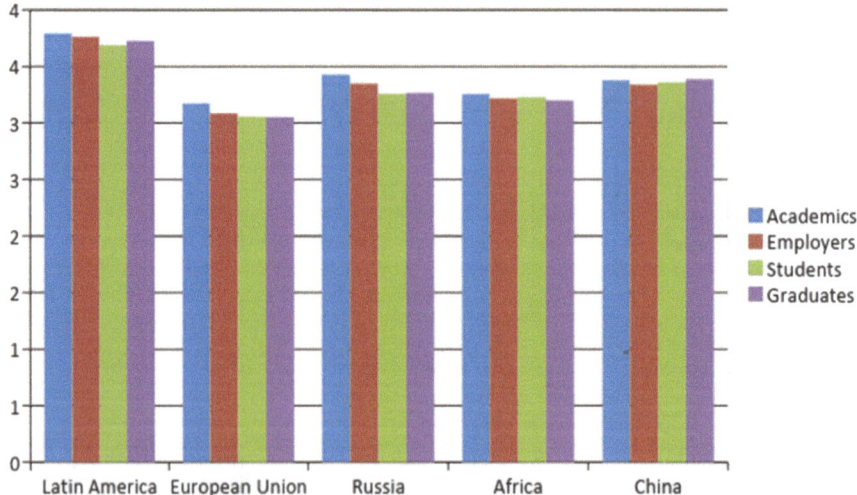

Graph 1 Regional views on the importance of the Ethical Commitment as a Generic Competence: comparing ratings of importance within projects

gaps are analyzed, the order that is produced is more associated with the stakeholders than with the regions (e.g., academics from all the regions analyzed are at the top of the gap).

4.2   Disciplinary Perspectives

At its heart Economics, Management, and Business Administration are dealing with production, distribution, and consumption of goods and value chain. The central theme is striving to resolve a basic contradiction between infinite human needs and limited resources to meet them.

Data collected during various Tuning consultations also permits us to speak of how Ethical Commitment, as a Generic Competence, is seen by stakeholders from the disciplines of Business, Economics, Management, and Business Administration, from different regions of the world. More specifically, such data is available for Latin America (Business Administration), China (Business), Africa (Economics), and Russia (Economics, Management).

Speaking of the perceived importance of Ethical Commitment from the disciplinary perspective (Table 5), four points appear worth making. Firstly, as can be seen in column "Rating (mean)," all groups of respondents from all the regions rate importance of Ethical Commitment Competence above 3 (out of 4), which does not happen for all the competences consulted. This suggests that Ethical Commitment is considered an important competence by academics who teach on undergraduate programs in Business Administration, Economics, and Management: students who are enrolled in these programs, as well as these programs' alumni ("graduates" in Tuning terminology) and employers who hire these graduates.

Secondly, comparing the means from the "same" groups of respondents (e.g., all academics, all employers, etc.) reveals certain regional differences, as well as patters (see Graph 2). Thus, for academics, university teachers from Latin America value the Ethical Commitment Competence the most (3.756), followed by their colleagues from China (3.52). Academics from the Management degrees in Russia are closer to the lower end of this continuum (3.38), while their counterparts teaching on programs in Economics—be it in Russia or in Africa—close the range (3.28).

For employers, the Latin American respondents are the most interested in students developing the Ethical Commitment Competence (3.751), followed by those from Russia—Management (3.42)—and China (3.41), with employers of Economics' graduates once again occupying the lowest position (Russia, 3.31; Africa, 3.21).

Students and graduates from Russia appear to value the Ethical Commitment Competence the least (in this sample), with African students and graduates close to them. The top position is once again occupied b y Latin American respondents (both in the case of students and in the case of graduates), with Chinese students and graduates situated between the two poles (slightly closer to Latin American respondents).

Thus, Latin American respondents could be said to value the Ethical Commitment Competence the most, regardless of the stakeholder group we look at (also

Table 5 Disciplinary views on the importance and level of achievement of the Ethical Commitment as a generic competence[a]

Region, discipline (year of consultation)	Number of respondents from the discipline	Stakeholder (number of respondents)	Importance		Achievement (mean)
			Rating (mean)	Ranking	
Latin America, Business Administration (2005)	8421	Academics	3.756	6/27	2.911
		Employers	3.751	4/27	3.016
		Students	3.667	9/27	3.088
		Graduates	3.703	5/27	3.181
China, Business (2013)	542	Academics	3.52	6/33	2.42
		Employers	3.41	10/33	2.80
		Students	3.39	25/33	2.71
		Graduates	3.58	15/33	2.89
Africa, Economics (2015)	1149	Academics	3.28	5/18	2.46
		Employers	3.21	7/18	2.54
		Students	3.18	4/18	2.66
		Graduates	3.32	5/18	2.60
Russia, Economics (2011)	1980	Academics	3.28	26/30	2.67
		Employers	3.31	24/30	2.75
		Students	3.16	28/30	2.85
		Graduates	3.0566	27/30	2.7821
Russia, Management (2011)	815	Academics	3.38	24/30	2.75
		Employers	3.42	22/30	2.97
		Students	3.16	26/30	2.84
		Graduates	3.10	27/30	2.89

[a]Data analysis in the case of Europe 2008 consultation on generic competences did not go to the level of particular subject areas. Therefore, the results of European region could not be included here

confirmed by the highest media across stakeholder group for this region—3.719). African and Russian respondents "take turns" in occupying the lowest position or share it (the lowest means across stakeholder groups are those of Russia, Economics (3.20), Africa (3.248), and Russia, Management (3.265)), while Chinese respondents most often find themselves in the second position (with mean across stakeholder group of 3.475), with the only exception of employers, where respondents from the Russian Management group are slightly above them.

It might also be interesting to comment on the difference in the answers of stakeholders from Economics and Management groups in Russia. Although coming from the same country and from two closely related disciplinary fields (in some countries "Economics and Management" is a single first-cycle degree), their responses are not always in the "same" position as compared to colleagues from other parts of the world. While for students and graduates the responses of the two Russian groups are closer to each other than to answers given by those consulted in other regions, Russian academics from Economics degrees and those employing Economics' graduates in Russia are closer to their colleagues from Africa than to

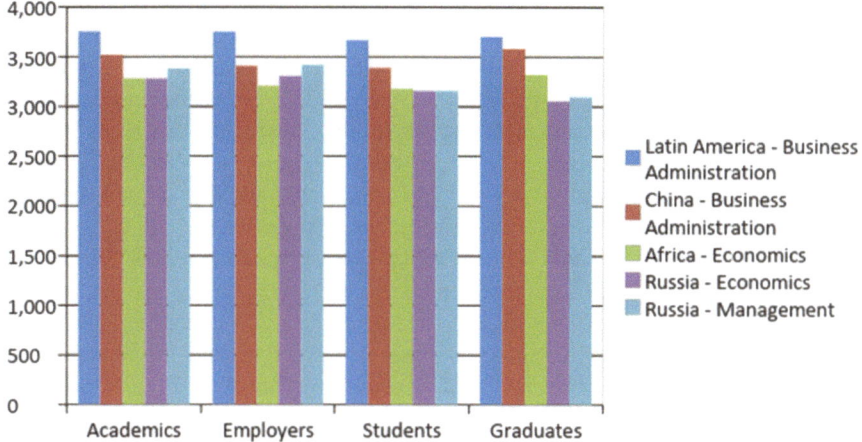

Graph 2 Disciplinary views on the importance of the Ethical Commitment as a Generic Competence: comparing ratings within groups of respondents

Table 6 Disciplinary views on the importance of the Ethical Commitment as a generic competence: relative position in importance among all generic competences consulted (in terms of the top/middle/bottom third and the exact position—e.g., first of the 27 for Academics in Latin America)

Stakeholders/ Region	Latin America	China	Africa	Russia (Economics)	Russia (Management)
Academics	Top third (1/27)	Top third (5/33)	Middle third (7/18)	Bottom third (21/30)	Middle third (18/30)
Employers	Top third (1/27)	Top third (10/33)	Bottom third (13/18)	Middle third (18/30)	Middle third (16/30)
Students	Top third (6/27)	Middle third (12/33)	Bottom third (13/18)	Bottom third (15/30)	Bottom third (23/30)
Graduates	Top third (4/27)	Top third (8/33)	Middle third (9/18)	Bottom third (25/30)	Bottom third (24/30)

their Russian counterparts from Management degrees/employing graduates of these programs.

Thirdly, the relative position of the Ethical Commitment Competence, in terms of rating, in the list of generic competences consulted in each region gives further insights (Table 6). Once the means for importance are calculated for each generic competence consulted, it is possible to sequence all the generic competences and see whether the rating given to the Ethical Commitment Competence places it among the most important ones, in the middle third, or among the competences perceived as the least important.

In this sense, the Ethical Commitment Competence is placed in the first third of the continuum in terms of importance by all the Latin American respondents, with academics and employers giving it the very first position. In China, it is situated in the second third if we consider academics', employers', and graduates' responses, and in the beginning of the lowest third for Chinese Students. For Africa, the Ethical Commitment Competence is found in the second third for academics and graduates, and at the top of the lowest third for employers and students. For Russian Economics respondents, the Ethical Commitment Competence is closer to the down edge of the second third for employers and in the lowest third for the other stakeholder groups. Finally, for Russian Management respondents, it is in the middle third for academics and employers, and in the lowest third for students and graduates.

Reading Table 6 at the level of stakeholder groups, we can see that academics from Latin America and China value the Ethical Commitment Competence most, followed by academics from Africa and Russian Management program, with academics from Russian Economics program place this competence in the lowest third. For employers, Latin American and Chinese respondents value the Ethical Commitment Competence most, Russian employers (of both Economics and Management graduates) place in the middle third, while African employers ascribe it the least importance. For students, Latin American respondents place the Ethical Commitment Competence in the top third, Chinese respondents—in the middle third, while all Russian and African students place this competence in the lowest third. For graduates, Latin American and Chinese respondents value the Ethical Commitment Competence most, African graduates place in the middle third, while Russian graduates (both those who completed a degree in Economics and those who did Management) situate this competence in the lowest third.

We can also observe that academics nearly always value the Ethical Commitment Competence higher than the other stakeholder groups, with the exception of Russia, where employers value it most, while academics are in the second position. Similarly, students, regardless of the region, seem to value this competence the least, with the only exception of the students who are enrolled in the Management degrees in Russia and who value the Ethical Commitment Competence slightly higher than the graduates of the same program. There is a greater variation in the employers' attitudes across regions: they are among the stakeholders who value the Ethical Commitment Competence the most in Latin America and Russia, but are in the third position only in China and Africa (with the third position being the last one in case of Africa).

For graduates, it can be observed that they tend to value the Ethical Commitment Competence less that students (in Latin America, China and Africa), with the exception of Russia, where for the Economics respondents the results are exactly the same for graduates and students, while for the Management respondents graduates place the competence slightly lower in importance than students do.

Fourthly, the ranking column of Table 5 completes the picture of "importance" of the Ethical Commitment Competence Tuning data can give. More specifically, comparing "Ranking" column of Table 5 with the data of Table 6, it is interesting to observe whether respondents place the competence higher/lower in importance when ranking—as compared to rating—or whether there is no significant difference. Thus, in Latin America, the Ethical Commitment Competence is ranked lower than it is rated. This is the case for all groups of respondents, even though the data are within the same top third of the continuum. In China, employers rank and rate the competence exactly the same; academics rank it slightly lower, while students and graduates rank the Ethical Commitment dramatically lower. In Africa, on the contrary, Ethical Commitment is ranked considerably higher by all respondents than it is rated: for academics and graduates, there is a change from the middle third to the top third, for employers—from lowest third to the middle third and for students—from bottom third to the top third. In Russia, ranking results are lower than the rating means, with sometimes a change of the third where the competence is placed (for employers of Economics and academics and employers of Management—with a descent from the mid-third to the lowest one).

The last column of Table 5 ("Achievement (mean)" column) contains the data for achievement, the third variable across all Tuning consultations (after rating and ranking, which both speak of the competence importance). Two aspects are of interest here: the mean for the perceived level of achievement as such (Table 5 data) and the difference between importance and achievement (Table 7).

First of all, the level of achievement is lower than the importance, which is common for all Tuning studies, but is still indicative. Table 5 shows as well that all stakeholders in all the regions believe that the Ethical Commitment is not developed to the highest level possible: the results are below three in most cases, with the only exception of Latin America, where employers, students, and graduates place it slightly above three.

As for the gap between importance and achievement (Table 7), the most visible finding here is that academics perceive this gap to be the largest. Looking at the "Mean per respondent category" column, we can note that employers also perceive quite a big gap, while students and graduates are more satisfied or perhaps less aware of the discrepancy. In terms of the regions, Chinese respondents seem to be the most critical ones, with consultation participants from Africa and Latin America being somewhat more positive (the gap they perceive is smaller), and Russian respondents closing the continuum as the most satisfied groups in the current sample.

To close this section, it can also be observed that in Latin America—the region where respondents ascribe the highest importance to the Ethical Commitment Competence—the perceived level of achievement is also the highest.

Table 7 Gap between mean of rating of importance and achievement across regions and stakeholder groups

Respondents/ Region	Latin America	China	Africa	Russia (Economics)	Russia (Management)	Mean per respondent category
Academics	0.845	1.1	0.82	0.61	0.63	0.801
Employers	0.735	0.61	0.67	0.56	0.45	0.605
Students	0.579	0.68	0.52	0.31	0.32	0.482
Graduates	0.522	0.69	0.72	0.27	0.21	0.482
Mean per region/project	0.67	0.77	0.68	0.44	0.40	

4.3   Comparing Regional and Disciplinary Perspectives

A potentially interesting angle of analysis is that of comparing the results in a region on the whole with the perspectives of respondents who come from the Business/ Business Administration/Economics/Management area in particular (comparing the data featured in Table 4 with those in Table 5). Such comparison could indicate how opinions of students, graduates, employers, and academics from these subject areas are different from what emerges at the level of the region in general. In the Tuning sample, however, the differences are minimal, and no clear patterns could be observed. For example, for Latin America the mean of importance is slightly less if only Business Administration data are considered, but the importance remains high—above 3.6 for all stakeholder groups. Similarly, in Africa, the rating of importance for Economics is slightly less than for the region on the whole, but is still above 3, with the exception of Economics graduates, who value the Ethical Commitment Competence slightly more than graduates of another program consulted. For China, the rating of importance results is slightly higher for all respondents in Business than the regional average, while in Russia it depends on the stakeholder group and the "shifts" observed are different for Economics and Management respondents.

The same uneven picture emerges for ranking of importance, which, depending on the stakeholder group, is sometimes exactly the same for the region on the whole and for the subject area group in particular (e.g., academics and employers in Latin America or academics in Africa or graduates in Management in Russia), sometimes decreases slightly (e.g., students in Latin America and China or employers in Africa), and sometimes increases slightly (e.g., students and graduates in Africa or employers in Management in Russia) or somewhat more visibly (e.g., academics, employers and graduates in China). Nonetheless, there is no single region where all stakeholders from the subject areas of interest here behave in the same way if compared to their respective region on the whole. Neither is there one single stakeholder group whose behavior can be described in exactly the same way when comparing regional and subject area data.

In terms of achievement, the following similarities can be observed, although the differences are too small to speak conclusively of strong patterns. Firstly, all respondents from Russian Economics are more critical of the perceived level of achievement of Ethical Commitment. Second, academics and students from Business, Business Administration, Economics, or Management groups in most regions are more critical than the total body of the respondents in the regions. Academics in Latin America and students in Africa are the only exceptions here—these two subgroups of respondents from subject area groups are more positive of the level of Ethical Commitment Competence development than the total body of respondents for the two regions. Finally, employers from the subject areas in question are more satisfied with the level of Ethical Commitment achieved by graduates in all regions except for Russia. These observations could be indicative of certain peculiarities of the degree program in question. Yet, to reiterate, the numerical differences are very small and should probably not be treated as revealing any definite patterns. More so, since comparison of the gap between means for importance and means for achievement seem to suggest other possible patterns. Thus, the gap is consistently smaller for all stakeholder groups in Latin America and consistently bigger across all stakeholder groups in China, while stakeholders in Russia do not fall under the same pattern, and neither does any stakeholder group across the regions for which the data is available.

5 Conclusions, Limitations, and Further Research

This chapter has tried to draw as a complete picture as possible of what Tuning data can tell us in terms of stakeholder, disciplinary, and regional perspectives on the importance and development of the Ethical Commitment Competence, with a particular focus on respondents from program in Business, Business Administration, Economics, and Management. However, as mentioned above, no data were collected specifically for this chapter, and the characteristics of the data available determined a number of limitations, which need to be acknowledged and which clearly indicate possible lines of further research.

First of all, the Tuning primary data this chapter builds on were collected in different regions at different moments and in one of the cases (Latin America) it happened more than 10 years ago. This means that more recent data need to be collected to update the analyses, and, in an ideal scenario, these will be collected simultaneously in all the regions.

Secondly, although the data reported come from four different continents—Latin America, Europe, Africa, and Asia—some key world regions are missing. None of the South-East Asian countries could be reported on and neither could India (their consultations have just finished or are currently underway). Nor are comparable data available, for example, for the USA. This, again, calls for additional data collection in order to further complete the picture in terms of geographical scope.

Thirdly, the data analyses reported in this chapter permits to formulate a number of hypotheses, which can guide further research and data collection initiatives (be it updating the data for the same regions or adding data from new regions). For example, available Tuning data suggest that Ethical Commitment comes forward as a very important competence for a graduate of any HE program in any country. All the stakeholders—academics, students, graduates, and employers—are unanimous of this opinion. Tuning data available today also indicate that there are no significant differences among stakeholder groups or regions. It will be interesting to test these hypotheses in further research—with new data and possibly additional data collection instruments and procedures.

Fourthly, further research is needed on the possible changes of the relevance of Ethical Commitment (and other competences) through political changes (e.g., trade war and other changes).

At a more general level, at least three more lines of further research seem both promising and desirable. To start with, qualitative research can be conducted to see how the Ethical Commitment Competence was contextualized in different regions and subject area groups and to analyze the processes associated with instrumentalizing the competence when incorporating it in concrete degree profiles and curriculum mapping. On the other hand, a separate study can look at the lists of subject-specific competences and see how the Ethical Commitment element appears or does not appear there and how subject-specific competences related to ethics feature in the consultations. Finally, similar studies can be strongly recommended for other global competences that might contribute to Humanistic Management Education.

References

Awono Onana, C., Bandele Oyewole, O., Teferra, D., Beneitone, P., González, J., & Wagenaar, R. (Eds.). (2014). *Tuning and harmonisation of higher education: The African experience.* Bilbao: University of Deusto.

Beneitone, P., & Bartolomé, E. (2014). Global generic competences with local ownership: A comparative study from the perspective of graduates in four world regions. *Tuning Journal for Higher Education, 1*(2), 303–334.

Beneitone, P., Esquetini, C., González, J., Marty Maletá, M., Siufi, G., & Wagenaar, R. (Eds.). (2007). *Reflections and outlook for higher education in Latin America.* Bilbao: University of Deusto.

Delamare le Deist, F., & Winterton, J. (2005). What is competence? *Human Resource Development International, 8*(1), 27–46.

Demchuk, A., Dyukarev, I., Karavaeva, E., Beneitone, P., González, J., & Wagenaar, R. (Eds.). (2013). *Towards comparability of higher education programmes: Information review.* Bilbao: University of Deusto.

Dierksmeier, C. (2016). What is 'humanistic' about humanistic management? *Humanistic Management Journal, 1*(1), 9–32.

González, J., & Wagenaar, R. (Eds.). (2003). *Tuning educational structures in Europe. Final report. Phase one.* Bilbao: University of Deusto.

González, J., & Wagenaar, R. (Eds.). (2008). *Universities' contribution to the Bologna process: An introduction* (2nd ed.). Bilbao: University of Deusto.

Melé, D. (2016). Understanding humanistic management. *Humanistic Management Journal, 1*(1), 33–55.

Villa Sánchez, A., & Poblete Ruiz, M. (Eds.). (2008). *Competence-based learning: A proposal for the assessment of generic competences.* Bilbao: University of Deusto.

Wagenaar, R., Gilpin, A., & Beneitone, P. (Eds.). (2015). *Tuning in China: An EU-China feasibility study into the modernisation of higher education.* Bilbao: Deusto University Press.

Part II
Humanistic Management

Integral Human Development Through Servant Leadership and Psychological Androgyny

Alejandro Amillano, Josune Baniandrés, and Leire Gartzia

1 Introduction

Humanistic management has emerged as a movement that aims at transferring humanistic principles to the management of organisations, promoting in business respect of human dignity, the consideration of ethical implications and corporate responsibility for a sustainable dialogue with the different stakeholders (Melé, 2016). This approach is closely associated with the concept of integral human development (IHD) and the broader consideration of human dignity as an essential factor for human development (Velisario, 2017). From this perspective human dignity is understood as a key element and requires that organizations are not only willing to provide individuals with development in relation to material dimensions (access to goods and services), but also in relation to the necessary social and cultural conditions for human development (see Melé, 2016).

Considering the diverse range of needs of human beings in organizations, including, for instance, the need of self-actualization, the promotion of appropriate human relations or the development of leadership styles that generate motivating workplaces, is a condition of human dignity (see Maslow, Frager, & Cox, 1970). As Retolaza, Aguado, and Alcaniz (2018) pointed out, however, previous economic theories have only partially incorporated this approach. From this perspective of integral human development, it has been suggested that 'firms that are engaged with preservation and promotion of human dignity will not simply offer decent jobs and salaries to their employees, but also will generate the necessary conditions for the

A. Amillano (✉)
Faculty of Psychology and Education, University of Deusto, Bilbao, Spain
e-mail: alejandro.amillano@deusto.es

J. Baniandrés · L. Gartzia
Deusto Business School, University of Deusto, Bilbao, Spain
e-mail: josune.baniandres@deusto.es; leire.gartzia@deusto.es

© Springer Nature Switzerland AG 2020   57
R. Aguado, A. Eizaguirre (eds.), *Virtuous Cycles in Humanistic Management*,
Contributions to Management Science,
https://doi.org/10.1007/978-3-030-29426-7_4

entire group of stakeholders to achieve self-actualization through their professional engagement with the firm' (Aguado, Retolaza, & Alcaniz, 2017, p. 10).

The aim of this chapter is to complement insights in this field by incorporating a critical psychological perspective focused on two particular antecedents of individual orientations towards common good in organizations: psychological androgyny and servant leadership. We argue that promoting a common good orientation in organizations is contingent on these two interrelated orientations. Servant leadership—a leadership style that is oriented to common good through service to others (Greenleaf, 1977)—has been consistently related to multiple positive behaviours and outcomes in organisations (see Van Dierendonck, 2011 for a review; see also Liden et al., 2015). Servant leadership also comprises a set of behaviours typically displayed at managerial that have been argued to be determined by levels of psychological androgyny (see Barbuto & Gifford, 2010; Gartzia, Amillano, & Baniandrés, 2016; Reynolds, 2011)—defined as the integration of both stereotypical masculine and feminine features, beyond gender roles associated with men and women. Our approach bridges these literatures, which have evolved in relatively separate dynamics, and provide support for an integrative approach of human development that takes into account how these two key dimensions are inherently associated with the development of common good in organizations. In short, we argue that androgyny is a necessary psychological variable for a common good orientation, and servant leadership is a specific behavioural approach through which such a common good approach can be implemented and have actual effects in organizations.

In the following pages, we provide detailed reviews about the servant leadership and psychological androgyny literatures as well as their connections, viewing them as potential antecedents of humanistic management and common good orientations at work. By underscoring the relevance of androgyny for psychological orientations towards common good and presenting servant leadership as a useful set of leadership behaviours through which such orientations can be materialized, we pave the way for new connections between the literature on integral human development and these more social and psychological dimensions of organizational behaviour. We conclude by pointing out how this approach can be a starting point to integrate insights from these different approaches and underscore some specific challenges that might be relevant for future research in the field.

2 Androgyny: A Psychological Condition for Common Good

Androgyny is generally defined as a combination of stereotypical masculinity (agency) and femininity (communion), considered on the level of behaviour, values, interests or personal orientation, as well as personality traits or identity features (see Bozionelos & Bozionelos, 2003; see also Bem, 1974). Agency and communion are important concepts in the notion of androgyny as they refer to basic dimensions about how humans see themselves and others in relation to both interpersonally oriented dimensions—communal or stereotypically feminine traits—and self-oriented dimensions, agentic or stereotypically masculine traits (Bakan, 1966). The agency dimension is based on the search for one's own benefit (Abele & Wojciszke, 2007) and represents stereotypical masculinity comprising traits such as 'independent', 'active' and 'self-confident' (Spence & Helmreich, 1980). For its part, the communion dimension, which is based on the search for benefit for others (Abele & Wojciszke, 2007), represents stereotypical femininity dimensions and qualities that capture interpersonally oriented traits such as 'kind' or 'aware of others' feelings (Spence & Helmreich, 1980).

In particular, what is known as 'psychological androgyny' (Bem, 1974) refers to the combination of stereotypically masculine and feminine personality features or traits. Broadly speaking, a person's psychological androgyny level depends on the extent to which his or her personality contains a series of features associated with both stereotypically masculine and feminine features, which requires overcoming gender roles and stereotypes about one's identity and behaviour. From this approach, a common good perspective would only be feasible if individuals are able to combine their agentic (self-oriented) and communal (other-oriented) orientations. In the androgyny literature, however, there is a major debate regarding the agency-communion combination that better defines psychological androgyny as well as their specific effects on health, well-being and behaviour (see Taylor & Hall, 1982 for a review; see also Ward, 2000).

Importantly, different models and perspectives can be found in relation to how both dimensions (communion and agency) contribute to different outcomes, such as generating more effective responses in the organisation or providing common good. For instance, the original concept put forward by Sandra Lipsitz Bem (1974) states that individuals with balanced levels of stereotypically masculine and feminine would be considered 'androgynous', irrespective of whether they obtain high or low scores in both dimensions. Later on, Spence, Helmreich, and Stapp (1975) propose differentiating between those representing high levels of stereotypical masculinity and femininity (androgynous) and low levels in both dimensions (undifferentiated). These complexities are described below and outlined in Table 1.

2.1   Additive or Main Effects Model

On the one hand and as described by Hall and Taylor (1985) in a complete review following the first years studying psychological androgyny, the additive or main effect model is taken into consideration, facilitated by the view introduced by Spence et al. (1975). This model considers the effects caused by the combination of stereotypical masculinity and femininity to be the result of adding the independent effects of both dimensions to the dependent variables being studied. In other words, the effects of androgyny are calculated by adding the effects of stereotypical

Table 1 Main androgyny models described in the literature

Additive or main effects model (Spence et al., 1975)	Differentiated additive model or main effects model dependent on domain[a] (Marsh & Byrne, 1991)
Balance model (Bem, 1974)	Emergent properties model (Hall & Taylor, 1985)

[a]Determined type of 'additive model' or its specific formulation that incorporates the assumption of 'dependence on domain' of the effects of pyschological androgyny

C communion, A agency

Source: Elaborated by authors

masculinity and femininity. In this respect, Marsh and Byrne (1991) also showed that the effects of each androgyny dimension might be dependent on the domain or dependent variable being studied in relation to the self-concept or its different facets, as well as being independent of each other. In the study conducted by the aforementioned authors, stereotypical masculinity helped predict certain aspects of the self-concept linked to other specific aspects different from that construct (Marsh & Byrne, 1991).

From the introduction to this conceptualization, a large proportion of those who defend the additive androgyny model incorporate the assumption that communion and agency have effects on different or specific facets of the self-concept. A distinction may be drawn between dependent variables of different types—some associated with communion and others associated with agency. Thus, from this assumption a certain type of additive model is constituted known as the differentiated additive androgyny model, which has a major repercussion on the literature (see, e.g. Ward, 2000). Specifically, it is important to point out the way in which this variety of additive model has tended to be related to the phenomenon of leadership and other types of behaviour in organizations. In this respect, some models referring to group and types of leadership behaviour that draw certain parallels with the differentiated structure of communion and agency that make up psychological androgyny need to be briefly reviewed. On the one hand, Parsons and Bales (1955; see also Bales, 1951) distinguish instrumentality from expressiveness as being two types of function that the members of a group may perform. Thus, instrumental functions would be 'oriented at good adaptation and optimal goal fulfilment of the group as part of a larger social system' (Abele & Wojciszke, 2007, p. 751). For their part, expressive functions would be 'directed at coherence, solidarity, and harmony within the group' (Abele & Wojciszke, 2007, p. 751). These functions are clearly distinguished in terms of types of leadership behaviour that are geared to a larger extent to one group function or another. Likewise, the leadership model proposed by different authors within the context of Ohio State University (see, e.g. Halpin & Winer, 1952; see also Stogdill & Coons, 1957), distinguish between task-oriented types of behaviour (or 'initiating structure') and individual-oriented types of behaviour (or 'consideration'). In other words, the first type of behaviour focuses on organization of work and is associated with group functions such as providing clear objectives to followers, whereas the second is related to aspects such as care and support for those followers via interpersonal relations with them (see Dansereau, Seitzb, Chiuc, Shaughnessyd, & Yammarinoe, 2013 for a review). Similarly, different authors of relevant leadership models (see, e.g. Hersey & Blanchard, 1974; see also Blake & Mouton, 1964) integrate this dual structure. Other recent leadership models such as transformational leadership style integrate dimensions such as what is referred to as individualized consideration, which clearly reflects the expressive dimension of behaviour.

In short, two dimensions associated with the concepts of communion and agency are observed, and these would be present in different forms at each different level of analysis, ranging from the most in-depth analysis of personality or identity traits to the most superficial level of behaviour. Korabik and Ayman (1987) explain this idea as follows: Bem (1974) sees the integration of these dimensions as taking place within the individual personality with the proportional representation of traits on each dimension representing the degree to which a person is sex-typed. Bales (1951), on the other hand, is interested in the representation of instrumental and expressive attributes within the small group and with the subsequent effects on group functioning. A small group, however, is composed of individual personalities and whether certain characteristics will be expressed in the group is a function of whether they exist in the individual members. Individuals who have been socialized to possess instrumental or expressive qualities will be likely to adopt either instrumental or expressive roles in group settings. Thus, if one takes an interactionist perspective, one would expect the concepts of androgyny and leadership style to be conceptually related (Korabik & Ayman, 1987, p. 1), given that communion and agency are related, respectively, with expressive and instrumental functions of leadership on a group level. From the explanation given by the same authors, it can be deduced that both dimensions—communion and agency—would supposedly be connected via the different levels mentioned. In this respect, leadership processes and group behaviour in organizations offer a scenario regarding this approach and the models described that is inclined towards the application of differentiated additive androgyny. Thus, different studies conducted within the organizational context that are referred to in the following section attempt to contrast whether stereotypical masculinity is related to instrumental behaviour or that of initiating structure, and whether stereotypical femininity is related to expressive behaviour or that of consideration. In this way, androgyny (stereotypical masculinity and femininity) would be related to the development of both types of behaviour and, therefore, to the performance of both group functions by the leader. Although this relation might appear evident and therefore of limited empirical interest, social psychology and specifically group psychology and the study of situational leadership models (see e.g. Hersey & Blanchard, 1974) show that traits and attitudes or aptitudes are not the only predictors of leadership behaviour (see House & Aditya, 1997 for a review). In other words, the development of certain roles or leadership styles is conditioned by a series of situational variables such as the possibility of expressing the aptitudes or features themselves of followers (Hersey & Blanchard, 1974; House & Aditya, 1997). Hence, an empirical contrast of the additive hypothesis dependent on domain which is considered in different studies regarding different dependent variables types of behaviour associated with communion or agency has a relevant function in clarifying relations and existing effects between the level of personal traits and behaviours.

2.2 Balance Model

From Bem's original conceptualization (1974), androgyny is viewed in other studies as referring to the balance between identifying masculine and feminine traits via the balance model (see Hall & Taylor, 1985). The effects of androgyny on the dependent variables taken into consideration would in this case result from that balance. Thus, this model sets out the fact that 'androgynous' subjects would evidence better conditions than subjects who are identified with a markedly masculine or feminine gender (sex-typed), without being concerned with the level of stereotypical masculinity or femininity in which the balance is found. In this way, individuals who are greatly identified with masculine or feminine traits and individuals with a low score in both dimensions would evidence a similar degree of androgyny, and we would therefore find similar levels in the dependent variables studied.

2.3 Emergent Properties Model

The two different models described in the previous paragraphs (additive model and balance model), which are mistakenly considered to be opposing or incompatible in some literature, conversely consider two independent hypotheses which are fully compatible and complementary to each other, as explained by Taylor and Hall (1982). This fact leads these same authors (Hall & Taylor, 1985) to define a new model known as the emergent properties model, which integrates both hypotheses or androgyny models. In this case, the effects of each dimension—i.e. agency and communion—and the effects of the balance between the levels of both dimensions, are taken into consideration separately. Greater effects emerge which are attributed to androgyny as emergent properties in cases in which stereotypical masculinity and femininity converge, being closely identified in both cases.

2.4 Studies on Androgyny and Its Effects on Leaders and Their Followers

As regard studies that analyse the effect of a combination of communion and agency—or androgyny—on different styles or types of behaviour of the leader, we find different approaches associated with the above-mentioned androgyny models. In sum, significant and positive relationships has been evidenced among psychological androgyny and diverse leaders' features and behaviours such as a broader range of leadership styles and behaviours (Korabik, 1981, 1982a, 1982b; Korabik & Ayman, 1987; see also Gartzia & Van Engen, 2012), rational emotive behaviour (Srivastava & Nair, 2011), higher levels of consideration in terms of leadership style Korabik and Ayman (1987), higher level of transformational leadership (Kark, Waismel-Manor, & Shamir, 2012), highest levels of conflict management integrative style (Brewer, Mitchell, & Weber, 2002) or higher levels of emotional intelligence (Gartzia, Aritzeta, Balluerka & Barberá, 2012).

Furthermore, there are very few studies that more specifically contrast the effects of androgyny of the leader on organizational outcomes via their followers. Thus, psychological androgyny of leaders has been shown as significantly and positively related to leadership effectiveness (Jurma & Powell, 1994; Kark et al., 2012; Srivastava & Nair, 2011), better quality decisions (Kirchmeyer, 1996) and personal effectiveness (Maheshwari & Kumar, 2008). Nonetheless, other studies have been conducted that fail to confirm the advantage of androgyny explained in terms of leadership effectiveness (Baril, Elbert, Maher-Potter, & Reavy, 1989; Korabik & Ayman, 1987). The existence thus far of major limitations in operationalizing and measuring androgyny (see Ward, 2000; see also Hall & Taylor, 1985) provides a plausible explanation for these inconsistencies found in the literature on the subject. In relation with servant leadership, and from a developmental and humanistic perspective, a particular conception of psychological androgyny is presented in the following pages. Thus, considering the integration of agency and communion as a consistent result of a person's development process (and discerning it from other forms of combination of both dimensions) may contribute to understand psychological androgyny and to state the adequate framework for the empirical analysis of its effects.

3 Servant Leadership

Servant leadership 'begins with the natural feeling that one wants to serve, to serve first. Then conscious choice brings one to aspire to lead' (Greenleaf, 1977, p. 7). This is how Robert Greenleaf (1977) coins the term that describes the phenomenon of leading towards the common good via service to others (Page & Wong, 2000). For his part Dirk Van Dierendonck (2011) integrates different ways of operationalizing servant leadership (e.g. Barbuto & Wheeler, 2006; Spears, 2003) by proposing six basic features of it: empowering and developing people, humility, authenticity, interpersonal acceptance, providing direction and stewardship.[1]

Servant leadership emerges as a phenomenon that meets the needs of current organizations as shown recent studies that evidence the link between servant leadership and different outcomes on an individual, team and organizational level (see Van Dierendonck, 2011 for a review; see also Liden et al., 2015). Furthermore, servant leadership has been proposed as an integrative style from a gender perspective (Reynolds, 2011), mostly as for the integration of agency and communion within it. In this sense, one the one hand, Barbuto and Gifford (2010) classify each of the servant leadership dimensions based on the model put forward by Barbuto and Wheeler (2006) as types of behaviour associated with communion or agency. Thus, the three dimensions[2] associated with the altruistic calling of the leader, their capacity to provide emotional healing where necessary and their commitment to the well-being of the community of which they form a part, would be related to communion in these authors' opinion (Barbuto & Gifford, 2010). In contrast, the same authors also maintain that the two remaining dimensions of the model that represent the wisdom of the leader and their capacity for persuasive mapping via an inspiring vision of the future would to a greater extent be related to the idea of agency.[3] Notwithstanding the aforementioned, these links between the different service leadership dimensions and communion or agency are not empirically contrasted in the study carried out by the authors referred to here (Barbuto & Gifford, 2010).

Likewise, in accordance with the servant leadership put forward by Spears (2002), Reynolds (2011) suggests distinguishing between dimensions which are especially linked to stereotypical masculinity and others to stereotypical femininity. Specifically, this points to the fact that the dimensions related to listening, empathizing, healing, serving the needs of others, exercising commitment to the growth of people

---

[1]Original names in English of the six dimensions: 'Empowering and developing people', 'humility', 'authenticity', 'interpersonal acceptance', 'providing direction' and 'Stewardship' (see Van Dierendonck, 2011).

[2]Original names in English of the dimensions referred to: 'altruistic calling', 'emotional healing' and 'organizational stewardship' (see Barbuto & Wheeler, 2006).

[3]Original names in English of the dimensions referred to: 'wisdom' and 'persuasive mapping' (see Barbuto & Wheeler, 2006).

Table 2 Summary of the relationship existing between the servant leadership dimensions and agency and communion

General servant leadership model (Van Dierendonck, 2011)	PAQ (Spence, Helmreich, & Stapp, 1974)
'Empowering and developing people'	Communion
'Humility'	Communion
'Authenticity'	Agency and communion
'Interpersonal acceptance'	Communion
'Providing direction'	Agency
'Stewardship'	Communion

and building community[4] are markedly *feminine* in nature. Dimensions linked to the capacities of the servant leader with regard to foresight, conceptualization, awareness and persuasion are in turn associated with stereotypical masculinity, according to the arguments set out by this author.[5]

Along these lines, Table 2 shows the results of the authors' own analysis that attempts to replicate the classification made by the aforementioned authors from the definitions of servant leadership dimensions provided by the general servant leadership model put forward by Van Dierendonck (2011).

As for agency and communion definitions are based on traits included in the PAQ (Spence et al., 1974). Like the classifications made by the aforementioned authors (Barbuto & Gifford, 2010; Reynolds, 2011), the presence of agency and communion may be observed via a definition of their dimensions based on the models referred to, although it is noted in this case that most dimensions of these models are mainly associated with communion.

In short and as described in the literature on the subject (Reynolds, 2011; see also Barbuto & Gifford, 2010) and expanded on in this section, it can be argued by studying different descriptions of servant leadership style that communion and agency form part of the same. It should be pointed out that this reasoning has been based on the *additive* androgyny model and specifically on the *differentiated additive* model that has already been explained. However, as noted in the introduction to this section, the integration of agency and communion into types of servant leadership behaviour may be formulated in another way, in keeping with a more complex understanding of androgyny that takes into consideration interaction effects between the two dimensions. This is described in greater detail in the following section via the literature on the role of agency and communion in the role of personal development and their relationship with servant leadership.

---

[4]Original names in English of the dimensions referred to: 'listening, empathising, healing, practicing stewardship (serving the needs of others), exercising commitment to the growth of people and building community' (Reynolds, 2011, p. 158; see also Spears, 2002).

[5]Original names in English of the dimensions referred to: 'foresight, conceptualization, awareness and persuasion' (Reynolds, 2011, p. 157; see also Spears, 2002).

4 Other Connections of Androgyny and Servant Leadership with Personal Development

People—that is human beings—are transformed throughout their life via psychological (e.g. Piaget, 1926; see also Erikson, 1956), moral (e.g. Kohlberg, 1969; see also Gilligan, 1982) or spiritual (e.g. Loder, 1998; see also Oser, 1991) development processes. As we have shown with our review of the psychological androgyny and servant leadership literatures, human development in organizations is also inherently linked to these two concepts, which bring relevant outcomes and orientations in organizations. In a relevant publication about servant leadership, Dirk Van Dierendonck (2011) determines three individual features for the development of servant leadership: self-determination, cognitive moral development and cognitive complexity. Van Dierendonck (2011) considers self-determination to be an essential condition for an individual to be able to act as servant leader and as a result of having met the basic needs of feeling competent, linked to others and separate. Thus, 'a self-determined person will be better in the use of personal resources, in building strong and positive relationships, and in helping others develop their self-determination. Therefore, instead of exerting power by controlling and directing people in an authoritarian way, self-determined leaders are able to work from an integrated perspective where power is not sought for its own sake' (Van Dierendonck, 2011, p. 1245). Van Dierendonck (2011) also explains the way in which an individual who has reached the highest states of moral development associated with a person's vital development and age will be more inclined to start behaving like a servant leader (Van Dierendonck, 2011). Finally, cognitive complexity would provide other capacities needed to develop a vision of a reality compatible with servant leadership (Van Dierendonck, 2011).

The three individual features described by Van Dierendonck (2011) can be seen as backgrounds to servant leadership and are in turn related to the maturing and personal development process of the leader (see, e.g. Kohlberg, 1969; see also Loevinger, 1976). Empirical evidence regarding the positive relationship existing between a leader's age and their tendency to develop servant leadership as recently described by Diehl (2015) is consistent with this relationship, and Beazley (2002) also finds a positive significant relationship between servant leadership and spirituality. Along the same lines, the PhD work by Boyer (1999) studies the relationship between certain key moments in life and the development of servant leadership in the case of men by discovering a pattern of experiences involving common vital development. In short, the literature on the subject shows a clear link between various aspects associated with different human or personal development processes and servant leadership.

Additionally, a review of the literature on androgyny in terms of the personal development process shows that the integration of agency and communion as basic guidelines for humankind plays a major role in this growth process. The idea of integrating masculine and feminine polarities as a phenomenon linked to an advanced state of development of the individual forms part of the traditional knowledge of different cultures and religions (see, e.g. Eliade, 1965). This approach has also been defended by major figures from the history of psychology such as Carl Gustav Jung, who, as Boyer (1999) explained, maintained that 'the full development of an individual (. . .) involves the surfacing, acceptance and expression of (rather than the projection of)' (Boyer, 1999, p. 41) the dimension (stereotypical masculinity or femininity) associated with the opposite sex. A large proportion of the main classic psychology models associated with human development (Erikson, 1956; Freud, 1992; Loevinger, 1976; Piaget, 1926) combine the need of all individuals to achieve a sense of their own identity, differentiation and personal independence with the need to develop their capacity to establish relationships and become integrated within a larger system. The evolutionary psychology models cited previously combine a part of development that is geared to the development of the individual themselves as an independent, separate entity from the rest and which facilitates identification via agency-based traits, with another part that is geared towards developing their capacity to establish relationships and become integrated within a large system, linked to identification of communion-based traits. Along these lines, the work by Bursik (1995) and Prager and Bailey (1985) show a positive relationship between the level of development of the self (see Erikson, 1956; see also Loevinger, 1976) and androgyny.

Note that development of individuals themselves as independent, separate entities from the rest—which is implicit in agency-related traits such as *independent*—also play an essential role in developing a suitable, healthy development of behaviour linked to communion. Thus, communion-related behaviour like the establishment of relationships with others, or in particular behaviour associated with help, needs to be integrated with aspects of the agency dimension that will enable the individual to maintain basic conditions such as one's mental health, independence or self-concept. Otherwise, some negative effects might arise from the resulting self-abandonment of unmitigated communion or lack of agency. Indeed, a certain sequentiality can be observed in the prior development of individualizing aspects and the subsequent development of aspects linked to communion, although such a sequence is considered more or less clearly, cyclically, or as being overlapped or interspersed successively depending on the theoretical model used (see, e.g. Erikson, 1956; Freud, 1992; Loevinger, 1976). Likewise, some of the main theories about moral development (e.g. Gilligan, 1982; Kohlberg, 1969) show a transition on the part of the individual from an individualistic orientation towards stances which are more closely connected with others. From this approach it is considered that types of behaviour linked to communion and emerging from the individual's psychological or moral development to be a suitable means for increasingly integrating agency elements (see Loevinger, 1976; see also Gilligan, 1982).

In this respect, the moral development model put forward by Carol Gilligan (1982) is especially illustrative of the aforementioned transition, as well a s he need on the part of the individual to integrate orientation or care towards themselves and towards others. This model emerges from criticism of the model proposed by Kohlberg (1969), which is anchored in a masculine view—according to the author—that pitches the ethics of care against the ethics of justice (see Gilligan, 1982, 1985).

A stance towards paying attention to the self would prevail during the first phase of the development process, which would subsequently be seen as being egoistical as it evolves into a phase involving connection with others linked to self-sacrifice, to end up in a phase that includes both the self and others in which care shown to both parties is well-balanced (Gilligan, 1982, 1985). Thus, suitable functioning of the individual would imply the integration of agency and communion, and it is to be hoped that any difficulties or shortcomings in evolutionary development will be linked to imbalanced, non-integrated personal traits and types of behaviour associated with negative (stereotypical) masculinity or femininity concepts or unmitigated agency and communion via aspects such as personality and attachment style (Helgeson & Fritz, 1998). It should be pointed out that there is evidence to suggest the apparently paradoxical combination of such negative dimensions, i.e. unmitigated agency and communion (Woodhill & Samuels, 2003) or the asymmetrical relationship between agency and community (see, e.g. Bozionelos & Bozionelos, 2003) as mentioned previously, thus reflecting the possible variety of androgynous forms of identification that can be deemed to be more or less positive for the individual and their behaviour.

Fundamental types of servant leadership behaviour such as serving others require the integration of attention to others linked to communion and care for the self linked to agency in order to be suitably developed and sustainable over time and to produce positive outcomes in both individuals and organizations. In this respect, as described by Greenleaf (2003) himself, different authors have tended to emphasize the distinction between servant leadership and other phenomena such as complacency—this difference being precisely owing to the fact that the latter is typical of unmitigated communion. In contrast, the integration of agency and communion would characterize the person as servant-leader. Thus, the description provided by Greenleaf (2003), as Reynolds (2016, p. 29) explains, maintains that 'the person who is by impulse a servant first and chooses not to take on the leadership role (...), is complacent'. Complacency should hence be interpreted by a lack of agency or the existence of unmitigated communion (see Helgeson and Fritz, 1998). Likewise, Van Dierendonck (2011) highlights the fact that servant leadership 'does not imply an attitude of servility in the sense that the power lies in the hands of the followers or that leaders would have low esteem' (Van Dierendonck, 2011, p. 1231), phenomena which are associated with unmitigated communion (Helgeson & Fritz, 1998).

In short, the literature on the field shows the relevance of the identity-shaping process via the identification of certain agentic traits (e.g. independent, self-confident) and communal traits, in addition to the integrative functioning of both dimensions at a motivational and behavioural level. Thus, both dimensions are related from earlier, more evolutionary phases to more advanced phases in the personal development and maturing process throughout the entire vital process, thus causing individual difficulties in terms of the level of integration they attain (see, e.g. Gilligan, 1982). Walker and Frimer (2015) recently studied the integration of agency and communion with regard to personal development by taking into consideration its true nature as the outcome of developing a major moral level: 'agency and communion may function dualistically for most people, but exemplars have overcome the tension by integrating their personal ambitions with their moral concerns. This suggests that the end-point goal for moral motivation is the integration of agency and communion in a form of enlightened self-interest. Morality can and should be self-regarding if it is to have motivational oomph (Walker, 2013)' (Walker & Frimer, 2015, p. 416). Hence, the individual who attains an advanced state of personal development will have integrated the search for their own good via the search for good for others and the common good. They will thus meet their own needs via service to others and the common good. These authors also find a link between this integration of agency and communion and people's age, considering this to be related to a person's vital development without disregarding individual differences (Walker & Frimer, 2015). At the same time and as explained in the previous section, these authors found that as the person's age increases, so does the presence of communion as a *terminal motive* accompanied by agency as an *instrumental motive*, coinciding with findings from previous studies (Frimer, Walker, Lee, Riches, & Dunlop, 2012).

Following these approaches, it can be seen that agency as an instrumental motive customarily permits and characterizes communion-oriented efforts and behaviour as a terminal motive, especially in the case of profiles with a high degree of personal and moral development such as those associated with servant leadership. Likewise, it is important to note that, in accordance with the model put forward by Gilligan (1982), communion typical of this high level of development would correspond to the third level of development which, unlike the previous level, should not be confused with self-sacrifice and caring for oneself and others. This integrated way of functioning coincides with the description of servant leadership types of behaviour (Van Dierendonck, 2011) explained previously. Similarly, the so-called *altruistic component* of servant leadership described by Barbuto and Gifford (2010), according to whom this would explain the reduction in gender barriers regarding the exercising of leadership, reflects the existence of communion as a *terminal motive* behind this leadership style. Servant leadership types of behaviour geared towards the empowerment or *accountability* of workers (see Van Dierendonck, 2011) are associated with communion in terms of their ultimate goal (to foster the collaborators' development) and may evidence behaviour linked to agency traits associated with their instrumental motives (e.g. not to give in easily when faced with difficulties that arise in the course of their collaborators' development or to be sufficiently self-assured to delegate major tasks).

These arguments highlight the existence of a type of integrated or androgynous functioning based on the integration of agency and communion via complex relations involving interaction between them. Hence, in contrast to that set out by the additive or main effects model, each dimension is needed to ensure the smooth running of the other in this case. A person might be highly identified with communion traits yet conversely not produce the positive outcomes expected (or at least not be able to maintain them over time), but rather have negative effects—at least for their own health and well-being (see Helgeson & Fritz, 1998; see also Woodhill & Samuels, 2003). On the other hand, the same agency would be needed to lead by communion, especially within certain contexts, by expressing the personal independence required and withstanding the pressure which leading in this way entails in many organizations, as shown in some studies described previously. Any analysis of types of servant leadership behaviour shows an association with both androgyny dimensions—agency and communion. Likewise, the properties of this leadership style that have been explained point towards genuine integration of the two dimensions that transcends their mere combination in terms of behaviour.

To conclude, all the arguments set out in this section clarify discrimination between a type of psychological functioning that combines agency and communion traits in an integrated manner as a result of a positive development process and its effects on behaviour, of the separate effects of each dimension and of other types of non-effective combination of elements from both of them (see Woodhill & Samuels, 2003). Thus, the limitations of the different models and methodology used to study androgyny that have been developed so far are made clear with a view to grasping the complex relations existing between them. In line with this, Hall and Taylor (1985) highlight the importance of discriminating the true nature of a *positive* type of androgyny beyond the mere coexistence of stereotypical masculinity and femininity in individual identity, in the following the words: 'we join Kaplan (1979) in urging attempts to develop more direct measures of integration, adaptability, and flexibility, the qualities claimed to exist among those who avoid narrow sex-role definition' (Taylor & Hall, 1982, p. 363; see also Martin, Cook, & Andrews, 2016). As argued in this section, servant leadership is a good example of behaviour that results from the genuine integration of both dimensions in the psychological functioning of the leader.

5 Concluding Remarks

In conclusion, this work shows some evidence in the literature that support the consideration of psychological androgyny and servant leadership as interrelated resources valuables for promoting integral human development in the organizational context. The literature on servant leadership has provided some relevant insights about how different components of this leadership style are related to higher states of psychological, moral and spiritual development. In the same way, the literature shows communion and agency as two basic psychological dimensions of human beings associated with richer human development processes, linking positively the level of integration of both dimensions (psychological androgyny) with richer human development (psychological, moral and spiritual). These developments match the theoretical concepts of 'integrality' of human beings and its development as a distinctive element of the integral human development literature (Velisario, 2017).

At an applied level, promoting common good orientations at work seems to be inherently linked to the development of more complex and creative responses from employees and leaders, as well as a richer understanding of the psychological determinants of such responses. First, given the specific connections of these dimensions of human development to servant leadership, this leadership style can be a particularly relevant concept to build an integrative approach of humanistic management. Servant leadership has not only been associated with employees' development, personal-realization and empowerment (see Van Dierendonck, 2011 for a revision) but also with the promotion of a 'servant culture' or behavioural tendencies in the organization (Liden, Wayne, Liao, & Meuser, 2014). In the same way, servant leadership serves to promote justice orientations (see Reynolds, 2016; see also Ferch, 2004). From this perspective, servant leadership can undoubtedly be important for the development of common good orientations in organizations that serve for integral human development.

Another challenge that organizations face to develop common good orientations is how to promote individual identities and behaviour that will incorporate a healthy integration of communal and agentic traits. As we have explained, generating positive environments that actually serve for the common good—such as servant leadership orientations from people who make decisions in organizations—involves deeper transformations into people's identities and the actual integration of communion and agency, which derives from a holistic personal development process. From a gender perspective, such positive integration of communal and agentic traits and behaviours requires challenging gender roles and implicit theories about leadership anchored in gender stereotypes, thus facilitating a model of change among employees that is aligned with gender equality actions and the integral development of men and women in organizations. Likewise, psychological androgyny, in its relation with servant leadership and IHD, is coherent with the consideration of the common good as the main goal of the firm, as it is stated by Christian Social Thought (CST; Aguado et al., 2017) as explained in the introduction of this chapter. In short, a feasible and realistic development of the common good requires integrating communion and agency in a transformative individual process of those who are leading the organization. Future research would benefit from more further investigating these questions with empirical studies that incorporate objective measures of common good and empirically test their connections to integral human development, leadership and gender traits. Such approach can productively complement analyses of these associations within the organization (e.g., in relation to internal processes and employees' attitudes) and outside the firm (e.g., in relation to other stakeholders). The latter approach is a particularly worthy endeavour if we take into account that relevant approaches in economic theory such as Stakeholder Theory (Freeman, 1984) has not paid sufficient attention to how organizations could be places whereby a common good approach is the main objective of the firm ('in relation with the principle of universal destination of goods'; see Retolaza et al., 2018, p. 2) or the consideration of human dignity as the base of human development at work (Aguado et al., 2017). Extending these approaches, our work brings new ideas about the contributing role of social and organizational psychology in envisioning ways to promote such necessary transformation towards the common good and integral human development inside and around organizations.

References

Abele, A. E., & Wojciszke, B. (2007). Agency and communion from the perspective of self versus others. *Journal of Personality and Social Psychology, 93*(5), 751–763. https://doi.org/10.1037/0022-3514.93.5.751

Aguado, R., Retolaza, J. L., & Alcaniz, L. (2017). Dignity at the level of the firm: Beyond the stakeholder approach. In M. Pirson & M. Kostera (Eds.), *Dignity and the organization*. London: Palgrave Macmillan.

Bakan, D. (1966). *The duality of human existence*. Reading, PA: Addison-Wesley.

Bales, R. F. (1951). *Interaction process analysis: A method for the study of small groups*. Chicago: University of Chicago Press.

Barbuto, J. E., & Gifford, G. T. (2010). Examining sex differences of the servant leadership dimensions: An analysis of the agentic and communal properties of the servant leadership questionnaire. *The Journal of Leadership Education, 9*(2), 4–21.

Barbuto, J. E., & Wheeler, D. W. (2006). Scale development and construct clarification of servant leadership. *Group and Organization Management, 31*(3), 300–326. https://doi.org/10.1177/1059601106287091

Baril, G., Elbert, N., Maher-Potter, S., & Reavy, G. (1989). Are androgynous managers really more effective? *Group and Organization Studies, 14*(2), 234–249. https://doi.org/10.1177/105960118901400210

Beazley, D. A. (2002). *Spiritual orientation of a leader and perceived servant leader behavior: A correlational study*. Doctoral dissertation. Minneapolis, Walden University.

Bem, S. L. (1974). The measurement of psychological androgyny. *Journal of Consulting and Clinical Psychology, 42*(2), 155–162. https://doi.org/10.1037/h0036215

Blake, R. R., & Mouton, J. S. (1964). *The managerial grid*. Houston: Gulf Publishing Company.

Boyer, G. B. (1999). *Turning points in the development of male servant-leaders*. Unpublished doctoral dissertation, The Fielding Institute.

Bozionelos, N., & Bozionelos, G. (2003). Instrumental and expressive traits: Their relationship and their association with biological sex. *Social Behavior and Personality, 31*(4), 423–429. https://doi.org/10.2224/sbp.2003.31.4.423

Brewer, N., Mitchell, P., & Weber, N. (2002). Gender role, organization status, and conflict management styles. *International Journal of Conflict Management, 13*(1), 78–94. https://doi.org/10.1108/eb022868

Bursik, K. (1995). Gender-related personality traits and ego development: Differential patterns for men and women. *Sex Roles, 32*(9/10), 601–615. https://doi.org/10.1007/BF01544214

Dansereau, F., Seitzb, S. R., Chiuc, C.-Y., Shaughnessyd, B., & Yammarinoe, F. J. (2013). What makes leadership, leadership? Using self-expansion theory to integrate traditional and contemporary approaches. *The Leadership Quarterly, 24*(6), 798–821. https://doi.org/10.1016/j.leaqua.2013.10.008

Diehl, S. (2015). *A gendered view of servant leadership*. Doctoral dissertation. Indiana University of Pennsylvania.

Eliade, M. (1965). *Mephistopheles and the androgyne* (J. M. Cohen trans.). New York: Sheed and Ward. https://doi.org/10.1177/000306515600400104

Erikson, E. H. (1956). The problem of ego identity. *Journal of the American Psycoanalytic Association, 4*(1), 56–121. https://doi.org/10.1177/000306515600400104

Ferch, S. R. (2004). Servant-leadership, forgiveness, and social justice. In L. C. Spears & M. Lawrence (Eds.), *Practicing servant leadership: Succeeding through trust, bravery, and forgiveness*. San Francisco, CA: Jossey-Bass.

Freeman, R. E. (1984). *Strategic management: A stakeholder approach*. Boston, MA: Pitman.

Freud, S. (1992). *Introducción del Narcisismo*. En S. Freud, *Obras Completas de Sigmund Freud*. (Vol. 14, pp. 65–98). Buenos Aires: Amorrortu editores.

Frimer, J. A., Walker, L. J., Lee, B. H., Riches, A., & Dunlop, W. L. (2012). Hierarchical integration of agency and communion: A study of influential moral figures. *Journal of Personality, 80*(4), 1117–1145. https://doi.org/10.1111/j.1467-6494.2012.00764.x

Gartzia, L., & Van Engen, M. (2012). Are (male) leaders 'feminine' enough? gender traits of identity as mediators of sex differences in leadership styles. *Gender in Management, 27*(5), 295–314. https://doi.org/10.1108/17542411211252624

Gartzia, L., Amillano, A., & Baniandrés, J. (2016). Women in Industrial Relations: Overcoming Gender Biases. In M. C. Euwema, L. Munduate, P. Elgoibar, E. Pender, & A. B. García (Eds.), *Building trust and constructive conflict management in industrial relations. Human resources management and constructive conflict management.* The Netherlands: Springer.

Gartzia, L., Aritzeta, A., Balluerka, N., & Barberá, E. (2012). Inteligencia emocional y género: más allá de las diferencias sexuales. *Anales de Psicología, 28*(2), 567–575. https://doi.org/10.6018/analesps.28.2.124111

Gilligan, C. (1982). *In a different voice: Psychological theory and women's development.* Cambridge, MA: Harvard University Press.

Gilligan, C. (1985). *La moral y la teoría: Psicología del desarrollo femenino.* México D.F: Fondo cultural económico de México.

Greenleaf, R. K. (1977, 2002). *Servant leadership: A journey into the nature of legitimate power and greatness.* Mahwah, NJ: Paulist Press.

Greenleaf, R. K. (2003). The servant as leader. In H. Beazley, J. Beggs, & L. C. Spears (Eds.), *The servant-leader within: A transformative path* (pp. 31–74). Mahwah, NJ: Paulist Press.

Hall, J. A., & Taylor, M. C. (1985). Psychological androgyny and the masculinity X femininity interaction. *Journal of Personality and Social Psychology, 49*(2), 429–435.

Halpin, A., & Winer, B. (1952). *The leadership behavior of the airplane commander.* Columbus: Ohio State University.

Helgeson, V. S., & Fritz, H. L. (1998). A theory of unmitigated communion. *Personality and Social Psychology Review, 2*(3), 173–183. https://doi.org/10.1207/s15327957pspr0203_2

Hersey, P., & Blanchard, K. H. (1974). So you want to know your leadership style? *Training and Development Journal, 28*(2), 22–37.

House, R. J., & Aditya, R. N. (1997). The social scientific study of leadership: Quo vadis? *Journal of Management, 23*(3), 409–473. https://doi.org/10.1177/014920639702300306

Jurma, W. E., & Powell, M. L. (1994). Perceived gender roles of managers and effective conflict management. *Psychological Reports, 74*(1), 104–106. https://doi.org/10.2466/pr0.1994.74.1.104

Kaplan, A. G. (1979). Clarifying the concept of androgyny: Implications for therapy. *Psychology of Women Quarterly, 3*(3), 223–230. https://doi.org/10.1111/j.1471-6402.1979.tb00539.x

Kark, R., Waismel-Manor, R., & Shamir, B. (2012). Does valuing androgyny and femininity lead to a female advantage? The relationship between gender-role, transformational leadership and identification. *Leadership Quarterly, 23*(3), 620–640. https://doi.org/10.1016/j.leaqua.2011.12.012

Kirchmeyer, C. (1996). Gender roles and decision-making in demographically diverse groups: A case for reviving androgyny. *Sex Roles, 34*(9), 649–663. https://doi.org/10.1007/BF01551500

Kohlberg, L. (1969). Stage and sequence: The cognitive developmental approach to socialization. In D. Goslin (Ed.), *Handbook of socialization theory and research.* Chicago: Rand McNally.

Korabik, K. (1981, marzo). *Androgyny and leadership: An integration.* Comunicación presentada en 'the annual meeting of the Association for Women and Psychology, Boston, MA'. (ERIC Document Reproduction Service ED208-274).

Korabik, K. (1982a). Sex-role orientation and leadership style. *International. Journal of Women's Studies, 5*, 328–336.

Korabik, K. (1982b, agosto). *Sex-role orientation and leadership: Further explorations.* Comunicación presentada en 'the annual meeting of the American Psychological Association, Washington, DC'. (ERIC Document Reproduction Service ED223-963).

Korabik, K., & Ayman, R. (1987, agosto). *Androgyny and leadership style: A conceptual synthesis.* Comunicación presentada en 'the annual meeting of the American Psychological Association, New York, NY'. (ERIC Document Reproduction Service ED291-032).

Liden, R. C., Wayne, S. J., Liao, C., & Meuser, J. D. (2014). Servant leadership and serving culture: Influence on individual and unit performance. *Academy of Management Journal, 57*(5), 1434–1452. https://doi.org/10.5465/amj.2013.0034

Liden, R. C., Wayne, S. J., Meuser, J. D., Hu, J., Wu, J., & Liao, C. (2015). Servant leadership: Validation of a short form of the SL-28. *The Leadership Quarterly, 26*(2), 254–269. https://doi.org/10.1016/j.leaqua.2014.12.002

Loder, J. E. (1998). *The logic of the spirit: Human development in theological perspective.* San Francisco: Jossey-Bass.

Loevinger, J. (1976). *Ego development: Conceptions and theories.* San Francisco: Jossey-Bass.

Maheshwari, N., & Kumar, V. (2008). Personal effectiveness as a function of psychological androgyny. *Industrial Psychiatry Journal, 17*(1), 39–45.

Marsh, H. W., & Byrne, B. M. (1991). Differentiated additive androgyny model: Relations between masculinity, feminity, and multiple dimensions of self-concept. *Journal of Personality and Social Psychology, 61*(5), 811–828. https://doi.org/10.1037/0022-3514.61.5.811

Martin, C. L., Cook, R. E., & Andrews, N. C. Z. (2016). Reviving androgyny: A modern day perspective on flexibility of gender identity and behavior. *Sex Roles. First on-line:* marzo, 2016. https://doi.org/10.1007/s11199-016-0602-5

Maslow, A. H., Frager, R., & Cox, R. (1970). In J. Fadiman & C. McReynolds (Eds.), *Motivation and personality* (Vol. 2). New York: Harper & Row.

Melé, D. (2016). Understanding humanistic management. *Humanistic Management Journal, 1*(1), 33–95. https://doi.org/10.1007/s41463-016-0011-5

Oser, F. I. (1991). The development of religious judgment. Religious development in childhood and adolescence. *New Directions for Child Development, 1991*(52), 5–25. https://doi.org/10.1002/cd.23219915203

Page, D., & Wong, P. T. P. (2000). A conceptual framework for measuring servant leadership. In E. S. Adjibolooso (Ed.), *The human factor in shaping the course of history and development* (pp. 69–109). Lanham, MD: American University Press.

Parsons, T., & Bales, R. (1955). *Family, socialization, and interaction processes.* Glencoe: Free Press.

Piaget, J. (1926). *The language and thought of the child.* New York: Harcourt Brace and Company.

Prager, K., & Bailey, J. (1985). Androgyny, ego development, and psychosocial crisis resolution. *Sex Roles, 13*(9–10), 525–536. https://doi.org/10.1007/BF00287759

Retolaza, J. L., Aguado, R., & Alcaniz, L. (2018). La Teoría del Stakeholder a través del Pensamiento Social Cristiano 2018. *Journal Business of Ethics.* https://doi.org/10.1007/s10551-018-3963-6

Reynolds, K. (2011). Servant-leadership as gender-integrative leadership: Paving a path to gender-integrative organizations through leadership education. *Journal of Leadership Education, 10*(2), 155–171.

Reynolds, K. (2016). Servant-leadership: A feminist perspective. *International Journal of Servant Leadership, 10*(1). Recuperado de: http://eprints.hud.ac.uk/21599/

Spears, L. C. (2002). Introduction: Tracing the past, present, and future of servant-leadership. In E. L. C. Spears & M. Lawrence (Eds.), *Focus on leadership: Servant-leadership for the twenty-first century* (pp. 1–16). New York: Wiley.

Spears, L. C. (2003). Introduction. En H. Beazley, J. Beggs, and L. Spears, (Eds.), The servantleader within: A transformative path (pp. 13-28). Mahwah, NJ: Paulist Press.

Spence, J. T., & Helmreich, R. L. (1980). Masculine instrumentality and feminine expressiveness: Their relationships with sex role attitudes and behaviors. *Psychology of Women Quarterly, 5*(2), 147–163. https://doi.org/10.1111/j.1471-6402.1980.tb00951.x

Spence, J. T., Helmreich, R., & Stapp, J. (1974). The Personal Attributes Questionnaire: A measure of sex role stereotypes and masculinity-femininity. *Journal Supplement Abstract Service Catalog of Selected Documents in Psychology, 4*, 43 (Ms. No. 617).

Spence, J. T., Helmreich, R., & Stapp, J. (1975). Ratings of self and peers on sex role attributes and their relation to self-esteem and conceptions of masculinity and femininity. *Journal of Personality and Social Psychology, 32*(1), 29–39. https://doi.org/10.1037/h0076857

Srivastava, N., & Nair, S. K. (2011). Androgyny and rational emotive behaviour as antecedents of managerial effectiveness. *Vision, 15*(4), 303–314. https://doi.org/10.1177/097226291101500401

Stogdill, R. M., & Coons, A. E. (1957). *Leader behavior: Its description and measurement.* Columbus: Bureau of Business Research, Ohio State University (Research Monograph 84).

Taylor, M. C., & Hall, J. A. (1982). Psychological androgyny: Theories, methods, and conclusions. *Psychological Bulletin, 92*(2), 347–366. https://doi.org/10.1037/0033-2909.92.2.347

Van Dierendonck, D. (2011). Servant-leadership: A review and synthesis. *Journal of Management, 37*(4), 1228–1261. https://doi.org/10.1177/0149206310380462

Velisario, R. (June, 2017). *Desarrollo Humano Integral vs. Enfoque del Desarrollo Humano y las Capacidades.* Paper presented at III Simposio UNIJES de Pensamiento Social Cristiano. Universidad de Deusto, Spain.

Walker, L. J. (2013). Exemplars' moral behavior is self-regarding. *New Directions for Child and Adolescent Development, 2013*(142), 27–40. https://doi.org/10.1002/cad.20047

Walker, L. J., & Frimer, J. A. (2015). Developmental trajectories of agency and communion in moral motivation. *Merrill-Palmer Quarterly, 61*(3), 412–439. https://doi.org/10.13110/merrpalmquar1982.61.3.0412

Ward, C. A. (2000). Models and measurements of psychological androgyny: A cross-cultural extension of theory and research. *Sex Roles, 43*(7), 529–552. https://doi.org/10.1023/A:1007171500798

Woodhill, B. M., & Samuels, C. A. (2003). Positive and negative androgyny and their relationship with psychological health and well-being. *Sex Roles, 48*(11), 555–565. https://doi.org/10.1023/A:1023531530272

Utilitarian Ethics in the Praxis of Companies: Challenges of Imposition and Duplicity

Andrzej Sarnacki

The appeal for a new way of thinking about business and organization has a solid basis in unresolved socioeconomic problems and appearance of new ones. These are often a side effect of business models, repeatedly blamed for dehumanizing our institutional environment. The primary level of disappointment comes from a global perspective of detrimental processes and a common perception of a massive technocracy; there is the overpowering role of allegedly scientific methods that rule modern management or even a growing gap between the income of top management and line workers. Corporations have acquired a bad name as a result of their way of operating, mostly in the third-world countries. A corporation in its worst could be compared to a pathological personality that has a destructive influence on both its members and its clients (Bakan, 2005). Corporations are often seen as ever power-gaining monsters that endanger the world democratic system through the acquisition of unlimited control and mafia-like praxis (Nace, 2003).

Another aspect of the skepticism comes from the experience of a disappointing leadership style, not just in scandalous worldwide known cases (Fortune, 2016).[1] Pfeffer claims that despite billions of dollars spent over years on leadership research and education, the results are tenuous and the situation in companies is *"disengaged, disaffected, and dissatisfied"* (Pfeffer, 2015, 10). Hardly a new leadership style emerged, and there are numerous cases of abusive behavior and intimidating work climate. Pfeffer sees the problem in an insufficient concept of leadership, in the divergence in the interest between individual leaders and their organizations, lack of an adequate measurement of the outcome, conceptual imprecisions, or focus on

---

[1]"The World's 19 Most Disappointing Leaders," Fortune 30.03.2016, Fortune Editors, http://fortune.com/2016/03/30/most-disappointing-leaders/ [accessed 3.12.2018].

A. Sarnacki (✉)
Jesuit University Ignatianum in Krakow, Krakow, Poland
e-mail: andrzej.sarnacki@ignatianum.edu.pl

© Springer Nature Switzerland AG 2020 77
R. Aguado, A. Eizaguirre (eds.), *Virtuous Cycles in Humanistic Management*,
Contributions to Management Science,
https://doi.org/10.1007/978-3-030-29426-7_5

inspiration instead of knowledge in actual leadership training. All that contributes to dehumanization of a workplace and reification of human activity. It seems that the logic and rules obtained in the material world with modern technical tools have been applied to the human world and conquered its uniquely hominine character. As the result many employees share a sense of being reduced to a functional or productive role, treated anonymously and in instrumental way. Though often acceptable, dehumanization brings negative effects in form of anti-sociality, aggression, hostility, low self-esteem, or demoralization (Christoff, 2014).

The process of reification of the human space could be certainly traced in history. The proposal of more human methods and practices has to take into account the underlying assumptions, which have been stored up over time. They have behind themselves two centuries of history of applying the model of mathematical mechanics to the entire discipline of economics, focusing on quantitative analysis and gradually separating itself from metaphysical, theological, and moral concern. Economics became a positivistic, value-free science, within self-imposed limitations of sheer profit maximization, utilitarianism based on subjectivism, maximization of commodity consumption, qualifying all categories outside the quantitative domain as unscientific (Dierksmeier, 2016, 11–13). The dark side of value-free and absolute profit dominance attitude is the submission and exploitation of employees and customers. The radical expressions of purely materialistic demeanor are visible in many forms of a soft violence, which reduces people to means of production and refuses open communication and partnership. Though sometimes it is not easy to draw the line between coercive practices and simple accountability. Even with best programs people might not take the opportunity to develop their own potential in a workplace, no matter how encouraged they would be.

The intention of this chapter is to explore if the shift toward more humane management style has been taking place and to what extent. The point of reference is the situation of a few companies in Poland. Some 30 years ago the bankrupt communist system left the country impoverished, with tremendous corruption of the work ethics and generation that was not taught to take responsibility of one's life, not to mention of an organization. A name for those who adopted such mentality was coined as *homo sovieticus*, a (wo)man unable to think for himself or herself, with learnt helplessness (Sarnacki, 2013, 56). Large corporations have been introduced to Poland since then, and undoubtedly they call the tune in the organizational environment (due to capital, knowledge, experience). A process of accelerated learning took place, with many outer signs of success. Undoubtedly, the change was introduced also in the field of organizational ethics. The concepts of training, coaching, motivating, or monitoring were transferred, when large companies started their *modus operandi*. Medium-sized organizations could compete with the large one in certain sectors, first studying their methods and matching their style. The initial premise of this paper assumes that there has been a substantial amount of copying the solutions, which first had proved to be successful in countries with a longer history of democracy and entrepreneurship. The thesis of this paper is expressed in a presumption that the corporate ethics are viewed with skepticism, due to Polish historical heritage and resistance, as well as a common opinion about the manipulative practices of large companies. Another part of this inquiry will address that issue of the utilitarian aspect of the work ethics, of what is regarded as ethical (subsequently as unethical) in the very complex business environment.

Ten interviewees were asked to share their observations in order to verify these organizational tendencies. They were chosen as representatives of a variety of companies (large-medium, state-private-owned, global-local, transferred-original concept, traditional-new), but also due to being known for their practices in the field, which could be regarded as humanistic management (HM). The comparative approach was applied in order to show the tendencies regarding possible changes in ethical practices. The information was gathered in September 2018 through a series of interviews, which I did in person. For the purpose of this chapter, qualitative, in-depth interviews, their design, and analysis have followed the general rules of such enquiry described here very briefly due to the size requirements (McMillan & Schumacher, 2014). The questions that explore the thesis of the paper were organized around three fundamental ones:

– Has the change after the collapse of the communism brought more humanistic approach or has it confirmed the feared dehumanizing effect in the work environment?
– Has the local character added something to the humanization of the environment or has it only absorbed the solutions already tested in other parts of the world?
– Is the ethics provided by new companies utilitarian or has it wider background?

The last question clearly could not be dealt in depth due to the limitations of the enquiry; therefore, it only outlines the issue. It could be undeniably stated that there has been a significant change regarding the managerial leadership style, which should be understood as a part of organizational culture (in a sense of Schein, 2017). The paper traces the organizational practices of HM and their perception, as presented by the interviewees. Anteriorly the premises of HM and the challenges of education are explored, while they create the context of the ethical approach.

1 Premises and Humanistic Management

Humanistic management is a proposal and attempt to accept intentionally a moral basis for managerial work, which is to reconstruct the actual model of organizational objectives toward people-oriented and holistic entrepreneurship that respects the dignity of a person and works within the framework of a common good (Melé, 2016). Sometimes it is perceived as a natural and obvious development, as a counter movement adopted for the recognition of values and human dignity in the workplace. Its content, extent, impact, advantages, and disadvantages form an interesting phenomenon in managerial trends. An organization is to take upon itself the responsibility of integrating the ethical premises with business decisions. The overemphasis hitherto put on productivity and profit is to be counterbalanced by a recognition of human values and human needs (Thompson, 2018). And there is already well-established responsibility of business for the rest of the society (Fried-man, 1970). Within that postulates managers are to embrace quite a complex reality and provide a conceptual framework for business. Naturally, such postulates stir a discussion about the allegedly unavoidable inhumanly structured market economy or possibility of humanistic goal-structuring economic activities (Loza Adaui & Habisch, 2013, 192). Nevertheless, the plausible intention of humanizing the labor environment would in practice imply a *paradigm shift away from the economistic views on market activities towards a humanistic approach.*[2] Such an intended shift is never an easy or self-driven affair, if possible at all. It also tackles more fundamental issues both of theoretical and practical nature.

The reflection and proposal of HM necessarily challenges axiomatic assumptions of the economics. Multiplication of reasons why there is a need for changing the paradigm opens also a vast area of theoretical problems of fundamental basis of the new approach. In fact, the question remains, how new this approach is. A number of authors considering that perspective refers to a normative perspective with its traditional values and in their argumentation occasionally takes into account also religious traditions (Habisch & Bachmann, 2016). The old problem of the moral imperative emerges every time one calls upon a conviction and motivation to do good and to avoid evil. Would that mean that in the era of innovation and always new discoveries we are to go back to the old values and partly (at least) rejected tradition? Is the proposal just a return or it is going to become a new synthesis? A serious religious tradition consists of not just techniques or good advices but pro-vides a set of anthropological approaches that demand cogitation. For instance, the basic Christian anthropology rejects the notion of human being as simply good, when the only problem is to organize a human environment for the use of his or her full potential. It regards such position as a simplification, naïve and utopian. On the other hand it does not see the human being placed on the opposite extremum. A proper ontological balance needs a more fundamental approach and serious theoret-ical background.

Another critical question concerns the final logic of the "paradigm shift." The shift means here putting human values and dignity in the center, beyond any means of instrumentalization. It proclaims the priority of a human being over the profit. The idea that humanization is to be introduced in a harmonious way, not at the expenses of productivity and profit, is understandable. It is an "obvious" and "realistic" requirement that any of the new concepts cannot lower productivity. Rather it has to promise an increase of value, otherwise would be dismissed. An epistle on human needs and aspiration has to lead to higher contentment, therefore engagement and productivity. Nevertheless, even if there are conceptual discrepancies, it does not negate a fact of a very positive development in managerial thought and practice. A

---

[2]The Three Stepped Approach to Humanistic Management, in: http://www. humanisticmanagement.org/cgi-bin/adframe/about_humanistic_management/the_three_stepped_ approach_to_humanistic_management/index.html [accessed 17.09.2018].

humanistic approach causes new problems of measurement and needs to be applied carefully (Kostera, 2015).

The situation and the output of modern organizations could be seen as already bringing better results in global scale. For instance, our political organizations and certain development of a thought about values, rights, or international co-responsibility have led to serious changes in the historical period of the last centuries and decades. The most important changes relate to the issue of violence and poverty. Steven Pinker claims that contrary to what could be perceived, violence statistically has declined in the developed world over the last centuries (2011). Walter Scheidel argues that there has been a major improvement of getting people out of poverty in recent decades (2017). And as always, there is a matter of a perspective. When evaluating behavioral patterns, some authors point out toward the loss of a moral horizon and decadence, when others perceive them as degenerated forms of a moral ideal, as a phase of a moral laxity or culture of narcissism, which eventually become a deeper source of morality (Taylor, 1991, 15, Gray, 2015). This macro-level, also connected to a certain type of mostly political management, has its multidimensional repercussion at lower levels of social and economic organization.

2 Educational Challenge

It is quite apparent that educational system with its framework of preconditions plays a decisive role in the orientation of future leaders. The postulates of HM would have to be introduced to a curriculum of business schools if the concept is to spread out. Sandra Waddock (2016) claims that the modern management is focused on technical, functional, and analytical skills, but much less on human environment. It runs the risk of producing quite a mechanical leadership style, which often fails in empowering people and bringing out the best of them. The prestigious MBA programs quite unilaterally endorse that model of education for business leaders and there is not much expectation that it could be changed. Waddock's proposal is to continue with this analytical and technical model of education intended for young entrepreneurs, while offering more humanistic approach for the next stage of education. That solution might be legitimate in a sense that "humanistic attitude" should not be a substitution for tangible skills. But the question remains if one who grows up only in technical, analytical environment will be willing to take into account something that will challenge his or her actual knowledge and convictions.

And it does not apply only to programs such as MBA. The expectations placed on formal education have achieved a wide recognition, already for a long time. Along with the increase in importance of technical development, humanities have been losing their position as "classical studies." The shift toward technicalization of all sectors of education, including humanities, has been perceived as a necessary step in ensuring the pragmatic and palpable skill apprentice at its best, creating nevertheless a side effect of reification (Kincheloe, 2011). At the same time, growing business production, service, or basically organizational environment have confronted a real danger of dehumanizing forces in the workplace, partly defined as a submission of ethics to the principle of profit maximization and efficiency. Therefore, the demand of introducing humanistic management to programs of studies goes against the common bias in modern education, with the fear of humans being replaced by machines (Brynjolfsson & McAfee, 2011), and needs to be dealt with accordingly.

The concept of solving the problem of dehumanization in the workplace through education faces at least a triple challenge. The first one is that the notion of values or humanization of the workplace could be too abstract, leaving students with a sense of wishful thinking and feeble arguments. The aspect of the theoretical background is not defined and could be too poor or could be grounded in ideology or populism. The realism of humanistic approach has to prove itself through meaningful examples from actual companies. The second challenge is the attitude of skepticism, claiming in-built hypocrisy in any ethical declaration of a firm or its moral champions. The discrepancy between promoted self-image and corporal practices could be quite significant and give the right to downgrading the hope for results of academic training. There are many examples of corporations that pride themselves on moral codes and social responsibility, when keeping employees from the third-world countries in misery, insanitary environment, and practical enslavement (Wagner, Lutz, & Weitz, 2009). The third challenge is somehow similar to the second one, yet quite distinct. It is the dilemma of practical choice between morality and efficiency, or a goodwill vs. economic pressure. Why would one choose a loss? Is not the perspective of the profit always the prevailing one? The idea that a situation of win-win is always possible seems quite utopian. But the dilemma is often between win less or win more at somebody's expenses. Are we to promote a semi-altruistic motivation that at times does not pay off? Or do we intend to employ a practical thinking, which regards the common good as a priority and in certain times is willing to scarify if it benefits the society? Is it not an attempt to go around the issue of the profit maximalization but at the end to come back to thinking: being ethical pays off?

This triple challenge cannot be simply discharged, while they are part of a common experience. In the classroom, it could be dealt with through a broad spectrum of cases and critical arguments. The question of the practical role of values appears to be of great significance, taking into account the renouncement of meta-physics and the introduction of relativism. The main point of this chapter would be the exploration if the tension between declarations and practice could be resolved against the spiritual background, which could give the ultimate reason for one's motivation. It would be important to show the necessity of the balance, while good intentions should not a substitute for knowledge. Preaching for more humanism in the business environment should involve the requirement of competence.

3   Practical Application: The Organizational Shift

The above theoretical approach has been verified during interviews with ten representatives of medium and large companies, operating for many years now in Poland. The cases need to be seen in the context of the shift from centralist, unwieldy and deeply dehumanizing communist system to the free market economy, with the transfer of Western managerial systems. The process has happened during less than 30 years, although it is probably more adequate to talk about visible changes during the last 15 years. Interviewee 5 (business consultant) claims that the mode of management, where an employee was only a cog in the machine belongs to the past. The concept of a central significance of a person is obvious and self-evident. This is an inevitable condition for a development. Care for human environment in the workplace has to support personal interactions. It is an indispensable element of personal progress. Aspects like an expression of joy (laughter), pride (self-confidence), and also kindness (respect) are in focus. A company allows to develop many personal aspects of life, like one's hobby (sport, music, theater) or one's contact with the family (working from home). Interviewee 2 (director and proprietor) makes an observation that the corporate style has affected Polish companies in a positive way. The realization that an ill-treatment of a worker badly influences his or her engagement or that a team works in an effective way only when good conditions are provided and a supportive attitude of a senior management is guaranteed, indelibly entered the organizational realm. Paying attention to enjoyment and satisfaction of the employees, security regulations, or time for relaxation have become a standard in relatively short time. Interviewee 2 ascribes this also to a low rate of unemployment and a new attitude of Millennials, the generation with high aspirations and high expectations. This new generation is better equipped for the job, in regard to their practical and linguistic skills, as well as the ability of integration and communication. It clearly marks a cultural change.

There are many examples of a practical application of this somehow anthropocentric organizational policy, enforced by ethical codes, CSR programs, rule of transparency, but also by offering programs that are designed in a personalized way. Interviewee 6 (IKEA manager) describes that in IKEA every employee is encouraged to understand his or her development in the company according to the motto "leading myself" or "leadership by example." There is therefore an assumption of a personal responsibility for one's own growth, strongly promoted by HR department. Certain attitudes and ambitions are encouraged, according to the company's mission: responsibility, for example, learning new skills, enterprise, resourcefulness, and gaining maturity. A substantial part of a personal evaluation must be based on not only productive results but one's attitude toward others, a willingness to share knowledge, a contribution to a shared culture. It is quite common nowadays for workers to have a full range of possibilities, starting with trainings, medical and insurance benefits, and comfortable work conditions (nap room, massage room, dining room, etc., furniture like sofa or games like a table soccer). The organizational environment is welcoming, and the values of diversity and respect emphasized.

Almost every interviewee was able to enlist many examples of supererogatory actions, taken by managers or staff in order to help a worker, somebody from their family or just somebody in need. In one of the companies, a very promising employee suddenly began to suffer from a schizophrenia. The superior took the freedom to provide some help for the medical treatment, but what is more, did not let the person to be dismissed. Instead, after achieving a mental balance through medical treatment, the job responsibilities were adjusted to the personal abilities, and the employee was able to function in the company having a regular supervision. In another case, an employee died leaving his wife without livelihood. The company took the widow and trained her in the workplace, till she was able to find her place in the labor market. Quite common is a help in cases of sickness or personal problems. Often the initiative comes from the employees themselves, once they assume a sense of solidarity. It also applies to regular or exceptional actions of helping, for example, the homeless or people who suffered from a catastrophe. These behaviors have become quite common, especially in large and medium companies in Poland over two last decades. Interviewee 1 (BP manager) asserts that although there is a saying that a satisfied client is the most important goal of the company, equally it could be said about an employee, who is a "pre-condition" for that satisfaction.

Therefore, the first observation takes note of positive aspects of corporate culture, which have influenced a significant part of the general organizational environment. This includes a decision and consciousness of the company's values, a creation of a friendly environment for employees, who are understood as the most important asset in an organization. It is a systemic shift, often forced by the standard practices of bigger companies, which came to Poland with their concepts of a balanced lifestyle and ethical codes. Also, the attitude of the foreign management has changed over the years. Interviewee 10 (board member in a big international company) mentions a situation from 20 years ago, when a French manager who was introducing 5S system for organizing documents allowed himself to throw documents from someone's desk, as a lesson. Today, says Interviewee 10, it would be unthinkable.

4 Practical Application: Change-Impaired Environments

Despite ubiquitous changes, many firms and companies continue considering their employees just as a labor force subservient to the overarching law of profit. Interviewee 5 claims that it is quite common that for small business profit is the emphasized and central value. But it also applies to traditional and large companies. Interviewee 9 (top management in a big state-owned company) confirms that profit-oriented strategy often disregards the human part of managerial practice. Interviewee 10 says that in his chain-store business the exploitation of the workers is quite obvious. A dehumanizing treatment is quite common, and the profit is gained at any price. Recently, due to the new state regulation about shops being closed every second Sunday, the chain store has introduced a post service, what allowed them to be open every Sunday. The main reason for this situation is that the chain was shortly acquired by an investment fund, which is very oriented toward profit. Top managers were hired to meet the fund's financial goals. The fund, therefore, took over an existing business with thousands of shops and developed it toward a financially successful enterprise. Interviewee 10 confirms that the company has its own ethical code and participates in many social initiatives, which is understood as an image-important CSR activity. But the superior purpose is own profit. A modern company could operate in this way mostly because its capital is anonymous, and the line workers do not know for whose benefit they work.

The pace of changes, as well as the fossilization of some companies, depend also on generational difference. The opinion about the work attitude is generally positive. Polish employees are seen as hardworking, very responsible, well-educated entre-preneurs, and focused on the results (Interviewee 6). Interviewee 9 shares this opinion but makes a distinction between generations. In her company the majority of workers qualifies as generation X (now 50-year-old and so) that came to the labor market with the attitude of total commitment to work, and readiness to sacrifice their family time working 10 hours a day or more. The older generation, which also forms a substantial part of the company, is difficult to motivate for participation in trainings and taking responsibility for personal development. In the course of their lives, they have developed survival tactics in an organizational leviathan and expect to stay there till their retirement. In the company there is very little of a genuine care for the people. What is more, due to the hiring policy there is a generational gap, and significantly less people from the Y generation, who come with a different attitude of establishing a balance between professional and family life. They do not take an authority for granted while it has to be earned. At the moment in companies like that there is no visible change and a focus on profit at the expenses of employees is predominant. Decisive, nevertheless, is the attitude of the top management. They are free to create a more friendly environment.

Sometimes there is also a need of a conceptual clarification. Humanistic man-agement does not always have a positive connotation. Interviewee 4 (managing director and chairman of the board in NEBI) reckons that the formula "humanistic management" is an erroneous one. So are declarations like "people are more important than profit," because they are just emotional. Profit, on the other hand, is a self-evident reality. Management is primarily based on skills and methods, what leads to the satisfaction of clients and staff. Management serves the well-being of all the groups. If the requirements of an effective management are fulfilled, concepts like "humanistic management" become unusable. When the management works properly, that is, optimizing companies processes with the method of the root cause analysis, the satisfaction from one's position in the organization comes automatically.

5   Practical Application: Ethical Considerations

The dignity of a human being in many cases is taken for granted (Interviewee 5). If someone is perceived as having poor qualities (e.g., in 360-degree feedback assessment), his or her abilities could be improved by special coaching. The companies by and large have a policy of worldview neutrality. Desire to make the world a better place does not necessarily come from religious convictions. Often, we do not know what motivates people. Interviewee 2 claims that having a chance of being a part of an interesting project has a great inspirational power. Finding a creative solution gives a lot of satisfaction, and this is felt to play a bigger role than the profit. Also, a sense of being treated justly, including an equality between men and women, has a substantial value for organizational atmosphere. Enormous value for everyone today is recognition, on a daily basis.

Interviewee 7 (president of xtech.pl) recalls the concept of turquoise management (Laloux) as an expression of the trend of humanistic approach to management. It is a very personal subject, while people are looking today for methods that are in agreement with their convictions, efficient and acceptable by the co-workers. There is an unavoidable conflict of interests in a company, as well as the pressure of profit, so it is an enormous challenge to find a harmony of the elements. The profit is always important, and making people happy without providing a tangible success will lead to a catastrophe. Interviewee 7 understands HM as a concept of full participation, which includes employees in the decision processes of a firm.

In many cases, it is not anymore possible to cheat on a client. A practical ethics would be to provide the products of best quality. For a responsible manager, the biggest pressure is the sense of responsibility not only for the employees, but their families. There is a religious neutrality in the company, although the majority of the workers are Catholics. The tolerance has its roots in Polish tradition. Also, a possible connection between religion and ethics is not noticeable and remains personal.

Despite the declared neutrality, companies are sensitive toward religious belief, not including it in work, but ensuring it is respected. Nevertheless, there is a question of symmetry. One international company has issued an instruction, which states that during the period of Ramadan, the workers should be delicate toward the Muslim workers who fast and could be irritated. Such sensitivity is, on the other hand, not present when it comes to Christian festivals or Lent.

A company ASTOR pursues a person-oriented policy in a very conscious way (Politańska et al., 2016). The inspiration is clearly Christian, thou it finds its expression in certain practices and not so much in statements or symbols. They do not call it humanistic but personalistic management. The conscious effort of finding ethical solutions to company rules and challenges derives from personal convictions and a study of Karol Wojtyła's thought, especially his book *The Acting Person* (Wojtyła, 1979). Some members of ASTOR set up even an Institute of Karol Wojtyła, and together with people from other companies, they study philosophical concepts of human actions. Their payroll system includes a basic salary, a bonus for experience and competences, and a premium. The premium comes from extra sell and is divided among all members of the company accordingly. Also, 27% of the share is offered to all employees, with possibility to become partners. Interviewee 8 (vice president for finances affairs of ASTOR) confirms that the participation of all in the profit is a very important part of personalistic management. Another part of the policy of the company is building a culture of transparency. Every year they give 2% of their profit to the charities, and the line workers decide to which one. The question about human dignity and the meaning of work is something that often appear during meetings. Yet the system is never stable, and Interviewee 8 sees the need of constant renegotiation.

6   The Final Paradox

This brief overview shows that the corporate practices have had a serious impact on many other organizations, also changing organizational culture and the style of leadership. It becomes convincible that in a long term, an employee has a more desirable value than an immediate profit. Also, other factors contribute to this attitudinal change, like a low unemployment rate or defined expectations of the newcomers. Interviewee 3 (manager and consultant, proprietor of a consulting company MAPRIT) claims that the HM takes place mostly in NGOs, where the members state clearly such expectations. There is also a growing awareness among managers that today's complexity of organizational environment makes a centralistic management obsolete and impossible. Only by exercising trust, a manager can empower an organization to match the complexity of the market. This finding has contradicted the initial thesis regarding skepticism toward ethical approach of corporate culture. The corporate policy of optimization, transparency, and work ethics seems to have a positive influence on many organizational environments.

The companies that refuse to participate in the "paradigm shift" represent usually bulky state-owned companies, small business, and enterprises owned by funds, which by definition are focused just on the profit and stay hidden behind the anonymity of the structure. The tasks performed by those firms and companies are usually repetitive and not very intricate. The turnover is usually high among younger generation, when the middle and the senior one are more willing to adapt to the circumstances. The decisive is the managerial style that continues the praxis of deliberate exploitation and ignorance.

The final paradox of the shift lies in its pragmatic motivation. As often argued, the shift from a profit-oriented to human-oriented logic allows employees to gain a better self-esteem, to have a sense of being a part of something important, and to be more creative and in return, treat other employees with respect. The goals are reached by people, so the people are the most important source of companies' strategy. Interviewee 6 confirms the accuracy of this logic. If we are focused only on the goal, we achieve nothing more. If on people, we achieve more than we have assumed. Not an employee comes to work, but a human being. There is no profit without a person. And a happy employee is a good employee (Interviewee 1). From that perspective an employee comes before a client and the profit. CSR is an investment. Engagement in good works liberates a positive energy and strength.

It is not a surprise that the conclusion drown from this experience predicates a harmony between ethics and money, and titles of many seminars could declare that the aim of being ethical pays off. Though in many cases it might be true, ethics in that perspective is treated as a means for the same purpose as always. It becomes therefore an unintended contradiction and could hardly be understood as a "paradigm shift," remaining in fact a calculated praxis. Sometimes an allegedly new method of "humanizing" certain practices of economic game looks very promising, yet at the end of the day it falls under the same dictate of profit and productivity maximalization, and the schema of utilitarian ethics that does not believe in unconditional gesture.

This pragmatic and rational attitude might also clash with the situation, when being ethical and committed to one's values might not be profitable, even in a long run. There are some more fundamental issues in the background, like the notion of values. Some of them might be ideological or fall at times in conflict with other values. There is always a question of the significance of the values. A company may decide that simplicity is a value, but without a hierarchy it is hard to determine how important this value is in comparison with others. On the other hand, a company does not need to be a school of a moral life. It still can search for convincing, historical examples (Freyer et al., 2018). Sometimes, says Interviewee 6, some practices may look like a substitute of religion. The workplace becomes a place of self-reflection and existential talks. As the confessional is a place of a personal progress in the church, so a company becomes a place of self-actualization.

Nevertheless, in spite of a danger of utilitarian ethics, the progress in anthropocentric organizational culture is a positive one. More sophisticated attitudes would demand an incorporation of a more complex and profound ethical thought, discussed for centuries in the history of philosophy. The practices introduced to Polish companies are mostly reproductive, operating in imitative mode of imported style. To substantial extend they provide a positive shift in still transitional period of work ethics environment. Yet there are some examples of original solutions. The example of a quest for better answers, which often means living a tension between idealistic principles and pressure of reality, was probably most visible in the practice of ASTOR. Interviewee 8 refers to their attitude toward personalism. Personalism takes its inspiration from Karol Wojtyla's philosophical work, but also from ideas of Viktor Frankl and logotherapy or from the concept of a transparent organization. Subjectivity in the workplace states a challenge and demands a constant effort of thinking and arguing. It could be expressed through a metaphor of striving to keep a ball on the mountain's top. There are thunderstorms and earthquake, but we try to keep the ball on the top despite all turbulence. It is not a Sisyphean task, but it does allow the individual to retain his or her personal integrity.

This brief research has confirmed that the practices of ethical attitude in Polish companies are mostly imposed by corporate policies. Though imitative they have brought positive changes and forced many traditional companies to adjust their praxis to international standards. The statements of the interviewees did not uphold the thesis that the organizational ethical practices are received with skepticism. They seem to play a positive role in work environment, with the exception of companies that refused to take into account the accomplishments of HM. The problem of the shortcomings of utilitarian ethics seems to abide in organizational environment in the predicted future.

Author's note To verify the point of the proliferation of humanistic management, I have interviewed 10 representatives from medium and big businesses. All of them have been working in the field for as many as 20 years, witnessing too many changes in the organizational environment, predominantly in Poland.

Alphabetical Listing of Interviewees Quoted in Text:

Interviewee 1: Dorota Adamska, Communication & External Affairs Manager, BP Europe

Interviewee 2: Marek Dyduch, director and proprietor of TEQUM (design engineering company in construction industry)

Interviewee 3: Wojciech Kmiecik, manager and consultant, proprietor of a consulting company MAPRIT, perennial vice president of a Foundation Iskierka

Interviewee 4: Piotr Pawela, managing director and chairman of the board of NEBI ltd.

Interviewee 5: Anna Walczowska, a business consultant in management and marketing, more than 20 years of experience

Interviewee 6: Katarzyna Warchał, Purchasing and Logistic Area Manager Central Europe at Inter IKEA Group

Interviewee 7: Antoni Wojtulewicz, president of xtech.pl (industry websites)

Interviewee 8: Michał Wojtulewicz, vice president for finances affairs of ASTOR (automation and industrial information technology)

Interviewee 9: Proprietary name of a top management person who works for a big State-owned company

Interviewee 10: Proprietary name of a board member of a big international chain store

References

Bakan, J. (2005). *The corporation: The pathological pursuit of profit and power.* New York: Free Press.

Brynjolfsson, E., & McAfee, A. (2011). *Race against the machine: How the digital revolution is accelerating innovation, driving productivity, and irreversibly transforming employment and the economy.* Lexington: Digital Frontier Press.

Christoff, K. (2014). *Dehumanization in organizational settings: Some scientific and ethical considerations.* Accessed September 27, 2018, from https://www.ncbi.nlm.nih.gov/pmc/articles/PMC4173804/

Dierksmeier, C. (2016). What is 'humanistic' about humanistic management. *Humanistic Management Journal, 1*(1), 9–32.

Freyer, B., Aversano-Dearborn, V., Winkler, G., Leipold, S., Haidl, H., Werner Brand, K., . . . Wallnig, T. (2018). Is there a relation between ecological practices and spirituality? The case of benedictine monasteries ecological practices in benedictine monasteries. *Journal of Agricultural and Environmental Ethics, 31*(5), 559–582.

Friedman, M. (1970, September 13). The social responsibility of business is to increase its profits. *The New York Times Magazine.*

Habisch, A., & Bachmann, C. (2016). Empowering practical wisdom from religious traditions: A Ricoeurian approach. *International Journal of Corporate Social Responsibility, 1*, 10.

John Gray. (2015, March 13). Steven Pinker is wrong about violence and war. *The Guardian.* https://www.theguardian.com/books/2015/mar/13/john-gray-steven-pinker-wrong-violence-war-declining

Kincheloe, J. L. (2011). Exposing the technocratic perversion of education: The death of the democratic philosophy of schooling. In J. L. Kincheloe, K. Hayes, S. R. Steinberg, & K. Tobin (Eds.), *Key works in critical pedagogy.* Sense Publishers: Rotterdam.

Kostera, M. (Ed.). (2015). *Metody badawcze w zarządzaniu humanistycznym* [Research Methods in Humanistic Management]. Warszawa: Wydawnictwo akademickie SEDNO.

Loza Adaui, R. C., & Habisch, A. (2013). Humanistic management. In B. Luigino & Z. Stefano (Eds.), *Handbook on the economics of reciprocity and social enterprise.* Cheltenham-Northampton: Edward Elgar.

McMillan, J. H., & Schumacher, S. (2014). *Research in education: Evidence-based inquiry.* Essex: Pearson New International Edition.

Melé, D. (2016). Understanding humanistic management. *Humanistic Management Journal, 1*(1), 33–55.

Nace, T. (2003). *Gangs of America. The rise of corporate power and the disabling of democracy.* San Francisco: Berrett-Koehler Publishers.

Pfeffer, J. (2015). *Leadership B S: Fixing workplaces and careers one truth at a time.* Sydney: HarperCollins Publishers.

Pinker, S. (2011). *The better angels of our nature: Why violence has declined.* New York: Penguin Books.

Politańska, A., Życzkowski, S., & Wojtulewicz, M. (2016). *Jeśli nie wiadomo, o co chodzi, to chodzi o ludzi.* Kraków: ASTOR Publishing.

Sarnacki, A. (2013). *Institutional changes for the Polish Church in facing new challenges (1989–2005). An enquiry from a social science and social philosophy perspective.* Kraków: Wydawnictwo WAM.

Scheidel, W. (2017). *The great leveler: Violence and the history of inequality from the Stone Age to the twenty-first century.* Princeton: Princeton University Press.

Schein, E. (2017). *Organizational culture and leadership.* Hoboken, NJ: Wiley.

Taylor, C. (1991). *The malaise of modernity.* Toronto: House of Anansi Press.

"The World's 19 Most Disappointing Leaders", *Fortune*, March 30, 2016, Fortune Editors. Accessed December 3, 2018, from http://fortune.com/2016/03/30/most-disappointing-leaders/

Thompson, S. *Challenges of humanistic management.* Accessed September 28, 2018, from Small Business – Chron.com, http://smallbusiness.chron.com/challenges-humanistic-management-64545.html

Waddock, S. (2016). Developing humanistic leadership education. *Humanistic Management Journal, 1*(1), 57–73.

Wagner, T., Lutz, R. J., & Weitz, B. A. (2009). Corporate hypocrisy: Overcoming the threat of inconsistent corporate social responsibility perceptions. *Journal of Marketing, 73*(6), 77–91.

Wojtyła, K. (1979). *The acting person.* Dordrecht: D. Reidel.

From Utility to Dignity: Humanism in Human Resource Management

Greg Latemore, Peter Steane, and Robin Kramar

1 Introduction

Human resource management (HRM) refers to the practices utilized to manage the people who do the work of organizations. This chapter proposes that there are a number of ways of conceptualizing HRM, including SHRM, humanistic management, and personalistic management. These three perspectives are based on different ontologies with varied assumptions about the people engaged in the work of organizations.

The objectives of this chapter are to define these three HRM perspectives: to examine their relative strengths and weaknesses, to integrate them (in Fig. 1), and to suggest further research for both HRM theory and practice.

One contribution of this chapter is to examine the assumptions within each HRM perspective in terms of the philosophy of Jacques Maritain (1882–1973) who distinguished between the "lower self" (the individual) and the "higher self" (the person). The chapter's second contribution is to propose an integral humanism which respects the whole person of the employee, who is not just a valuable resource but a valued person within a community of valued persons. We trust that the chapter is interesting and worth reading because it critiques the resource-centered assumptions within HRM, and it presents an alternative approach toward the conceptualization of those who do the work of organizations.

Our analysis reveals that a strategic perspective based upon SHRM emphasizes the lower self as a consequence of its focus on the "utility" of the individual. A personalistic perspective represents a characterization aligned with Maritain's (1947) view of respect for the "dignity" of the person as the higher self. However, while affirming their dignity as ends in themselves, the humanistic perspective at the same time, regards those who do the work of organizations as means to achieve organizational outcomes.

G. Latemore (✉) · P. Steane · R. Kramar
The University of Notre Dame Australia, Sydney, Australia
e-mail: gregory.latemorel@my.nd.edu.au

© Springer Nature Switzerland AG 2020
R. Aguado, A. Eizaguirre (eds.), *Virtuous Cycles in Humanistic Management*,
Contributions to Management Science,
https://doi.org/10.1007/978-3-030-29426-7_6

2   The Importance of Ontology to HRM Scholarship

The ontology of HRM is defined as how the nature of the human being is understood and regarded within the workplace. After the Greek words *ontos* meaning "being" and *logos* meaning "word" or "discourse," ontology refers to expressions of "what is" and is a branch of metaphysics concerned with the nature of being. René Descartes (1644) regarded metaphysics as the root of the tree of philosophy.

Greenwood (2013: 361) has pointed out that the HRM field "suffers from limited ontological assumptions." Delbridge (2006) concurs in that, while the word "ontology" is rarely used in the HRM literature, a consideration of ontology is fundamental in research. An examination of ontology surfaces a range of philosophical concerns "which have been muted within HRM," and that, to date, "philosophical introspection has been disappointingly absent in HRM" (Harney, 2014: 154 & 155). This situation is exacerbated by instrumental assumptions of human nature and ontological realism (Ferris, Hall, Todd Royle, & Martocchio, 2004). Some scholars have linked such an approach to human nature with the "narrow instrumentality of late capitalism" (Simons, 1995: 278), endorsing Habermas (1988) who saw in the extension of instrumental rationality the "colonization of the lifeworld," leading to an erosion of the very basis for social norms, solidarity, and the sense of community.

3   The Nature of Humanism

While the philosophical literature on humanism is extensive and will not be canvassed here, humanism has been defined as "a progressive philosophy of life that, without theism or other supernatural beliefs, affirms our ability and responsibility to lead ethical lives of personal annulment that aspire to the greater good" (AHA, 2018). The major document of the contemporary humanist movement is the Amsterdam Declaration 2002 which espouses eight principles: humanism is ethical; is rational; supports democracy and human rights; insists that personal liberty must be combined with social responsibility; is a response to the widespread demand for an alternative to dogmatic religion; values artistic creativity and imagination; and is a life-stance aiming at the maximum possible fulfillment (AD, 2002).

While there is both secular and religious humanism, humanists seem to agree that human dignity and well-being are to be affirmed. Humanism is understood as a way of life not just a way of thinking, and it is attained in the rational pursuit of virtues such as justice and benevolence.

4   Humanism Within HRM

Within HRM and its scholarship, the term "human" is usually combined with "resource." Greenwood (2013: 355) asks "what does it mean to us as humans to manage humans as resources?" Others lament the loss of the human in HRM (Janssens & Steyaert, 1999), and yet others assert that "taking up the research of and for the meaning of the 'H' in HRM is a core task for the discipline" (Steyaert & Janssens, 1999: 194).

This chapter focuses on those who do the work of organizations not only as human resources but as human beings and as persons. In that endeavor, two polarities will guide the approach: utility and dignity.

5   Two Polarities: Utility and Dignity

The concept of utility generally refers to usefulness and encompasses the "necessary knowledge, skills and techniques to be an excellent professional" (Aguado, Alcañiz, Retolaza, & Albareda, 2016: 13). Kahneman (2012: 273) postulates the view that "people's choices are based not on dollar value, but on the psychological values of outcomes, their utilities." Utility can, therefore, be defined as "the psychological value or the desirability of money" and refers to "the contribution of an anticipated outcome to the overall attractiveness or aversiveness of an option in a choice" (Kahneman, 2012: 272 & 446). Employees produce the "utility of wealth" as the desirable outcome of their individual and collective efforts. Pirson (2017c) has proposed that economism is predicated upon the same assumption regarding the value of the human contribution in creating wealth.

The concept of dignity is intrinsic to what it means to be human. Immanuel Kant (1724–1804) asserted that human beings can be described in terms of dignity as they are ends in themselves, above all price. He wrote:

> Everything has either a price or a dignity. Whatever has a price can be replaced by something else as its equivalent; on the other hand, whatever is above all price, and therefore admits of no equivalent, has a dignity. (Kant, 1785: 435)

Once the prerogative of exalted or royal persons (Waldron, 2009), all human beings now have (or should have) status, stature, and inherit worth (*dignitas*). People are neither superior nor inferior but equals, who merit respect and freedom (Hicks, 2011). It is this characteristic of freedom which modern authors regard as the foundation of human dignity (Aguado, Retolaza, & Alcañiz, 2017). Dignity has therefore been regarded as an intrinsic human quality, part of our human essence.

Dignity has also been viewed as "a moral obligation for humans as agents of free will" (Sen, 2002: 9) reflecting Hodson's (2001: 3) definition of dignity as "the ability to establish a sense of self-worth and self-respect and to appreciate the respect of others." To that extent then, "respect for dignity" signals an appreciation of the inherent worth of a human being. Combining both approaches, dignity is therefore defined as the moral obligation to appreciate one's own and others' intrinsic self-worth.

The concept of dignity is core to Maritain's understanding of the person and the common good, which shall next be examined.

5.1   The Person in Maritain's Philosophy

For Maritain (1947), the individual is the "lower self," the lower good of the human being, while the person can be defined as an expression of the "higher self," the higher good of the human being. Maritain contrasts individuality (the material component) with personality (the spiritual component) and highlights that the individual is but a narrow expression of the ego (to grasp for itself), while personality is an expression of the self (giving itself) (Maritain, 1947: 33–39).

Maritain acknowledges that "[t]his is no new distinction but a classical distinction belonging to the intellectual heritage of mankind [sic]" (1947: 33–34). Sison and Fontrodona (2012) source it to Aristotle and Thomas Aquinas with scholars asserting that this distinction is of major importance in Maritain's work (Capaldi, 2004; Evans, 1952). Melé's explanation of this distinction is as follows:

> Personalism differs from Individualism. The person is not seen as having an isolated existence, united to others only by social contracts. On the contrary, the person is seen as a social being with intrinsic relationships with others and an interdependent existence. (Melé, 2009: 229)

Maritain postulates that "the person is a whole … and only the person is free; only the person possesses, in the full sense of these words, inwardness and subjectivity" (1947: 68). He claims that "by the very fact that each of us is a person and expresses himself [sic] to himself [sic], each of us requires communication with other and the others in the order of knowledge and love" (Maritain, 1947: 41–42). Each person is "irreplaceable" (Maritain, 1947: 75). Viewing some human beings as inferior, such as slaves and women, might be permissible within the Aristotelian framework, but this is "clearly incompatible with Maritain's personalism" (Acevedo, 2012: 211). Acevedo summarizes Maritain's distinction as "individuality (uniqueness, diversity, deficiencies) and personality (interiority, spirituality, perfectibility)" (Acevedo, 2012: 208–209).

5.2   The Common Good in Maritain's Philosophy

The common good is "the end of the social whole" (Maritain, 1947: 49) and "the true ends of human persons" (Maritain, 1947: 48). Personality and the common good imply each other, and "[this implication] is at the core of Maritain's social and political philosophy" (Acevedo, 2012: 207). Maritain elaborates:

> The common good is common because it is received in persons, each of whom is a mirror of the whole. Among the bees there is a public good, namely, the good functioning of the hive, but not a common good, that is, a good received and communicated. The end of society, therefore, is neither the individual good nor the collection of the individual goods of each of the persons who constitute it . . . It is the good *human* life of the multitude, of a multitude of persons; it is their communion in good living. It is therefore common to both *the whole and the parts* into which it flows back and which, in turn, must benefit from it. (Maritain, 1947: 50–53 [his emphases]

The common good has more recently been seen as "a set of conditions enabling the members of a community to attain reasonable objectives" and as "a juridical order and social situation where opportunities . . . are maximized" (Arjoon, Turriago-Hoyos, & Thoene, 2018: 144 & 154). Maritain simply defines the common good as "the communion of persons in good living" (Maritain, 1947: 51).

The common good is attained through "integral humanism" (Maritain, 1936), a theocentric moral philosophy with a personalism offering a bridge between individualism with its initial freedom, on the one hand, and totalitarianism with its loss of freedom, on the other (Evans, 1952). Integral humanism proposes the freedom of autonomy, a radical self-determination within a community of persons who demonstrate intrinsic mutuality and reciprocity of interests. This theoretical approach of integral human development transcends the value creation within the stakeholder theory (see Retolaza, Aguado, & Alcañiz, 2018).

Maritain juxtaposes "integral humanism" with "anthropocentric or inhuman humanism" (Maritain, 1936: 45) and addresses contemporary forms of materialistic individualism in his day, namely, bourgeois individualism; communistic anti-individualism; totalitarian or dictatorial anti-communism; and anti-individualism, which "disregard the human *person* in one way or another, and, in its place, consider, willingly or not, the *material individual* alone" (Maritain, 1947: 91) [his emphasis].

Maritain's (1936: 279) concept of integral humanism transcends both individualism and imperialism to create a "personalistic democracy" which fosters a "popular civic consciousness." The ideal for a healthy civil society is for the realization of a "fraternal community" that "transcends both economism and politicism" (Maritain, 1936: 280 & 286). This viewpoint underpins the Universal Declaration of Human Rights, the first article of which states:

> All human beings are born free and equal in dignity and rights. They are endowed with reason and conscience and should act towards one another in a spirit of brotherhood. (UNDHR, 1948, Article 1)

Although Maritain's view of integral humanism has been criticized for its idealism (Battaglia, 2005), scholars have acknowledged Maritain's concept of the common good as the foundation of the stakeholder theory (Beer, Boselie, & Brewster, 2015) and as the basis for expanding the notion of value creation itself. Warren cites Maritain when urging a HRM that preserves employee dignity "without treating them in either a collectivist or a purely contractual fashion" (Warren, 2000: 181–182).

The principle of the common good has been adopted by Catholic social teaching (Retolaza et al., 2018; Turkson, 2017) where "the good of all people and of the whole person [is] the primary goal of society" (CSDC, 2004: 73). The principle of the common good has also been employed when challenging the HRM mantra to "attract, motivate and retain the best talent" as being "too limited and exclusive" in a case study where most of the employees were people with disabilities (Sison, 2007: 479). Maritain summarizes his own view of the common good as follows:

> We have emphasized the sociability of the person and the properly *human* nature of the common good. We have seen that it is a good according to the requirements of justice; that it must flow back upon persons, and that it includes, as its principal value, the access of persons to their liberty of expansion. (Maritain, 1947: 55) [his emphasis]

For Maritain, then, the person is the "higher self," endowed with and owed a "liberty of expansion," that is, personal growth and development. The seeds for civic growth and societal well-being are within the common good, and the common good itself fosters a "liberty of expansion" by ensuring that economic and social benefits "flow back" to citizens as persons.

Maritain's viewpoint on the person and the common good is now employed as a "lens" to examine three HRM perspectives.

6   The Strategic Perspective in HRM Scholarship

HRM can be defined as "the policies, practices and systems that influence the behaviors, attitudes and performance of those who do the work of organizations" (after Kramar et al., 2014: 6) and refers to the function within an organization focused on the management of the people who work for it. This broadens the view of Boxall and Purcell (2008) who defined HRM in terms of activities associated with managing employees. HRM now includes the management of all those who do the work of organizations, including full-time employees, subcontractors, consultants, and non-employed volunteers (Kramar, 2014). Nonetheless, in this chapter, "employee" has still been used as most HRM and SHRM scholars employ it.

The "strategic perspective" is our construct which combines strategic management and its derivative, SHRM. Strategic management refers to the formulation of goals and implementation of the initiatives taken by an organization's management on behalf of owners and investors, based on consideration of resources and an assessment of the internal and external environments in which they compete (after Nag, Hambrick, & Chen, 2007), while SHRM is "the pattern of planned HR deployments and activities intended to enable an organization to achieve its goals" (Wright & McMahon, 1992: 298). The strategic perspective in HRM is therefore defined as the approach whereby the formal management of people is undertaken to achieve organizational goals on behalf of owners and investors.

Five major theoretical frameworks have been identified in reviews of SHRM literature: the resource-based view (RBV); human capital theory; the behavioral perspective; the abilities, motivation, and opportunities (AMO) framework; and social exchange theory (Jiang & Messersmith, 2018). Consistently, RBV is regarded as the most important (Kaufman, 2015) or the most popular (Wright & Ulrich, 2017) among SHRM theories.

6.1 Strengths of the Strategic Perspective in Understanding the Human

In the strategic perspective, people at work are regarded as valuable assets, possessing work-related knowledge, skills, attributes, and other characteristics (KSAOs) essential for organizational outcomes (Barney & Wright, 1998; Beer et al., 2015; Ulrich, 2015). HRM architecture recognizes the resource-based view of the firm (Lepak & Snell, 1999) where resources which are valuable, rare, inimitable, non-substitutable, and organized (VRINO) are deployed (Barney, Wright, & Ketchen, 2001) to achieve competitive advantage for the organization (Kamoche, 1996).

The concept of human capital further supports the value of employee contributions. Human capital theory recognizes the collective contribution of the workforce as well as physical and financial assets (Becker, 1964). Lepak and Snell (1999) further affirm the value of HRM architecture in fostering employee contribution toward the value of a business enterprise.

High-performance work systems (HPWS) are important vehicles to achieve such organizational outcomes, and they are regarded as having universal application: "all else being equal, the use of high-performance work practices and good internal fit should lead to positive outcomes for all types of firms" (Huselid, 1995: 644). HPWS are now at the forefront of the current SHRM agenda (see Lv & Xu, 2018).

The strategic perspective also recognizes that employer and employee interests are aligned and that employers have employees' best interests at heart (Spencer, 2013). Such unitarism assumes that mechanisms to resolve conflict become unnecessary since common goals are automatically shared (Nankervis, Baird, Coffey, & Shields, 2017: 521).

Further, the strategic perspective provides HRM professionals with a clear direction for their role and how they spend their time, as it reinforces the importance of their adding value as business partners in managing talent and human capital (Pritchard, 2010; Ulrich, 2012, 2015).

6.2 Weaknesses of the Strategic Perspective in Understanding the Human

The strategic perspective exhibits a tendency of reducing those who do the work of organizations to instruments or commodities (De Gama, McKenna, & Peticca-Harris, 2013) and "treading dangerously close to placing [the] human in the same category with office furniture and computers" (Greenwood, 2002: 261). Such "mechanistic dehumanization" (Väyrynen & Laari-Salmela, 2018: 97), regarding people as machine-like, denies their humanity. In such a viewpoint, with its pursuit of productivity and efficiency, the "hard" model of HRM prevails (Guest, 1987), leading to increasing employee performance expectations, job insecurity, and lower job satisfaction (Kaye, 1999). Kaufman (2010) claims that greater motivation for the employee means work intensification, and more flexibility often means less job security.

The strategic perspective is prone to reify the person. György Lukács originally proposed the idea of reification to challenge ideologies where the products of workers' labor were independent of the social processes which created them. For Lukács, reification presents a false view of society and social relations, where

> [Man's] qualities and abilities are no longer an organic part of his personality, they are things which he [sic] can "own" or "dispose of" like the various objects of the external world. (Lukács, 1923: 100)

Axel Honneth revived Lukács' idea of reification in discussing modern forms of social life under capitalism and defined reification in terms of the various processes that promote a misrecognition, forgetting, or neglect of intersubjective recognition in the workplace and social relations (after Honneth, 1995, 2008).

Gazi Islam sees the reification of employees as "bearers or owners of traits, exemplars of categories … rather than as free agents whose self-expression is realized in and through such traits and categories" (Islam, 2012: 40). What reification leads to is "a kind of social pathology by which we forget the empathetic basis of our relations, turning our attention to instrumental uses of other people" (Islam, 2012: 43). The strategic perspective is prone to reduce people at work to bundles of discrete resources and capacities (Islam, 2012).

Within the strategic perspective, regarding people as "human capital" categorizes flesh and blood people (Fortier & Albert, 2015). While it is legitimate to refer to persons in general as "people," the aggregation and the meaning of "human capital" within HRM theory perhaps ignores the reality that humans are unique, that is, both similar and different from one another. Further, the concept of human capital was once alleged to be demeaning because it treated people as machines (Becker, 1996). While such hostility has waned, the risk remains that strategic HRM researchers may similarly treat human capital as a form of capital owned and controlled by the firm (Wright & McMahan, 2011).

The strategic perspective seems to be unclear about which HPWS lead to high performance. Despite attempts to distinguish between control-oriented and involvement-oriented HPWS (Ananthram, Teo, Connell, & Bish, 2017), such efforts do not illuminate what has been described as the "black box" of HPWS (Boxall, Ang, & Bartram, 2011). Kaufman (2015) asserts that Huselid's (1995) claim of the universal application of HPWS is fundamentally misspecified. Further, there are contradictory findings of HPWS which would question the claims in current HRM scholarship of beneficial outcomes for both employees and organizations of the strategic perspective (Van De Voorde & Beijer, 2015).

The strategic perspective's espousal of a unitarist view of the employment relationship might be a strength from the employer's viewpoint, but not necessarily from the employee's. Legge (1999) criticizes the tendency of SHRM to embody a unitarist view and that, until recently, the worker's perspective has been ignored (see also Edgar & Geare, 2014; Van Buren, Greenwood, & Sheehan, 2011). Williamson (1985) assumed that opportunistic behavior was more characteristic of employees than employers, and that SHRM seemed to be predicated on the assumption that controls had to be put in place to deal with employees' shirking of responsibility. Contrasted with this view is the assertion that "the idea that employers may be opportunistic and exploitative in their actions towards workers is not directly acknowledged [by economics]" (Spencer, 2013: 351).

The focus of the strategic perspective is upon the organization and employer interests. The strategic perspective adopts economism and financial wealth creation and underplays the need to pursue social value (Pirson, 2017c). Despite efforts to moderate its impact and attempts to integrate personalism and strategic management (Powell, 2014), the strategic perspective endorses Friedman (1962) in regarding the shareholder as the ultimate beneficiary of a business and that the responsibility of a firm is to its shareholders and to increase their profits, not to be morally responsible to wider beneficiaries.

The strategic perspective adopts an individualistic conception of the person and perhaps of an atomistic society (Ghoshal & Bartlett, 1998; Granovetter, 1985; Wilcox & Lowry, 2000). It legitimizes the casualization of the workforce, and the intensification of work, sometimes leading to employee harm (Mariappanadar, 2014) and the destruction of social inclusion (Sennett, 1999). The negative impact of SHRM upon employees has been summarized as "concerned with distancing, depersonalizing and dissembling, and acts in support of the . . . requirements of business, not of people" (De Gama et al., 2013: 97).

In the strategic perspective, HRM professionals are tools of management (Kinsey, 2012). While some HRM scholars advocate the importance of HRM being a credible business partner with management in adding strategic value (Barney & Wright, 1998; Ulrich, 2015), others see the role of the HRM professional as being a steward and the organization's conscience (Brown, Metz, Cregan, & Kulik, 2009; Macklin, 2006). The HRM profession appears to seek a balance between "value" and "values" (Wright & Snell, 2005) and whether it should be "guardians" or "gamblers" of well-being (Renwick, 2003).

In Fig. 1, the strategic perspective is identified as "individual resource" and "human capital." With its consideration of the person at work as a valuable asset and as a means of producing utility for organizational benefit, the strategic perspective is not aligned with Maritain's view of the person. The perceived strengths and weaknesses of the strategic perspective are now summarized in Table 1.

Table 1 Summary of the strengths and weaknesses of the strategic perspective

Strengths of the strategic perspective	Weaknesses of the strategic perspective
People are regarded as valuable assets for the organization	Tends to reduce people to instruments or commodities as "hard" HRM May regard "human capital" as a form of capital owned and controlled by organizations
As human resources and human capital, people are valuable, rare, inimitable, non-substitutable, and organized (VRINO) for competitive advantage	Prone to reify the person and reduce people at work to bundles of discrete resources and capacities Aggregation as human capital perhaps ignores the reality that humans are unique, not a category
High-performance work systems (HPWS) universally achieve positive organizational outcomes	The universal application of HPWS is perhaps misspecified There are contradictory outcomes of HPWS for both organizations and employees
Employer and employee interests are aligned in a unitarist viewpoint	Denies the plurality of interests between employers and employees
Adopts economism to pursue financial wealth creation for the organization	Underplays the need to pursue social value and legitimate outcomes for multiple stakeholders
	Adopts an individualistic conception of the person and perhaps of an atomistic society
	Legitimizes the casualization and intensification of work, perhaps leading to employee harm
Reinforces the role of HRM professionals as tools of management and business partners	Downplays the role of HRM professionals as employee advocates and guardians of employee well-being
	Is not aligned with Maritain's view of the person and the common good

7   The Humanistic Perspective in HRM Scholarship

Since Boethius, a human being has been regarded as a singular, rational entity (Gorman, 2011). Instead, Kitwood (1997) argues that all humans are properly regarded as persons with inherent dignity, even when they display diminished mental capacity as among children or adults with dementia. Therefore, a human (being) can be defined as an individual entity with physical, rational, nonrational, emotional, relational, and spiritual dimensions. This definition takes a holistic perspective, aligned with numerous scholars who advocate that "the human" refers to multiple dimensions beyond the purely biological.

The humanistic perspective is enshrined in humanistic management, which has been defined as "a management [theory] that emphasizes the human condition and is oriented to the development of human virtue, in all its forms, to its fullest extent" (Melé, 2003: 78–79). There is an increasing scholarship in this area with certain scholars being prominent including Aguado, Alcañiz, and Retolaza (2015), Dierksmeier (2015), Melé (2003), and Pirson (2017c).

7.1 Strengths of the Humanistic Perspective in Understanding the Human

The conception of the human being in humanistic management transcends the classical understanding of motives and needs about relatedness and satisfaction, to include transitive motives such as benevolence, as well as moral goods such as respect and flourishing (Melé, 2003). The humanistic viewpoint challenges the limited assumption of classical views that employee motivations are essentially self-interested, amoral, and non-spiritual (Guillen, Ferrero, & Hoffman, 2015).

In the humanistic perspective, the foundation of human nature is not wants, but needs, and its goal is not maximization, but balance (see Pirson, 2017c: 62). The additional human drives "to connect" and "to comprehend" are part of the humanistic perspective, not just the drives "to protect" and "to acquire" in the resourceful, evaluative, maximizing model [REMM] of economism (Pirson & Kimakowitz, 2010) which underpins the strategic perspective.

While the strategic perspective highlights the importance of utility, humanistic management highlights the importance of human dignity (Pirson, 2017c). Within the humanistic perspective, employees value and respond to managers who treat them with "respect, acceptance and communion" (Pirson & Lawrence, 2009: 553).

According to Dierksmeier (2015), the humanistic perspective recognizes the real *conditio humana,* not the fictional *homo economicus* of neoclassical economics. It broadens the conversation from the maximization of utility to a balance of interests (Pirson & Lawrence, 2009) and from the aspiration of wealth creation to well-being creation (Pirson, 2017a, 2017b). This paradigm shift from utilitarian economism to ecological capitalism has been expounded at length in the humanistic perspective (Aguado et al., 2015; Arnaud & Wasieleski, 2014; Dierksmeier, 2015; Fontrodona & Sison, 2006; Gassi & Habisch, 2011; Melé, 2008; Pirson, 2015; Spitzeck, 2011).

The common good is evident in humanistic management where a "community of persons embedded with an organizational culture . . . foster character" (Melé, 2003: 82) and that what characterizes a community is not "the multiplicity of subjects, but the unity of such multiplicity" (Melé, 2003: 83). The model of management in humanistic management is more conducive to societal value than the strategic perspective. Managers in the shareholder economy are stewards, while in the stakeholder economy, they are agents (Pirson & Lawrence, 2009). The mental model for humanistic management is that all business is "Human2Human business" (von Kimakowitz, 2017: 22). In such an approach, three characteristics of organizations, which strive to do as well as they do good, are "unconditional respect for human dignity, integration of ethical reflection in management decisions, and active ongoing engagement with stakeholders" (von Kimakowitz, 2017: 26).

The recognition of the humanity of the employee within a humanistic perspective successfully avoids the reification tendencies within the strategic perspective. Instead, recognition theory grounds social organization on the basis of individuals' needs for interpersonal recognition or affirmation and has a focus on "valorizing rather than the exploiting of employee capabilities" (Islam, 2013: 241). After Honneth and Margalit (2001), recognition can be defined as an affirmation of the basic personal bond between social actors, and their willingness to participate in society together. Recognition theory is useful for management, because it "does not constitute an anti-business view, claiming that all market relations are immoral" (Islam, 2013: 242). In the human-centered organization, people are valued for their humanness, and what they might deserve, not their resourcefulness, and what that costs (Keenoy, 1997: 386).

In the humanistic perspective, "the ultimate purpose of human existence is the notion of flourishing and well-being [*eudaimonia*]" (Pirson, 2017c: 75) rather than the wealth creation of the economistic, strategic perspective.

7.2 Weaknesses of the Humanistic Perspective in Understanding the Human

A surprising aspect of some advocates of the humanistic perspective is the apparent inconsistency in their endorsing the dignity of the human on the one hand while, on the other, claiming that the "view of other" is means and an end (Pirson & Lawrence, 2009: 555).

While the humanistic perspective challenges the economism of the strategic perspective with regard to its "view of other" as being means to an end, this "view of other" as means and an end, appears to be inconsistent with its own fundamental priority of affirming human dignity. Even if the intention is that the other person is a means and an end (as an object) and that only oneself retains the end (as a subject), this might be incompatible with the ideology of the humanistic perspective which seeks to transcend the economistic viewpoint which tends to objectify people. Accordingly, "one cannot trade off the dignity of one person in order to honor a greater dignity in two, ten, or a thousand persons" (Hill, 1980: 93). The Kantian "Formula of Humanity" (Kant, 1785) which embraces the principle that it is always wrong to treat others as a means must be affirmed, especially in a humanistic management discourse. Nonetheless, it might be possible to allow for a synthesis effect where those who do the work of organizations could be regarded as both means and ends, where their personal dignity is still upheld.

There is a vast literature on this Kantian "Categorical Imperative" and its interpretation, which is beyond the scope of this chapter. The point is that those who do the work of organizations must never be treated solely as a means: their dignity must always be affirmed, and they must never be exploited when voluntarily contributing to organizational wealth creation (thereby displaying usefulness and utility). This imperative and its reasonable application in practice appear to be unclear within the humanistic perspective.

Further, the humanistic perspective might be idealizing employees in its quest to overcome economism and to make a convincing case for an alternative approach. The positivity of comparative views of human nature therefore seems to be emphasized in various taxonomies. For example, economism espouses maximization and status, whereas the humanistic view espouses balance and well-being (Pirson, 2017c: 62).

The humanistic perspective perhaps also downplays the importance of the managerial prescription (Johnsen & Gudmand-Høyer, 2010) and the responsibility of the employer to manage viable, competitive organizations. As agents of the organization, managers are still legally required to work toward shareholder value. While this might not reflect the desired ideology of the humanistic perspective, it still seems to be the predominant viewpoint in practice.

The humanistic perspective is identified in Fig. 1 as "human being" and "community." With its consideration of the employee as a human being with dignity, as both means and end, the humanistic perspective then is reasonably aligned with Maritain's view of the person (as solely an end). The perceived strengths and weaknesses of the humanistic perspective are now summarized in Table 2.

Table 2 Summary of the strengths and weaknesses of the humanistic perspective

Strengths of the humanistic perspective	Weaknesses of the humanistic perspective
Challenges the view that employee motivations are essentially self-interested, amoral, and non-spiritual	That people are both means and ends appears to be inconsistent with its own fundamental priority of affirming human dignity
Defines the foundation of human nature as not wants but needs and that its goal is not maximization but balance	Perhaps idealizes employees in its quest to overcome the limitations of economism in the strategic perspective
Avoids the reification tendencies of the strategic perspective	Perhaps downplays the importance of managers as organizational agents and their managerial prerogative
Recognizes the importance of human dignity and of the community	
Asserts the ultimate purpose of human existence as human flourishing and well-being.	
Is reasonably aligned with Maritain's view of the person and the common good	

8   Bridging the Humanistic and Personalistic Perspectives

The concepts of the common good in relation to stakeholder theory and the corporation being understood as a community of persons (Melé, 2016) represent the pillars of a possible bridge between the humanistic and the personalistic perspectives. Retolaza et al. (2018) highlight that the key features of the stakeholder theory include: value creation for all stakeholders is the aim of the firm; a complex view of human nature is recognized; property rights are shared; and governance is in favor of multi-stakeholder interests.

The stakeholder theory recognizes that there are other beneficiaries to be considered apart from shareholders, a view consistent with Maritain's (1947) personalistic perspective, in that the benefits of organizations should "flow back" to citizens and provide a "liberty of expansion" to employees as well as to organizational owners and investors. Corporate social responsibility (CSR) also recognizes the same imperative, namely, that a business has social and environmental obligations which transcend the financial interests of shareholders. Michael Beer (Beer, Spector, Lawrence, Mills, & Nalthon, 1984), the original advocate of the so-called "soft" or "Harvard" model of HRM, has recently reiterated his multi-stakeholder advocacy for HRM theory and practice (Beer et al., 2015).

Helen Alford (2010) advocates that the human being is to be seen as a duality, both self-interested and self-giving. She challenges the view of humans as purely self-interested maximizers as not being inaccurate, but as being incomplete. Similarly, Naughton, Alford, and Brady (1995) challenge the purely economic purpose of the firm and they reinforce the notion that the common good provides an orientation, or a moral compass in favor of human development and generosity.

While Drucker (1954) once argued that the purpose of a business was to create and keep a customer, he also insisted that, while profitability was the crucial oxygen that kept any business alive, profit maximization was a dangerous myth which was not only detrimental to society, but also self-destructive for the organization itself. Rather, he advocated that a business was an "organ of society."

Other scholars have taken up this same point. Weisbord (1987) depicted the purpose of an organization as to foster dignity, meaning, and community. Melé (2016: 52) sees the business firm as "a community of persons, to be built up by reinforcing the sense of belonging, the awareness of common purposes, the links among those who form the community, and the willingness to cooperate to achieve common goals." Freeman and Ginena (2015) view a business as a human institution based upon "social cooperation" (page 17) and that it is "part of the community, not separated from it" (page 11). Similar narratives espouse "conscious capitalism" and the "economy of communion" (Frémeaux & Michelson, 2017).

Retolaza, San-José, and Ruíz-Roqueñi (2016) have even advocated the concept of "shapeholder" to extend the limits of the stakeholder theory. Shapeholders can be understood as stakeholders who do not represent their own interests, but those of excluded third parties. Shapeholders help organizations align the common good of the firm with social well-being.

9   The Personalistic Perspective in HRM Scholarship

While Acevedo (2012: 197) regards humanistic management as "inherently person-alistic," the personalistic perspective presents an alternate approach for HRM scholarship.

There is no dogma or unified doctrine that specifies a personalistic ideology (Whetstone, 2002): "personalism is not a system, but a perspective, a method, an exigency" (Mounier, 1951: 150). Personalism transcends individualism, with socia-bility and dignity as its inherent characteristics (Alford, 2010; Retolaza et al., 2018).

Five fundamental themes have been identified within the personalistic perspective: centrality of the person, subjectivity, and autonomy; human dignity; the person within community; and participation and solidarity (Gronbacher, 1998). The personalistic perspective is defined as a viewpoint about the nature of humanity which emphasizes the significance, uniqueness and inviolability of the person, as well as the person's essentially relational or communitarian dimension (after Williams & Bengtsson, 2016).

The personalistic perspective therefore integrates two key ideas: the "person" and the "common good," endorsing the approach of Maritain. Aspects of the person typically include the nature of the person, the person is an end not solely a means, and the person exists in relationship, which shall now be addressed.

9.1   The Nature of the Person

In a personalist perspective, a person is regarded as the author of their own destiny and possessing individual agency. The person is a "process not a product" (Rogers, 1961: 122). This "becoming a person" includes getting behind the mask of inauthenticity, allowing for the experience of feeling, and discovering the self (Rogers, 1961: 108–114). Personhood implies both a quest for, and the discovery of the self, "to become that self which one truly is" (Rogers, 1961: 163). The proper disposition toward a person is solicitude for the "I–Thou" not just concern for an "I–It" (Buber, 1958, 1975). For Buber, rather than concern for a problem in a calculating way, the proper relationship with a human being is care for a person in a reflective way. Citing Buber, Malloy and Hadjistavropoulos (2004) similarly propose that, when dealing with persons with dementia, one should move from the calculative "I–It" relationship to the calculative–reflective "I–Thou" relationship.

Holley (1978) enumerated the five essential qualities as a mind, a body, a social presence, autonomy, and a multidimensional harmony. Self-determination theory asserts that there are three innate psychological needs: competence, autonomy, and relatedness (Deci & Ryan, 2000). Arnaud and Wasieleski (2014) enumerate five aspects: liberty and self-determination with the right to develop one's potential; moral autonomy; dignity; the need to be socially integrated, recognized, and con-sidered as a unique and singular person; care for others; and a concern for the common good.

Such representative personalistic views espouse dignity, uniqueness, interiority, and freedom as being essential to the nature of personhood. These views are aligned with Maritain's viewpoint on the nature of the person.

9.2   The Person Is an End Not Solely a Means

The personalistic perspective adopts Kant's second formulation of the Categorical Imperative:

> Act in such a way that you always treat humanity, whether in your own person or in the person of any other, never simply as a means but always at the same time as an end. (Kant, 1785: 429)

The conditions for, and the implications of this principle are complex and have been explored elsewhere (Hill, 1980). In describing a "kingdom of ends," Kant distinguishes relative or personal ends from ends in themselves, in that the latter have dignity, whereas the former only have price (Kant, 1785). This idea may be a key to understanding the sense in which humanity is supposed to be an end in itself. Autonomy is said to be "the ground of dignity, not fear or hope of rewards" (Kant, 1785: 103), and that dignity is the fundamental reason why humanity is to be honored in word and gesture as well as in deed. Therefore, any disrespect and mockery of others is to be as opposed as is any self-disparagement or servility toward others (Hill, 1980).

9.3   The Person Exists in Relationship

A person is always "being-with" or *co-esse* other human beings, that is, identity and status as a person is a matter of intersubjectivity (Hill, 2013). Both *dasein* (being there) and *mitsein* (being with) are understood in the nature of a person. This idea of being-with echoes the old African concept of *ubuntu,* "I am because we are" (Gade, 2012).

Warren (2000) notes the strong individualistic orientation in SHRM philosophy. Western scholars typically emphasize the individualistic nature of the person, while Eastern (Li, 2012) and African (Obioha, 2014) scholars typically emphasize a more communal personhood. Obioha (2014) argues for a moderate communalism where mutuality and reciprocity occur between the individual and the community. Obioha (2014: 263) states that "communal consciousness helps to avoid the excesses of extreme individualism and makes room for the achievement of the common good necessary for social flourishing." He concludes by summarizing that "communal personhood is germane for the realization of this all important destiny, human well-being" (Obioha, 2014: 265). So, the person is a person with other persons.

Overall, the person is self-aware, self-determined, in process, has inherent dignity, is a subject not an object, is an end not solely a means, is relational, and seeks communion.

9.4   Strengths of the Personalistic Perspective in Understanding the Human

The personalistic perspective is aligned with Maritain's views on the nature of the person and on the importance of the common good.

The personalistic perspective endorses the humanistic perspective in recognizing human dignity, where the employee is a subject not an object (Fortier & Albert, 2015).

This personalistic perspective also challenges the strategic perspective in that employees are not "resourceful, evaluative maximizers" (Jensen & Meckling, 1994), a challenge shared with humanistic management (Pirson, 2017c). Rather, employees are persons with inherent altruism and connectedness.

The personalistic perspective, especially under Kant and Maritain, corrects the notion of some scholars in the humanistic perspective by asserting that human beings are not means and ends, but ends in themselves, and that they should never be treated solely as a means. That people are useful in contributing to organizational goals is acknowledged in both strategic and humanistic perspectives: the personalistic perspective perhaps offers an emphasis which is implicit in these two HRM perspectives.

The personalistic perspective challenges the view of the strategic perspective where employees are tradeable individuals, short-term commodities to "turn on and off like a tap" (Legge, 1999: 251). While individuals might be replaceable, the person is unique and irreplaceable (Maritain, 1947), of incomparable worth (Kant, 1785), with innate self-determination (Deci & Ryan, 2000).

The personalistic perspective overcomes both the social aggregation and collectivist orientation of human capital in the strategic perspective, and strengthens the humanistic perspective in that persons are not "a category,", but unique "flesh and blood" beings (Fortier & Albert, 2015: 3) who are at once similar and different from each other.

The personalistic perspective also addresses the possible social atomization (Granovetter, 1985), reductionism (Fortier & Albert, 2015), and reification (Honneth, 2008) of the individual within a strategic perspective. It presents a nuanced view of both human nature itself, and of society.

The personalistic perspective recognizes the understanding of "community of persons" (Melé, 2003: 77) and the "social community" (Pirson & Lawrence, 2009: 555) within the humanistic perspective, but strengthens it when endorsing Maritain's

(1947) viewpoint on the "common good," where persons engage in both the "liberty of expansion" and the sharing or "flowback" of prosperity to all.

The personalistic perspective presents a view which is respectful of people with diminished capacity. Person-centered caring for dementia patients (Kitwood, 1997) suggests guidelines for HRM in relating to employees with diminished capacity, notwithstanding that the concept of "person-centeredness" was first employed in a health-care context. For example, recent research by Cavanagh et al. (2017) on employing workers with disabilities provides evidence that enhanced knowledge and support overcomes employer discrimination and negative attitudes.

The personalistic perspective offers a supportive narrative for HRM professionals who adopt an employee-centered approach to their HRM activities (Brown et al., 2009; Macklin, 2006).

9.5   Weaknesses of the Personalistic Perspective in Understanding the Human

The personalistic perspective might presume that unique self-determination and freedom in the employment relationship are desired and achievable by all those who do the work of organizations. Indeed, the employment relationship has paradoxes and dilemmas (Kramar & Holland, 2015) that are not easily resolved by simply specifying optimum freedom, discretion, and voice.

The personalistic perspective might be appropriated to diminish the importance of the employer in the employment relationship, to diminish the managerial prerogative (Johnsen & Gudmand-Høyer, 2010) and managers' legitimate responsibility of ensuring performance from employees (Spencer, 2013).

While efforts are being made to transcend the profit-making emphasis of businesses within the personalistic perspective and consider human value (Neesham, Hartel, Coghill, & Sarros, 2010), it is unclear how people actually contribute toward "human value" if they are not meant to be a means to an end, but ends in themselves (after Kant, 1785). More work needs to be done in ensuring that employees are not treated solely as means, notwithstanding the voluntary nature of their contributing KSAOs for organizational benefit.

In Fig. 1, the personalistic perspective is identified as "person" and "common good." With its consideration of the employee as a valued person with dignity, and as an end and not solely as a means, the personalistic perspective is aligned with Maritain's view of the person. The perceived strengths and weaknesses of the personalistic perspective are now summarized in Table 3.

Table 3 Summary of the strengths and weaknesses of the personalistic perspective

Strengths of the personalistic perspective	Weaknesses of the personalistic perspective
Transcends individualism with dignity and sociability as its inherent characteristics	Might presume that unique self-determination and freedom in the employment relationship are desired and achievable
Emphasizes the significance, uniqueness, and inviolability of the person and their essential relational or communitarian nature	Might be appropriated to diminish the importance of the employer in the employment relationship
Asserts that a person is the author of their own destiny possessing individual agency and self-determination	Might be unclear how people actually contribute toward "human value"
Espouses the view that the person is unique and irreplaceable, not a short-term, tradeable commodity as in the strategic perspective	
Perhaps corrects the notion in the humanistic perspective that human beings are not "means and ends" but "ends" in themselves and reinforces that people should never be treated solely as a means	
Overcomes both the social aggregation and collectivist orientation of the concept of human capital in the strategic perspective	
Addresses the possible social atomization, reductionism, and reification tendencies of the strategic perspective	
Strengthens the community focus in the humanistic perspective by emphasizing the liberty of expansion and the flowback of prosperity with its notion of the common good	
Presents a view of humanity which is respectful of people with diminished capacity	
Offers a supportive narrative for HRM professionals who adopt an employee-centered approach	
Is clearly aligned with Maritain's view of the person and the common good	

10 Overall Summary of the Three Perspectives for HRM Scholarship

Figure 1 now represents an overall summary of these three perspectives for HRM scholarship. The horizontal dimension contrasts the three perspectives according to their respective viewpoints about employees being valuable with utility, and their being valued with dignity. The vertical dimension juxtaposes the macro- and micro-foundations of strategic management.

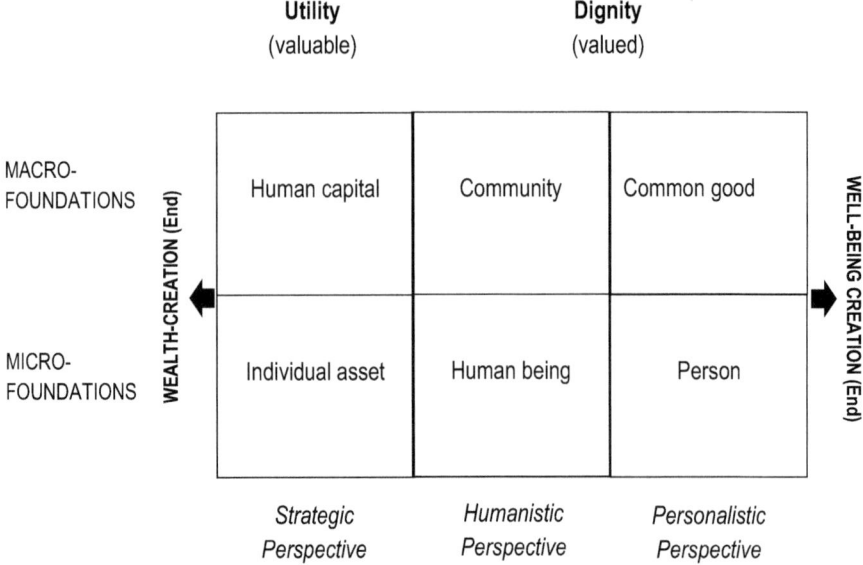

Fig. 1 Three HRM perspectives

10.1 The Vertical Dimension: Macro- and Micro-foundations of Strategic Management

In the social sciences, micro-foundations and macro-foundations explore methodological individualism or methodological collectivism, respectively (Barney & Felin, 2013). Specifically, micro-foundations in strategic management refer to domains such as HRM at the individual and group level, while macro-foundations refer to organization-level or firm-level considerations (Molina-Azorin, 2014). This distinction in strategic management is employed here to assist in integrating our research on these three perspectives for HRM.

On macro-foundational grounds, and within the strategic perspective, people are considered as "human capital." At the other pole of the macro-foundational dimension is the "common good" with communal harmony attained through integral humanism.

In Fig. 1, and adopting the distinction of Maritain (1947), micro-foundations are represented as the "individual resource" within the strategic perspective, as "person" within the personalistic perspective, with "human being" as the bridging descriptor within the humanistic perspective. In the strategic perspective, the goal of human nature is maximization (Jensen & Meckling, 1994); in the humanistic perspective, it is balance (Pirson, 2017c); and in the personalistic perspective, it is human flourishing (Arjoon et al., 2018). In both humanistic and personalistic perspectives, the focal point of human nature is both relational and communal.

10.2 The Horizontal Dimension: Three HRM Perspectives

In Fig. 1, the poles of the horizontal axis depict the contrasts between wealth creation through HPWS and well-being creation through recognition and respect.

The strategic perspective in the left-hand column of Fig. 1 is characterized by the deployment of HPWS, where KSAOs are bundled to form a valuable resource (Lepak & Snell, 1999). The strategic perspective acknowledges that those who do the work of organizations are a valuable means, possessing utility to achieve organizational outcomes.

The humanistic perspective in the middle column of Fig. 1 recognizes the inherent dignity of those who do the work of organizations (Pirson, 2017b). They are valued human beings and both "means and an end" (Pirson & Lawrence, 2009: 555) in the pursuit of well-being. Collectively, people are understood as a "social community" (Pirson & Lawrence, 2009: 555) or as a "community of persons" (Melé, 2003: 82) where multiple stakeholders benefit from their endeavors in the workplace (Pirson, 2017b, 2017c).

The personalistic perspective in the right-hand column of Fig. 1 also recognizes the dignity of those who do the work of organizations, that they are valued as persons, and regards them as ends in themselves and not simply as means (after Kant, 1785). Persons have optimum discretion and self-determination, who cooperate toward the common good and whose benefits are "fully shared" (Maritain, 1947). The personalistic perspective respects their uniqueness as persons, fostering communal harmony toward the common good.

11 Conclusion

11.1 Implications for HRM Scholarship

In the light of an examination of these three HRM perspectives, a number of considerations for further HRM research are proposed:

Firstly, to what extent are these three perspectives the only or the main ones in current HRM and SHRM research, and to what extent are they contested among HRM scholars?

Secondly, to what extent does the personalistic perspective add significant value to the perspective of humanistic management in understanding those who do the work of organizations, or is such a distinction problematic? Specifically, how does Maritain's notion of "the common good" extend (if at all) the notions of "social community" (Pirson & Lawrence, 2009) and of "community of persons"

(Melé, 2003) within humanistic management theory? Would personalism then, be viewed as true humanism, rather than as an alternative perspective for HRM theorists?

Thirdly, apart from Maritain's philosophy of person and the common good, what other approaches might provide useful theoretical "lenses" for examining HRM theories about those who contribute to organizations?

Fourthly, to what extent does the personalistic perspective itself exhibit a tendency to reify certain abstract concepts such as "resource," "human," and "person" while seeking to correct the reification and commodification tendencies within the strategic perspective?

Fifthly, what factors contribute to the apparent persistence of the strategic perspective in HRM theory when other narratives exist about the human condition and society itself?

Sixthly, to what extent do HPWS exhibit instrumental assumptions of human nature and reinforce a strategic perspective within HRM scholarship? How well does HRM scholarship investigate the impact of HPWS upon persons and community well-being in the quest for organizational productivity?

11.2   Implications for HRM in Practice

A number of suggestions for implementing a personalistic perspective are also offered:

Firstly, devise personalized employment contracts which are not only linked with staff vacancies and current role descriptions, but also linked with each person's unique skill sets, recognize employee self-determination, and their drives to connect and to comprehend. For HRM practitioners, autonomy is to be fostered, so those who do the work of organizations have the power to "set their own ends" as persons (after Kant, 1797: 51).

Secondly, encourage forms of voice and participation as in worker councils and ensure fair and equitable reward schemes such as profit sharing where the benefits of their efforts "flow back" (after Maritain, 1947).

Thirdly, create leadership development programs which encourage autonomy-supportive leadership of staff rather than merely compliance-supportive leadership.

Fourthly, implement reward and recognition programs which are geared toward self-determination and development, rather than contingent reward and performance.

Fifthly, craft HRM policies which foster healthy and nontoxic cultures, where the dignity of people is respected, and where they are treated as ends, not solely as means.

Sixthly, support people in the workplace in contributing toward the common good, and set up programs where a healthy, civil society can be developed and actualized.

The objectives of this chapter were to identify and define three HRM perspectives: to examine their relative strengths and weaknesses, to integrate these three perspectives (Fig. 1), and to offer suggestions for further research for both HRM theory and practice. The main contribution of this chapter was to examine the assumptions within each HRM perspective in terms of the philosophy of Jacques Maritain who distinguished between the "lower self" (the individual) and the "higher self" (the person).

Words do matter, and the meaning of words is found "in their use" (Wittgenstein, 1953, para 43). It is in language that concepts are both created and conveyed: as Karen Legge concludes, "the representation we make of employees is not just an exercise in rhetoric" (Legge, 1999: 260). Those who do the work of organizations have been variously described here as resources, as humans, and as persons. While acknowledging the contribution of the strategic perspective, this chapter sought to guide HRM discourse with the contributions of humanistic and personalistic perspectives.

References

Acevedo, A. (2012). Personalist business ethics and humanistic management: Insights into Jacques Maritain. *Journal of Business Ethics, 105*, 197–219.

AD [Amsterdam Declaration]. (2002). *The fundamentals of modern humanism.* International Humanist and Ethical Union. Accessed September 9, 2018, from https://iheu.org/about/human ism/the-amsterdam-declaration

Aguado, R., Alcañiz, L., & Retolaza, J. L. (2015). A new role for the firm incorporating sustainability and human dignity: Conceptualization and measurement. *Human Systems Management, 34*, 43–56.

Aguado, R., Alcañiz, L., Retolaza, J. L., & Albareda, L. (2016). Jesuit business education model: In search of a new role for the firm based on sustainability and dignity. *Journal of Technology, Management and Innovation, 11*(1), 12–18.

Aguado, R., Retolaza, J. L., & Alcañiz, L. (2017). Dignity at the level of the firm: Beyond the stakeholder approach. In M. Kostera & M. Pirson (Eds.), *Dignity and the organization*. London: Palgrave Macmillan.

AHA [American Humanist Association]. (2018). *Definition of humanism.* Accessed September 9, 2018, from https://americanhumanist.org

Alford, H. (2010). The practical wisdom of personalism. *Journal of Management Development, 29* (7–8), 697–705.

Ananthram, S., Teo, S. T., Connell, J., & Bish, A. (2017). Control and involvement HR practices in Indian call centres: Still searching for answers. *Asia Pacific Journal of Human Resources, 35*(1). Accessed December 12, 2017, from https://doi.org/10.1111/1744-7941.12153

Arjoon, S., Turriago-Hoyos, A., & Thoene, U. (2018). Virtuousness and the common good as a conceptual framework for harmonizing the goals of the individual, organizations, and the economy. *Journal of Business Ethics, 147*, 143–163.

Arnaud, S., & Wasieleski, D. M. (2014). Corporate humanistic responsibility: Social performance through managerial discretion of the HRM. *Journal of Business Ethics, 120*, 313–334.

Barney, J. B., & Felin, T. (2013). What are microfoundations? *The Academy of Management Perspectives, 27*(2), 138–155.

Barney, J. B., & Wright, P. M. (1998). On becoming a strategic partner: The role of human resources in gaining competitive advantage. *Human Resource Management, 37*(1), 31–46.

Barney, J., Wright, M., & Ketchen, D. J., Jr. (2001). The resource-based view of the firm: Ten years after 1991. *Journal of Management, 27*, 625–641.

Battaglia, V. (2005). Building a new Christendom. *Australian eJournal of Theology, 5.* Accessed December 6, 2017, from http://aejt.com.au/__data/assets/pdf_file/0011/395516/AEJT_5.14_ Battaglia.pdf

Becker, G. S. (1964). *Human capital*. New York: Columbia.

Becker, G. S. (1996). *The economic way of looking at behavior: The Nobel lecture*. Essays in Public Policy, No. 69. Palo Alto, CA: Hoover Institution, Stanford University.

Beer, M., Boselie, P., & Brewster, C. (2015). Back to the future: Implications for the field of HRM of the multi-stakeholder perspective proposed 30 years ago. *Human Resource Management, 54* (3), 427–438.

Beer, M., Spector, B., Lawrence, P., Mills, Q., & Nalthon, R. (1984). *Managing human assets*. Boston, MA: Harvard Business Press.

Boxall, P., Ang, S. H., & Bartram, T. (2011). Analysing the 'black box' of HRM: Uncovering HR goals, mediators, and outcomes in the standardized service environment. *Journal of Management Studies, 48*(7), 1504–1532. Accessed September 20, 2018, from https://doi.org/10.1111/j.1467-6486.2010.00973.x

Boxall, P., & Purcell, J. (2008). *Strategy and human resource management*. Hampshire: Palgrave Macmillan.

Brown, M., Metz, I., Cregan, C., & Kulik, C. T. (2009). Irreconcilable differences? Strategic human resource management and employee wellbeing. *Asia Pacific Journal of Human Resources, 47* (3), 270–294.

Buber, M. (1958). *I and Thou* (R. G. Smith, Trans.). Edinburgh: T & T Clark.

Buber, M. (1975). *Between man and man*. New York, NY: Macmillan.

Capaldi, N. (2004). Jacques Maritain: La vie intellectuelle. *The Review of Metaphysics, 58*(2), 399–421.

Cavanagh, J., Bartram, T., Meacham, H., Bigby, C., Oakman, J., & Fossey, E. (2017). Supporting workers with disabilities: A scoping review of the role of HRM in contemporary organizations. *Asia Pacific Journal of Human Resources, 55*, 6–43.

Compendium of the Social Doctrine of the Church (CSDC). (2004). *Pontifical council for justice and peace*. Vatican City.

De Gama, N., McKenna, S., & Peticca-Harris, A. (2013). Ethics and HRM: Theoretical and conceptual analysis. *Journal of Business Ethics, 111*, 97–108.

Deci, E. L., & Ryan, R. M. (2000). The 'what' and 'why' of goal pursuits: Human needs and the self-determination of behavior. *Psychological Inquiry, 11*(4), 227–268.

Delbridge, R. (2006). Extended review: The vitality of labor process analysis. *Organization Studies, 27*(8), 1209–1219.

Descartes, R. [1644] (2009). *Letter of the author to the French translator of the principles of philosophy serving for a preface* (J. Veitch, Trans.), *Selections from the principles of philosophy*. Michigan: Ezreads Publications LLC, & Hatfield, G. (2016). 'René Descartes'. Edward N. Zalta (Ed.), *The Stanford encyclopedia of philosophy* (Summer 2016 edition). Retrieved May 31, 2016, from https://plato.stanford.edu/archives/sum2016/entries/descartes

Dierksmeier, C. (2015). Human dignity and the business of business. *Human Systems Management, 34*, 33–42.

Drucker, P. (1954). *The practice of management*. New York, NY: Harper Collins.

Edgar, F., & Geare, A. (2014). An employee-centered analysis: Professionals' experiences and reactions to HRM. *The International Journal of Human Resource Management, 25*(5), 673–695.

Evans, J. W. (1952, April). Jacques Maritain's personalism. *The Review of Politics, 14*(2), 166–177.

Ferris, G. R., Hall, A. T., Todd Royle, M., & Martocchio, J. J. (2004). Theoretical developments in the field of human resources management: Issues and challenges for the future. *Organizational Analysis, 12*(3), 231–254.

Fontrodona, J., & Sison, A. J. G. (2006). The nature of the firm, agency theory and shareholder theory: A critique from philosophical anthropology. *Journal of Business Ethics, 66*(1), 33–42.

Fortier, M., & Albert, M.-N. (2015). From resource to human being: Towards persons management, *SAGE Open, 5*(3), 1–15. Accessed May 31, 2017, from http://journals.sagepub.com/doi/pdf/10.1177/2158244015604347

Freeman, R. E., & Ginena, K. (2015). Rethinking the purpose of the corporation: Challenges from stakeholder theory. *Notizie di Politeia, XXXI, 117*, 9–18.

Frémeaux, S., & Michelson, G. (2017). The common good of the firm and humanistic management: Conscious capitalism and the economy of communion. *Journal of Business Ethics, 145,* 701–709.

Friedman, M. (1962). *Capitalism and freedom.* Chicago: University of Chicago Press.

Gade, C. B. N. (2012). What is 'ubuntu'? Different interpretations among South Africans of African descent. *South African Journal of Philosophy, 31*(3), 484–503.

Gassi, W., & Habisch, A. (2011). Ethics and economics: Towards a new humanistic. *Journal of Business Ethics, 99*(1), 37–49.

Ghoshal, S., & Bartlett, C. (1998). *The individualized corporation.* London: Heinemann.

Gorman, M. (2011). Personhood, potentiality and normativity. *The American Catholic Philosophical Quarterly, 85*(3), 483–498.

Granovetter, M. (1985). Economic action and social structure: The problem of embeddedness. *American Journal of Sociology, 91*(1), 481–510.

Greenwood, M. R. (2002). Ethics and HRM: A review and conceptual analysis. *Journal of Business Ethics, 36*(3), 261–279.

Greenwood, M. R. (2013). Ethical analysis of HRM: A review and research agenda. *Journal of Business Ethics, 114,* 355–366.

Gronbacher, G. (1998). The need for economic personalism. *The Journal of Markets and Morality, 1*(1), 1–34.

Guest, D. (1987). Human resource management and industrial relations. *Journal of Management Studies, 24*(5), 503–521.

Guillen, M., Ferrero, I., & Hoffman, W. M. (2015, February). The neglected ethical and spiritual motivations in the workplace. *Journal of Business Ethics, 128*(4), 803–816. Accessed September 20, 2018, from https://doi.org/10.1007/s10551-013-1985-7

Habermas, J. (1988). *The theory of communicative action* (Vol. 2). Boston: Beacon Press.

Harney, B. (2014). Researching HRM to enhance understanding: The neglected role of ontology. In C. Machado & J. P. Davim (Eds.), *Work organization and human resource management* (pp. 153–163). Bern: Springer.

Hicks, D. (2011). *Dignity: Its essential role in resolving conflict.* Pennsylvania: The Maple Press.

Hill, T. E. (1980). Humanity as an end in itself. *Ethics, 91*(1), 84–99.

Hill, C. D. (2013). *Who am I? Experience as the unity between the person and the world in the philosophy of Gabriel Marcel (1889–1973),* an unpublished dissertation for the degree of Doctor of Philosophy, The Catholic University of America.

Hodson, R. (2001). *Dignity at work.* Cambridge: Cambridge University Press.

Holley, R. (1978). *Religious education and religious understanding: An introduction to the philosophy of religious education.* London: Routledge & Kegan Paul.

Honneth, A. (1995). *The struggle for recognition: The moral grammar of social conflicts.* Cambridge: Polity Press.

Honneth, A. (2008). Reification and recognition: A new look at an old idea. In M. Jay (Ed.), *Reification: A new look at an old idea* (pp. 17–96). Oxford: Oxford University Press.

Honneth, A., & Margalit, A. (2001). Recognition. *Proceedings of the Aristotelian Society, 75,* 111–139.

Huselid, M. A. (1995). The impact of human resource management practices on turnover, productivity and corporate financial performance. *Academy of Management Journal, 38*(3), 635–672.

Islam, G. (2012). Recognition, reification, and practices of forgetting: Ethical implications of human resource management. *Journal of Business Ethics, 111,* 37–48.

Islam, G. (2013). Recognising employees: Reification, dignity and promoting care in management. *Cross Cultural Management, 20*(2), 235–250.

Janssens, M., & Steyaert, C. (1999). The inhuman space of HRM: Sensing the subject. *Organization, 6*(2), 371–383.

Jensen, M., & Meckling, W. H. (1994). The nature of man. *The Journal of Applied and Corporate Finance, Summer,* 4–19.

Jiang, K., & Messersmith, J. (2018). On the shoulders of giants: A meta-review of strategic human resource management. *The International Journal of Human Resource Management, 29*(1), 6–33.

Johnsen, R., & Gudmand-Høyer, M. (2010). Lacan and the lack of humanity in HRM. *Organization, 17*(3), 331–344.

Kahneman, D. (2012). *Thinking fast and slow.* London: Penguin Books.

Kamoche, K. (1996). Strategic human resource management within a resource-capability view of the firm. *Journal of Management Studies, 33*(2), 213–233.

Kant, I. [1785] (1964). *Groundwork of the metaphysics of morals* (H. J. Paton, Trans.). New York: Harper & Row.

Kant, I. [1797] (1964) *The doctrine of virtue* (M. J. Gregor, Trans.). New York: Harper & Row.

Kaufman, B. E. (2010, April). SHRM theory in the post-Huselid era: Why it is fundamentally misspecified. *Industrial Relations, 49*(2), 286–313.

Kaufman, B. E. (2015, May–June). Evolution of strategic HRM as seen through two founding books: A 30th anniversary perspective on development of the field. *Human Resource Management, 54*(3), 389–407.

Kaye, L. (1999). Strategic human resources management in Australia: The human cost. *International Journal of Manpower, 20*(8), 577–587.

Keenoy, T. (1997). HRMism and the language of re-presentation. *Journal of Management Studies, 34*(5), 825–841.

Kinsey, S. (2012). *Professional partner or management's bitch?* A discourse analytic study of the identity construction of HR practitioners in English local government, PhD thesis, The University of Nottingham.

Kitwood, T. (1997). *Dementia reconsidered: The person comes first.* Buckingham: Open University Press.

Kramar, R. (2014). Beyond strategic human resource management: Is sustainable human resource management the next approach? *The International Journal of Human Resource Management, 25*(8), 1069–1089.

Kramar, R., Bartram, T., De Cheri, H., Noe, R. A., Hollenbeck, J. R., Gerhart, B., & Wright, P. M. (2014). *Human resource management: Strategy, people, performance, 5e.* North Ryde, NSW: McGraw Hill.

Kramar, R., & Holland, P. (2015). *Capstone HRM: Dynamics and ambiguity in the workplace.* Prahan, VIC: Tilde University Press.

Legge, K. (1999). Representing people at work. *Organization, 6*(2), 247–264.

Lepak, D. P., & Snell, S. A. (1999). The human resource architecture: Toward a theory of human capital allocation and development. *The Academy of Management Review, 24*(1), 31–48.

Li, Y. (2012). The philosophical underpinnings of Western HRM theory. *Frontiers of Philosophy in China, 7*(2), 317–346.

Lukács, G. [1923] (1971). Reification and the consciousness of the proletariat. In *History and class consciousness* (pp. 83–222) (R. Livingstone, Trans.). Cambridge, MA: MIT Press.

Lv, Z., & Xu, T. (2018). Psychological contract breach, high-performance work system and engagement: The mediated effect of person-organization fit. *The International Journal of Human Resource Management, 29*(7), 1257–1284.

Macklin, R. (2006). The moral autonomy of human resource managers. *Asia Pacific Journal of Human Resources, 44*(2), 211–221.

Malloy, D. C., & Hadjistavropoulos, T. (2004). The problem of pain management among persons with dementia, personhood, and the ontology of relationships. *Nursing Philosophy, 5,* 147–159.

Mariappanadar, S. (2014). Stakeholder harm index: A framework to review work intensification from the critical HRM perspective. *Human Resource Management Review, 24,* 311–329.

Maritain, J. [1936] (1996). *Integral humanism: Freedom in the modern world and a letter on independence – The collected works of Jacques Maritain,* Volume II, O. Bird (Ed.), (O. Bird, J. Evans, & R. O'Sullivan, Trans.). Notre Dame, IN: University of Notre Dame Press.

Maritain, J. [1947] (1966). *The person and the common good* (J. J. Fitzgerald, Trans.). Notre Dame, IN: University of Notre Dame Press.

Melé, D. (2003). The challenge of humanistic management. *Journal of Business Ethics, 44,* 77–88.

Melé, D. (2008). Integrating ethics into management. *Journal of Business Ethics, 78,* 291–297.

Melé, D. (2009). Integrating personalism into virtue-based business ethics: The personalistic and the common good principles. *Journal of Business Ethics, 88*(1), 227–244.

Melé, D. (2016). Understanding humanistic management. *Humanistic Management Journal, 1*, 33–55.

Molina-Azorin, J. (2014). Micro-foundations of strategic management: Toward micro-foundational research in resource-based theory. *BRQ Business Research Quarterly, 17*(2), 102–114.

Mounier, E. (1951). *Be not afraid: A denunciation of despair* (C. Rowland, Trans.). London: Sheed and Ward.

Nag, R., Hambrick, D. C., & Chen, M.-J. (2007). What is strategic management really? Inductive derivation of a consensus definition of the field. *Management Journal, 28*(9), 935–955.

Nankervis, A., Baird, M., Coffey, J., & Shields, J. (2017). *Human resource management: Strategy and practice, 9e*. South Melbourne: Cenage.

Naughton, M. J., Alford, H., & Brady, B. (1995). The common good and the purpose of the firm: A critique of the shareholder and stakeholder models from the Catholic social tradition. *Journal of Human Values, 1*(2), 221–237.

Neesham, C., Hartel, C. J., Coghill, K., & Sarros, J. C. (2010). Profit-making vs. human value: Philosophy's contribution. *Equality, Diversity and Inclusion: An International Journal, 29*(6), 593–608.

Obioha, P. U. (2014). A communitarian understanding of the human person as a philosophical basis for human development. *The Journal of Pan African Studies, 6*(8), 247–267.

Pirson, M. (2015). Conceptualizing humanistic management as an alternative to managing in a post-crisis world. *Human Systems Management Journal, 34*, 1–4.

Pirson, M. (2017a). *Dignity and well-being as cornerstones of humanistic management*. Humanistic Management Association. Research paper series no. 17-19. Gabelli School of Business, Fordham University Research Paper No. 2916454. Accessed May 10, 2016, from https://doi.org/10.2139/ssrn.2916454

Pirson, M. (2017b). *Working alternatives: From capitalism to humanistic management?* (May 1). Humanistic Management Association. Research paper series no. 17-25. Accessed May 10, 2016, from https://ssrn.com/abstract=2961559

Pirson, M. (2017c). *Humanistic management: Protecting and promoting well-being*. Cambridge: Cambridge University Press.

Pirson, M., & Kimakowitz, E. (2010). Towards a human-centered theory and practice of the firm. *SSRN Electronic Journal*. Accessed September 20, 2018, from https://doi.org/10.2139/ssrn.1654827

Pirson, M., & Lawrence, P. R. (2009). Humanism in business – Towards a paradigm shift? *Journal of Business Ethics, 93*, 553–565.

Powell, T. C. (2014). Strategic management and the person. *Strategic Organization, 12*(3), 200–207.

Pritchard, K. (2010). Becoming an HR strategic partner: Tales of transition. *Human Resource Management Journal, 20*(2), 175–188.

Renwick, D. (2003). HR managers: Guardians of employee wellbeing? *Personnel Review, 32*(3), 341–359.

Retolaza, J. L., Aguado, R., & Alcañiz, L. (2018). Stakeholder theory through the lenses of Catholic social thought. *Journal of Business Ethics*. Accessed September 10, 2018, from https://doi.org/10.1007/s10551-018-3963-6

Retolaza, J. L., San-José, L., & Ruíz-Roqueñi, M. (2016). *Social accounting for sustainability: Monetizing the social value*. New York, NY: Springer.

Rogers, C. R. (1961). *On becoming a person*. Boston, MA: Houghton Mifflin.

Sen, A. (2002). *Rationality and freedom, 2e*. Cambridge, MA: Harvard University Press.

Sennett, R. (1999). How work destroys social inclusion. *New Statesman, 31st May, London*, 25–27.

Simons, R. (1995). Rediscovering the common good. In S. Rees & G. Rodley (Eds.), *The human costs of managerialism: Advocating the recovery of humanity* (pp. 271–284). Leichardt, NSW: Pluto Press.

Sison, A. J. G. (2007). Toward a common good theory of the firm: The Tasubinsa case. *Journal of Business Ethics, 74*(4), 471–480.

Sison, A. J. G., & Fontrodona, J. (2012). The common good of the firm in the Aristotelian-Thomistic tradition. *Business Ethics Quarterly, 22*(2), 211–246.

Spencer, D. A. (2013). Barbarians at the gate: A critical appraisal of the influence of economics on the field and practice of HRM. *Human Resource Management Journal, 23*(4), 346–359.

Spitzeck, H. (2011). An integrated model of humanistic management. *Journal of Business Ethics, 99*(1), 57–62.

Steyaert, C., & Janssens, M. (1999). Human and inhuman resource management: Saving the subject of HRM. *Organization, 6*(2), 181–198.

Turkson, P. K. A. (2017). Pope Francis' integral human development: An inclusive growth proposal. *Humanist Management Journal*. Accessed December 20, 2017, from https://doi.org/10.1007/s41463-017-0030-x

Ulrich, D. (2012). HR talent and the new HR competencies. *Strategic HR Review, 11*(4), 217–222.

Ulrich, D. (2015). Are we there yet? What's next for HR? *Human Resource Management Review, 25*, 188–204.

UNDHR. (1948). *The United Nations Declaration of Human Rights*. General Assembly Resolution, 217-A. Accessed December 10, 2017, from http://www.un.org/en/universal-declaration-human-rights

Van Buren, H. J., III, Greenwood, M., & Sheehan, C. (2011). Strategic human resource management and the decline of the employee focus. *Human Resource Management Review, 21*, 209–219.

Van De Voorde, K., & Beijer, S. (2015). The role of employee HR attributions in the relationships between high-performance work systems and employee outcomes. *Human Resource Management Journal, 25*(1), 62–78.

Väyrynen, T., & Laari-Salmela, S. (2018). Men, mammals, or machines? Dehumanization embedded in organizational practices. *Journal of Business Ethics, 147*(1), 95–113.

von Kimakowitz, E. (2017). *An introduction to humanistic management*. Accessed December 10, 2017, from https://www.soka.ac.jp/files/ja/20170419 14025.pdf

Waldron, J. (2009). *Dignity, rank, and rights*. The Tanner Lectures on Human Values, University of California, Berkeley, April 21–23. Accessed September 20, 2018, from https://tannerlectures.utah.edu/_documents/a-to-z/w/Waldron_09.pdf

Warren, R. C. (2000). Putting the person back into human resource management. *Business and Professional Ethics Journal, 19*(3 & 4), 181–198.

Weisbord, M. R. (1987). *Productive workplaces revisited: Organizing and managing for dignity, meaning and community*. San Francisco, CA: Jossey-Bass.

Whetstone, J. T. (2002). Personalism and moral leadership: The servant leader with a transforming vision. *Business Ethics: A European Review, 11*(4), 385–392.

Wilcox, T., & Lowry, D. (2000). Beyond resourcefulness: Casual workers and the human-centered organization. *Business and Professional Ethics Journal, 19*(3 & 4), 29–53.

Williams, T. D., & Bengtsson, J. O. (2016) Personalism. In E. N. Zalta (Ed.), *The Stanford encyclopedia of philosophy* (Summer ed.). Accessed December 11, 2017, from https://plato.stanford.edu/archives/sum2016/entries/personalism

Williamson, O. (1985). *The economic institutions of capitalism*. New York: Free Press.

Wittgenstein, L. (1953). *Philosophical investigations*, G. E. M. Anscombe & R. Rhees (Eds.), (G. E. M. Anscombe, Trans.). Oxford: Oxford University Press.

Wright, P. M., & McMahon, G. C. (1992). Theoretical perspectives for strategic human resource management. *Journal of Management, 18*(2), 295–320.

Wright, P., & McMahan, G. C. (2011). Exploring human capital: Putting human back into strategic human resource management. *Human Resource Management Journal, 21*(2), 93–104.

Wright, P. M., & Snell, S. A. (2005). Partner or guardian? HR's challenge in balancing value and values. *Human Resource Management, 44*(2), 177–182.

Wright, P. M., & Ulrich, M. D. (2017). A road well-travelled: The past, present, and future journey of strategic human resource management. *Annual Review of Organizational Psychology and Organizational Behaviour, 4*, 45–65.

Part III
Humanistic Management in Practice

Managing for Good Work: Principles and Practices of Humanistic Management Based on Catholic Social Thought

Benito Teehankee and Yolanda Sevilla

1 Introduction

What conditions at work would be considered just and good for people? What working conditions would enable people to develop themselves properly as befits their nature as human beings? What is the role of business leaders in designing organizations and instituting management practices which bring such conditions about? What does Catholic social thought (CST) have to say to guide the reflections and practices of humanistic managers?

These are important questions for business leaders, in general, but especially so in today's economic realities where poverty and profound inequalities exist even when substantial amounts of wealth are being generated for a minority of the members of societies. The co-authors, an advocate of CST in management at De La Salle University's Management and Organization Department (Teehankee) and a business owner-manager (Sevilla), partnered to explore these questions in this chapter. They were prompted to write this chapter by a challenge posed by Pope Francis during the World Economic Forum conference in Davos a few years ago. Pope Francis presented this challenge to the assembled business leaders:

> . . .the successes which have been achieved, even if they have reduced poverty for a great number of people, often have led to a widespread social exclusion. Indeed, the majority of the men and women of our time still continue to experience daily insecurity, often with

B. Teehankee (✉)
Ramon V. del Rosario College of Business, Business for Human Development Network – Center for Business Research and Development, De La Salle University, Manila, Philippines
e-mail: benito.teehankee@dlsu.edu.ph

Y. Sevilla
The Leather Collection, Inc., Las Piñas, Philippines
e-mail: yoling@leathercollection.ph

© Springer Nature Switzerland AG 2020
R. Aguado, A. Eizaguirre (eds.), *Virtuous Cycles in Humanistic Management*,
Contributions to Management Science,
https://doi.org/10.1007/978-3-030-29426-7_7

> dramatic consequences. . . .Those working in these sectors have a precise responsibility towards others, particularly those who are most frail, weak and vulnerable. It is intolerable that thousands of people continue to die every day from hunger, even though substantial quantities of food are available, and often simply wasted. . . . Without ignoring, naturally, the specific scientific and professional requirements of every context, I ask you to ensure that humanity is served by wealth and not ruled by it. (Vatican Radio, 2014)

The challenge of Pope Francis is a core challenge of humanistic management that resonates in CST: How can management practice be oriented toward serving human dignity and flourishing? In light of the Pope's challenge, this paper addresses the questions posed above and aims to:

- Explain the normative basis for good work and humanistic management emerging from CST.
- Present management applications and reflections of one of the authors (Sevilla), a practicing manager and head of Philippine firm, The Leather Collection, on how she endeavors to manage her firm humanistically based on indigenous concepts and CST.

2 Work and Integral Human Development: The Perspective of Catholic Social Thought

In the encyclical *Centesimus Annus*, Saint John Paul II asserted a core argument of humanistic management based on CST with respect to the business organization: "the purpose of a business firm is not simply to make a profit, but is to be found in its very existence as a community of persons who in various ways are endeavoring to satisfy their basic needs, and who form a particular group at the service of the whole of society" (John Paul II, 1991). While the need for a firm to provide some value to society is immediately recognizable as a business goal even in mainstream management literature, the assertion that such firms must also build community and meet the basic needs of its human members is less obvious and comprises a characteristic component of the Catholic vision for the firm (Teehankee, 2008).

With respect to poverty, on the other hand, traditional concern regarding the role of business organizations has revolved around the importance of providing for people's material goods. The vision of CST for the satisfaction of human needs is much broader; however, in the encyclical *Mater et Magistra*, Saint John XXIII argued that:

> Justice is to be observed not only in the distribution of wealth, but also in regard to the conditions in which men are engaged in producing this wealth. Every man has, of his very nature, a need to express himself in his work and thereby to perfect his own being. (82)

Thus, those who manage business organizations need to be alert that persons may be impoverished in many ways apart from materially if they are not able to develop to their full potential as human beings. CST argues for the role of organizations in facilitating this multidimensional aspect of human development as a core goal of all organizational work. It is referred to as the "subjective" dimension of work to distinguish it from the "objective" aspect which refers to the production of output through work. The Vatican document, *The Vocation of the Business Leader*[1] (Pontifical Council for Justice and Peace, 2012), further explains the role of the subjective dimension of work as a critical element of not only productive but also *good* work:

> The worker, the subject of work, is also greatly affected by his or her own work. Whether we think about the executive, the farmer, the nurse, the janitor, the engineer, or tradespeople, work changes both the world (objective dimension) and the worker (subjective dimension). Because work changes the person, it can enhance or suppress that person's dignity; it can allow a person to develop or to be damaged.

The importance of work as a means for dignity was emphasized by Saint John Paul II in the encyclical *Laborem Exercens* (John Paul II, 1981):

> While work is not the source of human dignity, it is the means by which persons express and develop both being and dignity. Persons are the subjects of work and are not to be looked upon simply as a means of production or a human form of capital. Work must be organized to serve the workers' humanity, support their family life, and increase the common good of the human community—the three purposes of work.

Employees are, therefore, not to be construed as merely means in a production process but also as themselves the end of productive work. Sound work must be organized and managed in ways that not only ensures productivity but also the promotion of human flourishing in all its aspects—integral human development. Through the concepts of the objective and subjective dimensions of work, CST effectively challenges managers to think beyond the traditional lens of productivity and efficiency and always consider the many impacts of work on the workers themselves—including the managers (Alford & Naughton, 2001).

Explicit references to good work in the CST sense have been slowly entering management literature. Alford and Naughton (2001) elaborated on the various dimensions of human development at work that managers need to give attention to (Table 1).

Alford and Naughton (2001) show that the promotion of good work by managers does not have to be an abstract affair. In fact, for the most part, the various dimensions of human development are influenced by very concrete managerial actions. Some of these dimensions have been addressed in secular management literature for some time. For example, the field of ergonomics promotes worker's interactions with others and with the physical environment in support of health and well-being (Wilson, 2000). The fields of organization development and learning organizations (Argyris & Schon, 1978; Schein, 1999; Senge, 2006) have argued for engaging the thinking and emotional commitment of workers through various modes

---

[1]"The Vocation of the Business Leader: A reflection" was released by the Vatican Pontifical Council for Justice and Peace in 2012, and later updated, to synthesize Catholic social teachings for effective communication to practicing business leaders. The document explains practical principles intended to advance human dignity and the common good. It seeks to do this based on the promotion of the good and the sustainable creation of wealth and its just distribution, without forgetting the fundamental value of solidarity, especially for the poor and vulnerable.

Table 1 Human development at work (Alford & Naughton, 2001)

1. Bodily development—The physical structure of the workplace and the design of work processes and equipment are calculated to protect employee's health and to respect their overall, physical well-being
2. Cognitive development—Employees' expected contributions to the work process are made intelligible to them; jobs are kept "smart" to exercise and develop employees' talents and skills; overall, employees' cognitive abilities are matched to proportionately challenging work
3. Emotional development—Through the freedom to take initiative without fear of reprisal, employees exercise responsibility and accept accountability for their work
4. Aesthetic development—Craftsmanship is encouraged, and within the limits prescribed by their uses, products are designed and manufactured with an eye for beauty, elegance, and harmony with nature; services are conceived and delivered in ways that honor the human dignity of both the provider and the receiver
5. Social development—Internally, the organization encourages appropriate expressions of collegiality; the organization exhibits a "social conscience," encourages the same in employees, and supports employees' initiatives in the direction of service to the wider community
6. Moral development—The firm's managerial practices and work rules recognize that human acts are as such moral acts; working relationships of every kind should demonstrate respect for the human dignity of each party to them
7. Spiritual development—Work is understood as a vocation, and valued as collaboration, in the presence of God, for the good of one's fellow human beings

Source: Alford and Naughton (2001, p. 75)

of participation and dialogue. What CST brings uniquely to the literature on work is that all the various dimensions of human development constitute an integrated whole which cannot be dealt with piecemeal—a complete vision of the human person which organizations are ethically bound to respect and to nurture. Human beings have inherent worth as such but also because they are, ultimately, spiritual beings created by God.

In the promotion of work that dignifies people and promotes their total development, CST deploys a critical principle for good work—subsidiarity. The *Vocation of the Business Leader* explains, "The principle of subsidiarity is rooted in the conviction that, as images of God, the flourishing of human beings entails the best use of their intelligence and freedom. Human dignity is never respected by unnecessarily constraining or suppressing that intelligence and freedom."

An implication is that managers are not to unduly impose their will or interpretation of situations on their subordinates but instead must allow the latter to study, appreciate, and exercise judgment with respect to realities that they observe at their level of the organization—as long as this always takes into account the common good or, specifically, the need for development of all other affected parties. The appropriate application of subsidiarity in an organization promotes almost all dimensions of human development at once. Employees who are trusted to make decisions within the proper scope of their responsibility and enabled (through proper tools and training) to make such decisions at their own levels are better able to develop confidence (emotional development), prudence (moral development), attend to their health needs (bodily development), think and reason (cognitive development), pursue their work as a craft (aesthetic development), work with others and for others (social development), and align their work with their own sense of transcendental purpose (spiritual development).

3 Case in Practice: Organizing Good Work at The Leather Collection (TLC)

The Leather Collection (TLC) is a 27-year-old first-generation Filipino-owned small enterprise engaged in the design, manufacture, and distribution of genuine leather accessories to the corporate gifts and private label markets. It is owned and managed by couple Federico Sevilla, Jr. and Maria Yolanda Capistrano (aka Yolanda Sevilla). The company flourished and experienced double-digit growth in its early years, after which it experienced challenges in the wake of the Asian financial crisis, the influx of cheap goods from China, the global recession, the European recession, and the ups and downs of the Philippine economy.

Throughout its history, TLC has reorganized its workforce and reengineered its systems and processes in response to the times, seeking to survive and remain true to its mission and values. Average tenure is in the vicinity of 25 years. The three longest-serving employees have been with the company from its birth; its managing account officer has been with the company for 27 years. Including owner-managers, the current head count is 36 members referred to as "TLCkers" (from "seekers").

The rest of this section cites passages from *The Vocation of the Business Leader* (VBL) (as they are numbered in the original) and narrates the author's related management experience and reflections in the first-person voice. Individuals are referred to by initials.

TLC uses a number of indigenous Filipino interpersonal and organizational concepts and principles which are intended to appeal to the workers' cultural values and which are in line with CST. These are summarized in the table below with approximate English translations:

Filipino concept or principle	English translation
Hanap-buhay	The search for life—life in its fullness
Magkabalikat sa hanap-buhay	Community of workers and teamwork
Hindi pwede ang pwede na	Searching for excellence. Good enough is not good enough

VBL passage 31: ". . .each of us has a duty. . .to promote that flourishing (of others) for we are all really responsible for all."

Example #1
Since TLC is positioned in our domestic market as corporate gifts specialists, our Chairman (also our product master was invited by a Philippine foundation to partner with a group of marginalized women who were artisanal weavers of mats and market baskets. Their idea was to produce corporate gift items (e.g., meeting folders,

passport wallets) handwoven in indigenous fibers, which TLC would trim with leather. Their objective was to provide these mothers and grandmothers with a sustainable source of income.

Our chairman did not think this a workable idea and instead offered to visit the community to assess its level of weaving mastery and openness to learning how to weave with a different material.

Now on its fifth year, the partnership between the Sibaltan Women Weavers Association (SWWA) and TLC is beginning to flourish. SWWA has become part of TLC's value/supply chain, providing the latter with handwoven leather panels for an assortment of gift items which are now being manufactured for private label brands based in the European Union.

Not only has the income of the artisanal weavers multiplied tenfold so has their self-esteem and mastery of the new medium (leather), mastery of new weaves and weaving techniques (designed by TLC's industrial designer), increased productivity, and consistency of quality (TLC provides them with jigs and molds and continuous training).

Example #2

I (Sevilla) am an active member of the Women's Business Council of the Philippines and an advocate of WEE (women's economic empowerment) and women helping women up the value chain. Through the GREAT Women (Gender-Responsive Economic Action for the Transformation of Women) Initiative, TLC (with over 50% women in its workforce and management) became a member of the GREAT Women collective and was partnered with a group of women tribal weavers of abaca (Manila hemp) fibers. TLC designed a collection of bags and accessories in leather accessorized with their handwoven textile. These products are now being distributed through private label brands based in the European Union.

Just like the women in Example #1, the women of the Tribal Women Weavers Association (TWWA) now enjoy increased income and self-esteem (they were both awed and delighted to see the finished products of our collaboration). In addition, we are part of an effort to preserve our cultural heritage, and the initial success of these aboriginal women is inspiring younger women to take up the art and craft of backstrap weaving.

VBL passage 44: "The way human work is designed and managed has a significant impact...on whether people will flourish through their work."

Hanap-buhay (trans. TLC Guiding Principle: The search for life—life in its fullness)

We in The Leather Collection (TLC) perceive work as more than what one does to earn a living and as a vehicle for experiencing life in its fullness, for actualizing one's full potential, and for developing the whole human being—mind, heart, body, and spirit.

My husband and I started our first enterprise (grandmother to The Leather Collection) when we wed, in response to the need to provide for our growing family and our need to find meaningful and fulfilling work where we could employ and develop our talents and skills.

In the course of time, we came to realize that we were in a position to provide the same opportunity to those who worked with us.

". . .today the decisive factor (for production) is increasingly man himself, that is, his knowledge. . ., his capacity for interrelated and compact organization. . ."— *Saint John Paul II*

Magkabalikat sa hanap-buhay (trans. TLC Guiding Principle: Community of Workers)

We see ourselves as a community of co-workers with a common purpose—to build a Filipino company that is a showcase of excellence in product quality and customer service.

We emerged from a company-wide visioning workshop held in our second year of existence with the battle cry: "World class, *gawang Pinoy!*" (trans. made by Filipinos!). We also came up with our objectives, the first one of which was to foster mutually nurturing relationships with all our stakeholders.

This was first advocated in the relationship between and among employers and employees. Attendance is a core value. Attendance means not just physical presence in the workplace, but each employee is expected to be attending to his work (his role and function) during work hours. Tardiness and habitual absences are sanctioned.

The rationale behind this is the concept of being *magkabalikata (community of workers)*. We work in teams, and each team's output is computed based on total man-hours per workday. This being the case, each member of the team must be attending to his work and generating the expected output for the team to meet its daily target.

3.1   Values Reformation

This requires not just values formation but values reformation. In most workers' perspective, one fulfills the attendance requirement simply by clocking in the required number of work hours per day. Through general assemblies, meetings with team leaders, and one-on-one counseling sessions, we explain that this does not fulfill the employment contract. One must be working or at work during work hours, not timing in at the start of work hours and timing out at its end. The same rule applies for break times. Habitual tardiness and absenteeism are sanctioned and can be cause for termination.

Example #3

Worker JJA, while a competent worker with output that met both quality and quantity standards, was habitually tardy and/or absent. Over a period of 3 months, he was either late or absent for work 50% of the time during the peak season when it was critical that all team members be present to fulfill orders on time. Furthermore, he did not seek approval for "vacation" leaves but simply informed his supervisor by text in the morning that he was not coming in that day for activities that could have been pre-planned (e.g., transferring the cremains of his mother from one town to another). His other absences were for "sick" leaves when he reports "*masama ang pakiramdam ko*" (I'm not feeling well).

He was served a first notice asking him to explain why he should not be terminated for habitual absenteeism and tardiness. In conference he admitted that he had neglected his duty due to family problems (he was "not feeling well" because he felt rejected and ostracized by his family). He also claimed he was "not fit to work" hence his frequent absences (he was previously diagnosed with pulmonary tuberculosis for which he had received treatment and was given a "fit to work" certificate).

After reviewing the case, our managers and team leaders agreed that there was cause to terminate JJA.

In the course of making a final decision, our chairman assessed JJA's performance over the length of his tenure with TLC. JJA's disposition was also examined—was he contrite, did he seek to make amends and change his ways? The answer to this was yes. My husband and I (Chairman and CEO) decided, in consultation with team leaders to give JJA another chance—he would be put on probation for 3 months with very clear expectations regarding changes in behavior, particularly in his attendance.

I called a general assembly of all TLCkers to discuss the case and how it was handled and how management proposed to resolve it. It was made clear that this decision implied that all TLCkers were expected not only to respect and accept management's decision, but were duty bound, as *kabalikat*, a community of workers, to enable JJA to reform and meet the conditions of his probation. The entire work community felt it was a good decision and congruent with our corporate values.

3.2 Advocating Mutually Nurturing Relationships with Other Stakeholders

Putting this value into practice is most challenging in the relationship with our customers, many of which are large and/or multinational corporations with purchasing and payment standard operating procedures (SOPs) that are designed to optimize their profit and increase their internal efficiencies at the expense (hopefully not deliberate) of their suppliers and/or service providers.

Example #4
Customers dictate terms of payment (30/60/90/120 days from "goods receipt" of deliveries) yet negotiate prices down to exclude cost of money. There are designated check release days, and should that day be a holiday, checks are released the following week.

How have we addressed this? We make the effort to include terms of payment in the negotiation process, with prices calculated based not just on order quantity but also on terms of payment.

Some customers are sneaky. They request a quote for 12,000 units, say at 15-day payment term, then issue a purchase order for 3000 units at the price of 12,000 units reasoning that they will order a total of 12,000 units within the year and that this is just the first of several purchase orders. We make the effort to explain that the price at 12,000 units assumes the efficiencies of scale gained when one has a "long-run" vs. a "short-run" job, to no avail.

We recently did not accept such an order and held our ground—either they ordered 12,000 units in one lot at the price quoted, or 3000 units at the recalculated price for the lower quantity. Our reason? We need to have win-win contracts for our relationship to be sustainable.

Their response, after several phone calls and threats of losing the business, was to issue a new purchase order for 3000 units at the recalculated price.

This time around they adhered to the 15-day payment term. In the past they have calculated the 15 days (workdays, not calendar days) based on the date the "Goods Receipt" is received by purchasing from their warehouse (which has taken as long as a week). In the price negotiations with the buyer, we categorically stated that this kind of "abuse" was no longer acceptable to us since it was costing us and had gone on long enough.

We hope that in advocating mutually nurturing relationships with our other stakeholders, particularly our customers, we are also promoting "good work" in their companies.

VBL passage 45: *Foster dignified work:* "... the grandeur of one's work not only leads to improved products and services but develops the worker [as a person] himself... work changes both the world and the worker...Because work changes the person, it can enhance or suppress the person's dignity. It can allow the person to develop or to be damaged."

VBL passage 46: "Work is for [the person] man and not [the person] man for work.... Good work...'s context promotes social relationships and real collaboration... This requires from leaders the ability to develop the right person in the right job and the freedom and responsibility to do just that. ... Moreover, reward structures should make sure that those workers who do engage their labor in a sincere way also receive the necessary esteem and compensation from their companies."

Our recruitment, hiring, and assessment process includes a fourfold assessment of the applicant's profile to ensure a job and organizational fit: skills, personality, inclination, and character (SPIC). Skills are based on previous training, experience, and previous job descriptions. Personality identifies the applicant's presenting persona. Inclination surfaces her interests, dreams, plans, preferred work, and learning style. Character reveals the person's value set.

While the job description for similar functions would be the same, each worker would be assigned to a task that would best fit his unique "SPIC" profile and would be given special assignments that would allow him to employ his other talents.

Together with the employee, we also assess whether he/she is assigned to a function where he/she is rendering his/her "highest value added" to the work community. When this level is reached, and he/she has found his/her niche, he/she is allowed to flourish there.

Example #5
GFJ started out as our security guard. His skill set was appropriate for his function. However, when drawing up his SPIC profile, we found that he was technically inclined, that he had a pleasant personality, was a good team player, and had analytical skills and leadership potential. We started training him on-the-job to do minor repairs and maintenance until he reached mastery level. He rose to the challenge and is now head of repairs and maintenance.

3.3 Skills Training

One becomes a member of Team TLC with a set of skills needed for the enterprise to fulfill its objective. In the course of his work, the TLCker's (from "seeker for excellence," another core value) skills are developed and enhanced. She starts off usually with a single skill at the acceptable level of mastery and graduates to become a master at that particular task. She is also cross-trained and becomes multiskilled.

3.4 Continuous Learning and Improvement

Core values—fostering mutually nurturing relationships, team work (*magkabalikat sa hanap-buhay*), searching for excellence (*hindi puede ang puede na*, trans. "Good enough is not good enough"), responsibility and accountability, transparency, and integrity—were promoted, advocated, and ingrained initially in general assemblies and team building activities and in "walking our talk."

Example #6
Sometime in 2000, a multinational corporate customer rejected our delivery (the first time this had happened) claiming that the material used was substandard. We immediately pulled out the delivery to their claim. To our chagrin, we found out that he was right! Despite our quality assurance online and sign-off/sign-on protocols, the substandard material went unnoticed by the entire production line from materials preparation to assembly, finishing, and packaging! What did we do? We replaced the customer's order, tightened protocols, and—most important of all—invited all our craftsmen and women to destroy the substandard products with stripping knives. This is a lesson no one has forgotten and was the first and last time an order has been rejected.

3.5 Justice with Mercy

While we have rules and regulations, policies and practices, workers who violate such at the expense of the company (understood as Team TLC) are treated with justice tempered by mercy.

Example #7

Manager MTM went on sudden and emergency leave in the middle of the peak season after an altercation with her husband. It was found that she had been having an affair with the company driver and that the entire organization, except for my husband and myself, were aware of this. All were scandalized but did not know how to address their concern about the appropriateness of the relationship and its impact on company operations. No one thought to bring it up to the owners and general managers.

This threw company operations into disarray. MTM was a key person—she was in charge of manufacturing operations. However, she could not discharge her duties due to her psycho-emotional state. She filed an emergency leave. The knee jerk reaction was to ask her to resign for causing "moral scandal."

My husband, our chairman and manufacturing director, her direct supervisor, met her regularly, counseling her and accompanying her through her crisis. She was thrown out of her home, and her husband threatened to keep her children away from her.

We both prayed over her case and discerned what might be the right response to the situation. Consultations with key personnel were held. All the employees filed a request for clemency. After several counseling sessions with MTM and in the interest of giving her a chance to pick up the pieces of her life (her work was very important to her; in the midst of a troubled marriage, it was one area of her life that gave her fulfillment), she was reintegrated with very clear objectives: to help her start over, to accompany her, and to help her fulfill her resolve to move forward.

MTM is back at work and is more effective and efficient than she was in the past. She has found inner peace and calm. She lives apart from her family but talks to her children (a boy and a girl, aged 5 and 7 years) daily, monitors their activities, attends their school functions, and has them sleep over on weekends (whenever their father allows them to). She has turned to God, goes to mass, and spends time in the Adoration Chapel as often as she can. She offers all her trials and tribulations to God and thanks him for what consolations she now enjoys—the embrace of her *kabalikat sa hanap-buhay* (work community), the support of her family of origin, and the love of her children. She also values her role and function as their mother more now than she did before. They are now her top priority, not work nor her personal "happiness."

VBL passages 47 and 48: "The principle of subsidiarity recognizes that in human societies, smaller communities exist within larger ones."

"The principle of subsidiarity applies to the structure of. . .business organiza-tions. . .We develop in our work best when we use our intelligence and freedom to achieve shared goals and to create and sustain right relationships with one another and with those served by the organization. . . .This fosters initiative, innovation, creativity and a sense of shared responsibility."

Example #8

The Leather Collection's organization is made up of work units or cells. The Manufacturing Department is made up of the following work units: Product

Research and Development, Materials Preparation, Assembly (composed of several lines or cells whose size and composition varies according to work-in-process), Finishing, Packaging and Packing, and Dispatching. Each work unit acts as a team and is responsible for contributing their share to meeting the department's targets.

Production planning is done by the operations manager together with the work unit and line leaders to determine output per man hour for each step in the production process of a particular product model and plan work schedules and work unit composition to optimize productivity and efficiency.

Quality assurance is every craftsman's responsibility. Following the *kanban* principle of "sign off, sign on," worker A passes on his "finished product" to worker B after ensuring that it is of good quality; worker B checks the product before accepting it to verify that it is of good quality and is ready for the next step in the production process.

VBL passage 49: "...subsidiarity provides business leaders with three practical steps:

- Clearly define the realm of autonomy and decision rights to be made at every level of the company...
- Teach and equip employees, making sure that they have the right tools, training, and experience to carry out their tasks.
- Accept that the persons to whom tasks and responsibilities have been given will make their decisions in freedom and, thereby in full trust, the risks of their decisions...nurture mutual respect and responsibility..."

VBL passage 50: "Under the principle of subsidiarity... [co-workers] are indeed 'co-entrepreneurs.'"

Each *kabalikat (community mate)* or TLCker is expected to ensure that costs are kept reasonable and profit optimized.

Example #9
Sales officers are provided with order quantity-based price guides and are expected to negotiate the best prices and terms of payment for the company and to resist the temptation to sell at the lowest possible price just to bag the order. Commissions are a percentage of transaction value, so desired performance is rewarded commensurately.

To optimize operating profit:

- Materials Control ensures leather hides ordered and delivered are of the optimum size and quality to ensure maximum yield and reduce spoilage.
- Materials Preparation cuts components with the end in view of maximizing yield and minimizing spoilage further.
- Assembly organizes its work teams for each step in the process to ensure maximum productivity, assigning the right craftsman for the right process and reengineering process to increase productivity

After-action reviews are conducted after each major project is completed to analyze best practice for each step in the business process (from inquiry to order fulfillment), the objective of which is to increase productivity and efficiency while ensuring product and service quality. This fosters continuous learning and improvement with a focus on our multiple bottom lines.

3.6 Sevilla's Practitioner Reflections

As we continue managing our enterprise, leading our community of workers *kabalikat* in the search for life in its fullness (*hanap-buhay*) and advocating sustainable (mutually nurturing) relationships with all our stakeholders, we are growing more convinced that work is a vehicle for salvation of human flourishing (transformation, conversion).

We have also learned that our circle of influence of promoting integral human development is not limited to ourselves and our *kabalikat community mates* in TLC. Instead our circle has grown to include both SWWA and TWWA, now integral parts of our value chain. We are committed to spreading the gospel of good work—work that is a vehicle for the full flourishing of (wo)man, reading the signs of the times and responding to the call of the times.

Before our involvement with De La Salle University's Management and Organization Department (MOD) and its advocacy for the practice of CST in the workplace, we were not aware that this was in fact the framework for our leadership style. While both my husband and I were born into Catholic families and studied in Catholic schools, we did not consciously strive to practice Catholic social teaching as business leaders. We simply practiced what we believed was right, guided by the Christian principles we had imbibed as we were growing up. We were very vocal about our values, and one of the gifts of being entrepreneurs is being able to "walk our talk" and advocate our deepest held values.

Our involvement with De La Salle's MOD has resulted in our active engagement in training business students to make socially responsible decisions, telling our story and sharing our experiences in the hope of contributing toward building God's kingdom in the world of business.

4 Conclusion

The challenge for managers to organize work for human development is a daunting one, given the demands of global competitiveness. Fortunately, the normative bases for good work and humanistic management are fully explained. Considerable intellectual resources have been generated by CST and VBL, particularly on the nature of work and its relationship to human dignity and development. These resources are accessible for the guidance of prudent managers of good will everywhere.

However, the use of such knowledge resources requires disciplined prudence and practical creativity, as shown by the example of The Leather Collection. Business organizations do not become humane places for people to work in by default. In fact, the opposite is the natural tendency. Thus, business leaders must actively manage in order to provide conditions for workers to flourish to their full potential in terms of health, emotion, thinking, relationships, morality, aesthetics, and transcendent purpose. The business leaders of The Leather Collection enable such conditions through culturally relevant language, values-based communication practices, collaboration, and sensitive policy enforcement.

We recommend that other managers likewise conscientiously pursue practice guided by principles of human development, the common good, and subsidiarity. They will have to apply their creative abilities to adapt their practices to the principles. Their task will be assisted not only by deep and reflective study of the principles but also through collaborations with researchers and teachers on CST. Finally, the task of advancing humanistic management and good work becomes more feasible if business educators and committed practitioners will work alongside each other, as the authors have done in writing this chapter.

References

Alford, H. J., & Naughton, M. J. (2001). *Managing as if faith mattered: Christian social principles in the modern organization.* Notre Dame, IN: University of Notre Dame Press.

Argyris, C., & Schon, D. A. (1978). *Organizational learning: A theory of action perspective.* Reading, MA: Addison-Wesley.

John Paul II. (1981). *Laborem exercens.* Retrieved from http://www.vatican.va/holy_father/john_paul_ii/encyclicals/documents/hf_jp-ii_enc_14091981_laborem-exercens_en.html

John Paul II. (1991). *Centesimus annus.* Retrieved from Vatican: http://www.vatican.va/holy_father/john_paul_ii/encyclicals/documents/hf_jp-ii_enc_01051991_centesimus-annus_en.html

Pontifical Council for Justice and Peace. (2012, April 5). *Vocation of the business leader: A reflection.* Retrieved from Pontifical Council for Justice and Peace: http://www.pcgp.it/dati/2012-05/04-999999/Vocation%20ENG2.pdf

Schein, E. H. (1999). *Process consultation: Building the helping relationship.* Reading, MA: Addison-Wesley.

Senge, P. (2006). *The fifth discipline: The art and practice of the learning organization* (Revised ed.). New York: Doubleday.

Teehankee, B. L. (2008). Humanistic entrepreneurship: An approach to virtue-based enterprise. *Asia-Pacific Social Science Review, 8*(1), 89–110.

Vatican Radio. (2014, January 21). *Pope Francis' message to World Economic Forum in Davos.* Retrieved from News.va: http://www.news.va/en/news/pope-francis-message-to-world-economic-forum-in-da

Wilson, J. R. (2000). Fundamentals of ergonomics in theory and practice. *Applied Ergonomics, 31*(2000), 557–567.

Promoting Greater Levels of Employee Health and Well-Being in the UK: How Much Worse Do the Problems Have to Get?

Robin Roslender, Lissa Monk, and Nicola Murray

1 Introduction

It is now almost four decades since Peters and Waterman reminded managers that their employees are their most valuable assets (Peters & Waterman, 1982). In so doing they provided support for those within the human resource management profession who argued that there was a necessity to view human resources as strategic assets in need of a new approach to people management, namely, strategic human resource management. Similar thinking was evident in the identification of human capital as the most crucial component of intellectual capital by Edvinsson after the mid-1990s (Edvinsson, 1997; Edvinsson & Malone, 1997; Roslender & Fincham, 2001). By this time, however, customers were being touted by many observers as the key organizational asset, providing a fillip to the marketing management function and its own strategic ambitions. Like employees, customers were also identified as a key constituent of intellectual capital, forming a major part of its relational capital component. Although intellectual capital's third generic component, structural capital, has not attracted the same level of support in respect of its value to organizations as people and customers, there has been a growing awareness of the need to recognize the role which the environment and natural capital plays in ensuring the long-term sustainability of the planet and everything that it encompasses.

What employees, customers, the environment, and most constituents of structural capital have in common is that each of them poses a major challenge to the accounting profession. For generations the profession has been able to incorporate the

R. Roslender (✉)
Department of Business and Management, Aalborg University, Aalborg, Denmark
e-mail: r.roslender@dundee.ac.uk

L. Monk · N. Murray
School of Business, University of Dundee, Dundee, Scotland, United Kingdom
e-mail: e.a.monk@dundee.ac.uk; n.z.murray@dundee.ac.uk

© Springer Nature Switzerland AG 2020
R. Aguado, A. Eizaguirre (eds.), *Virtuous Cycles in Humanistic Management*,
Contributions to Management Science,
https://doi.org/10.1007/978-3-030-29426-7_8

organization's key assets, normally designated fixed and current, within the financial statements that constitute its professional jurisdiction, alongside a variety of liabilities, within the balance sheet or statement of financial position. For the most part, this has been accomplished by means of identifying the financial values of such assets and liabilities and inserting them into the basic accounting equation: *assets less liabilities equals equity*. The continued robustness of this exercise has been accomplished in large part because those outside of the accounting profession accept the premise that it is only prepared to accept *objective* financial values. Unfortunately, the array of assets identified in the previous paragraph permits only the attribution of subjective valuations, hence the challenge to the profession's traditional jurisdiction. It is not for the want of trying that the profession has been unsuccessful in this direction. For example, accounting for people has a history that dates back to the 1920s (Roslender & Monk, 2017), while environmental accounting has been one of the most widely subscribed accounting research topics since the later 1980s. Within the structural capital designation, some intellectual properties (assets) have long been successfully taken into account, although the profession continues to struggle with such key assets as a global management succession program. Some progress has also been evident in valuing brands, but customer valuation remains a sparsely populated space. In recent time integrated reporting has been promoted as a means of revivifying corporate reporting (Aguado, Alcaniz, & Retolaza, 2015; IIRC, 2013; Roslender & Nielsen, 2018), although to date its reception on the part of practitioners continues to be modest.

Within the UK, the accounting profession's dominance within the hierarchy of organizational management functions continues to prevail despite concerns about some of the behavior of the external audit function. A pecking order also persists among accounting practitioners employed with organizations, with many of the most influential posts being filled by members of the Institute of Chartered Accountants in England and Wales (ICAEW) or its Scottish counterpart, the Institute of Chartered Accountants of Scotland (ICAS). It would be naïve to claim that practitioners affiliated with the Chartered Institute of Management Accountants (CIMA) or the Association of Chartered Certified Accountants (ACCA) are not also to be found in these positions and to a greater extent than ever before. This state of affairs is simply more than an example of intra-professional rivalry, however, as it essentially ensures that management accounting continues to be regarded as a lesser form of accounting than financial accounting. This in turn results in a greater acceptance of the approach to accounting and reporting that faces considerable difficulty in taking employees, customers, the environment, and sustainability into account. By contrast, contemporary management accounting and reporting evidences a greater willingness to explore how it might be possible to accommodate them by being prepared to abandon the underlying cost and value calculus of financial accounting and reporting. It is important not to overstate this prospect; however, although as Nielsen and Roslender (2015) assert, many of those seeking to advance financial reporting should be prepared to take a look at what three decades of "relevant" management accounting development has to offer.

The continuing dominance of financial accounting within the UK has ensured that accounting for people has found very little support, even following its resurgence within the intellectual capital field from the mid-1990s. Although it would be unfair to suggest that there has been a similar level of disinterest in intellectual capital in general in the UK, the greater part of the resulting research has focused on the (limited) development of intellectual capital reporting. Theoretical and conceptual work from UK researchers remains scarce, with only three of the thirty chapters in the 2017 *Routledge Companion to Intellectual Capital* originating in the UK (interestingly all based in Scotland) (Guthrie, Dumay, Ricceri, & Nielsen, 2017). Roslender and Stevenson (2009) document how the UK accounting profession succeeded in smothering the Labour Government's 2003 *Accounting for People* initiative, much to the disappointment of the Chartered Institute of Personnel and Development (CIPD). Although the 2010 coalition government initially flirted with the idea of requiring the reporting of a very modest amount of people information in the annual report, with the benefit of hindsight, it is possible to recognize that the CIPD has found itself a spectator to a progressive worsening of the workplace experiences of the majority of the UK workforce since the financial crisis of 2008.

In view of the above observations and assertions, there is little to suggest that in the UK employees are regarded by managers and the accounting profession as anything other than a source of expenditures, a cost that should be reduced or removed wherever possible in the pursuit of increased shareholder value. Viewing employees in a more holistic way, including as highly valuable assets, is largely alien to the narrative of employment current within most corporations. This is greatly at odds with how employees are enrolled in the chairman's report within the annual financial statements. For many UK employees, the workplace has provided a highly negative experience in recent times, although the main thrust of public statements regarding work is that unemployment levels are at their lowest since the mid-1970s as a result of which there are now more people in work in the UK than ever before.

Largely absent from view (and debate) are the conditions that provide the motivation for his essay, namely, the extent, nature, and consequences of compromised work health and well-being presently evident among UK employees. The continued persistence of such conditions underlines the absence of humanistic management practices within UK organizations and highlights a scant regard for the dignity of workers and the attributes they are prepared to gift to those who employ them. The chapter has been organized as follows: initially the UK's continued sickness absence problem is documented. Section 3 considers the broader implications of this sickness absence problem, while the fourth section explores how it contradicts the assertions of recent human capital theory. An indication of how some employers have attempted to respond to continuing work health and well-being challenges is provided in Sect. 5, while the sixth section provides evidence from a recent empirical study that corroborates the largely effete nature of these interventions. The chapter concludes by briefly reviewing two current opposing interventions designed to combat compromised workplace health and well-being, before affirming the need for fashioning more ambitious initiatives as part of a new narrative of business.

2   The Continuing UK Sickness Absence Problem

At the turn of the century, the CIPD began an absence management survey that it has continued to date, providing an immensely valuable source of information on sickness absence in the UK. There is no comparable information set available elsewhere in the UK and, indeed, until recently provided, is the only robust source available to researchers, management, and government alike. The 2016 survey reported that during the past 12 months, the mean number of days lost to sickness absence reduced by 8.7% to 6.3 days, the equivalent of 2.8% working time lost overall (CIPD, 2016). This fall continues the downward trend evident over the past 6 years, although this has not been completely smooth. Compared with position at the turn of the century, present levels of sickness absence are relatively low, an observation that applies equally to the UK's Scandinavian neighbors. Significant variations persist, however, with lowest levels evident in the private sector, very similar for manufacturing and services. The public services sector evidences the highest level of days lost to sickness absence, with an average of 3 days more absence than for all sectors, with health and central government exhibiting the highest levels. The nonprofit sector lies between the public and the private sectors, having significantly improved its profile over recent years. Manual workers continue to lose more days per employee than nonmanual workers.

Translating the above into the cost of sickness absence arguably provides a starker representation of the problem. Several years ago, CIPD elected to move to reporting median cost information rather than mean cost information, which makes longer-term comparisons more difficult. In the 2016 survey, the £522 median cost per employee is reported to have fallen slightly from the 2015 level, continuing the overall downward trend since 2010. There is again significant variation between different sectors, with the public sector employee costing £835 per annum (60% above the overall median), while manufacturing sector employees cost a little over £450 per employee. In 2010 it was possible to estimate that the total cost of sickness absence was in the region of £17 billion per annum, continuing to slowly edge upward over time and in real terms. CIPD itself reported that PricewaterhouseCoopers estimated that these costs were significantly higher in 2013, at an estimated £29 billion. The Office for National Statistics estimated that in the region 137 million working days were lost in 2016, which translates to a figure of £17 billion, although according to their statistics, the average number of days lost per employee was 4.4 days compared with CIPD's 6.3 days. Taken together this suggests a probable current minimum annual cost in the region of £20 billion. This figure should be understood to be the base cost of employee sickness absence, before the addition of further amounts consequent upon the absences themselves. In this context, it is interesting to note that a decade ago, the Black Report estimated that the cost of sickness among working people in the UK was around £100 billion (Black, 2008).

The most common causes of short-term absence reported for 2016 were minor illnesses; stress; musculoskeletal conditions and back pain; extra-work responsibilities; and mental health conditions. The CIPD comments that many employers believe that a significant proportion of such short-term absences, sometimes referred to as "sickies," may not be genuine. Musculoskeletal and back problems are more common among manual workers, while stress and mental health issues are more common among nonmanual workers. Stress and mental health issues are more pronounced in the public services, particularly among nonmanual workers. Nonmanual workers in the private services sector seem slightly more prone to short-term episodes but comparatively little stress or mental health issues. Stress and acute medical conditions such as heart, strokes, and cancers are the two top causes of long-term (over 4 weeks) absence, followed by mental health issues, musculoskeletal conditions, and back pain. Stress and mental health issues are again more common among nonmanual employees, with the levels of stress and acute medical conditions reported for nonmanual public sector employees as the most arresting numbers in Table 7 (CIPD, 2016).

Although CIPD completed a further survey in 2017, again in partnership with Simplyhealth, its subsequent report evidences a major shift in emphasis, as evident in its title, *Health and Well-being at Work*, and in its content (CIPD, 2018). For example, there is no cost information provided, possibly because the limitations of the earlier move to median figures have become more obvious. Overall, the report indicates that the situation documented for 2016 has not improved, the headline figure of average days lost actually rising slightly to 6.6 days (Fig. 16, p. 28). The report focuses attention on *presenteeism* and *leaveism*, both of which are strongly asserted to be likely major longer-term problems linked with the growth of stress and mental illness. For several years and indeed in parallel to the decline in days lost to sickness absence, the level of presenteeism believed to exist within the workforce has been on the increase. In 2016 CIPD reported that almost three quarters of their survey respondents had observed presenteeism, understood as employees presenting for work when they are unwell (Chandola, 2010; Hemp, 2004; Johns, 2010). The figure for 2017 has risen to 86% with over a quarter of survey respondents indicating that it had increased in extent during the previous year. CIPD acknowledges that presenteeism is recognized to be closely associated with a long-hours culture (CIPD, 2017: 43), an attribute of UK workplaces that it seeks to encourage employers to tackle. Emphasis is also placed on the observation that in many instances presenteeism is a rational response to the fear of losing one's job, a threat that has increased in the UK in recent years. Equally it is possible that some employees experiencing the onset of mental health conditions may not actually recognize their evolving illness, continuing to work as best they can and in many instances possibly hastening it.

Leaveism is a related development noted among employees in recent times, documented by Hesketh, Cooper, and Ivy (2014, 2015) in the case of the UK police service (see also Hesketh & Cooper, 2014, 2018). It is recognized to take a number of forms. In the context of sickness absence, employees may take holidays in an effort to mask their ill health rather than taking a sickie or engaging in presenteeism. Taking holiday entitlement in order to work at home in an effort to keep up with a debilitating pace of work is another variant of leaveism as is the practice of working for some time when formally on holiday (however, much of the individuals may enjoy this). The longer-term prognosis for some employees prepared to practice leaveism may not be positive and is readily associated with the "burnout" phenomenon (Hesketh & Cooper, 2018; Schaufeli & Bakker, 2004).

Reviewing CIPD surveys published for over a decade, although there is a case to be made that the present situation is an improvement on that evidence existed during the noughties, behind the positive headlines lies a worrying, worsening scenario. Long-term sickness absence is now more prevalent than previously, while within this designation, there has been a shift in the profile of medical conditions from those that might be termed traditional, such as musculoskeletal and back pain, to those aptly captured by the term well-being—stress and kindred mental health conditions. Acute medical conditions remain prevalent, although there are some grounds to speculate that nowadays well-being-related conditions are more implicated in their causation than in previous generations. Viewed from the perspective of the broader changes in the jobs profile of societies such as the UK and Scandinavian countries, all of which have experienced the transition to a postindustrial and subsequently a knowledge society status, it appears that the worst manifestations of the broad sickness absence phenomenon in the UK are evident among those occupations that characterize the essence of the new order. If this is so, it raises the issue of the sustainability of this order and its underlying processes from which there presently seems little possibility of retreating.

3   UK Sickness Absence in Context

For most employees, being unwell and thereby unable to work is a distressing situation in which to find themselves. While the financial consequences of enforced sickness absence may no longer be as desperate as in the past, again for the majority, they certainly continue to be present, particularly for those who experience long-term absence. Employers also experience a range of negative financial consequences as they endeavor to accommodate to the disruption that sickness absence produces, as does the broader society, initially as taxpayers and indirectly as customers or clients who are expected to take their share of increased costs. In the case of private enterprises, investors, individual or institutional, are also impacted by the costs of absence, while taxpayers cannot avoid footing the bill for public sector employees where they remain stubbornly high in the UK.

The persistence of acute medical conditions accounts for a significant proportion of the costs of sickness absence, as do recurring chronic conditions. These conditions are experienced by everyone, not simply employees, and are sometimes referred to as general health conditions. To some degree they are unavoidable in the sense that the human body, in all its complexity, can malfunction and does so increasingly with age. The continual advance of medical science has meant that nowadays many general health conditions can be controlled effectively, as a consequence of which many employees can remain in the workforce, although perhaps more susceptible to absence due to ill health. In recent times the role of lifestyle factors in increasing the extent of general health conditions has been hotly debated, while a greater focus on preventative medicine has documented the dangers of obesity, alcohol and substance abuse, and a worrying lack of physical exercise, in addition to smoking, in relation to ill health. Although employers sometimes overstate the impact of lifestyle factors on absence statistics and not least in tandem with observations on the growth of a sickies culture, it would be naive to discount such factors.

Stripping away these layers of general health conditions allows the development of a focus on work health issues, especially those identified as stress and mental ill health conditions. They now present the principal work health challenges of the modern era, the incidence of which promises to worsen in the medium term. It would be disingenuous to suggest that both stress-related and mental ill health conditions are or have ever been solely related to the workplace, and it seems likely that a sizable proportion of employees' stress and kindred conditions are driven by extra-work factors to some degree. Equally, both are increasingly part of the current public discourse in the UK, resulting in a measure of contagion. After taking these factors into account, however, the conclusion seems to be that work currently appears to provide a negative experience for many employees who are absent themselves due to illness. Ironically it seems to be the case that having successfully tackled long-standing safety concerns in the workplace, the health and well-being couple has emerged to replace it.

Having announced that "stress is now the most common cause of long-term absence," in Table 13 the CIPD report provides a textbook headline analysis of what its survey's respondents recognize to be its principal causes (CIPD, 2016: 28–9). It is noteworthy that largely the same factors have been rehearsed within previous reports. By far the most common cause is identified as workloads/volume of work, which seem most pronounced in the public services. Nonwork factors associated with relationships and management style are identified next. If the two organization change issues are combined, this would rank second, again being a particular problem in the public services. Personal health and illness factors and relationships at work, which might be understood as a euphemism for workplace bullying, figure next. Also mentioned are long hours and pressures to meet targets, with private sector services in the vanguard here. Conversely, job insecurity is not reported to be a major issue nor financial worries. It should be remembered, however, that survey respondents are senior human resource managers, many of whom might be reluctant to admit to reality of such factors while commonly having little influence on them in practice.

Leaving aside nonwork factors, the prevailing workplace culture would seem to be one of widespread understaffing exacerbated by seemingly continuous change which is both widely misunderstood and badly managed. The majority of the UK's current workforce would be unlikely to disagree with this picture. The early chapters of Hesketh and Cooper (2018) provide a chilling characterization of the conditions of work within the public sector in the UK and beyond, leaving the reader with the clear message that more discomfort and distress is likely to characterize the medium term in the UK. Acknowledging a growing health and well-being problem that cannot be denied, Hesketh and Cooper's position is that given the unlikely event of an imminent reversal of a catalogue of external factors, it is necessary that concerted efforts to protect and ideally enhance the health and well-being of employees should now be pursued, for the benefit of all stakeholders.

4 Employee Worth: Theory or Rhetoric?

The widespread absence of employees from their places of work as a consequence of factors that are in some part addressable contradicts the much rehearsed assertion that was mentioned at the beginning of this chapter, namely, that "our employees are our most valuable assets." An assertion that had long attracted substantial support in some quarters, it was thrust firmly back into the discourse of management in the early 1980s in the *In Search of Excellence* text (Peters & Waterman, 1982), thereby providing a sound platform for the development of human resource management as a major management function within a rapidly changing competitive marketplace. Although it was only one of a series of business aphorisms advanced by Peters and Waterman, it resonated with several aspects of the resource-based view of strategic management (Barney, 1991; Rumelt, 1991; Wernerfelt, 1984), if not Porter's competitive advantage theory (Porter, 1980, 1985). The emergence of knowledge management in the early 1990s affirmed the crucial role that employees played in securing and sustaining the competitive advantage of business enterprises.

The emergence of the intellectual capital (IC) concept in the mid-1990s further strengthened the need to recognize the importance of employees and the damage done by the persistence of long-term sickness absence trends. Three generic forms of IC were quickly identified: human capital; relational capital; and structural capital. While all three are prerequisites for successful value creation and delivery, as Edvinsson's seminal 1997 paper intimates, human capital assets should be recognized as of the greatest importance. Roslender and Fincham (2001) subsequently designate human capital as primary IC and the other two capitals as secondary IC, being the creation of human capital itself. The resulting imperative is that enterprises seeking to sustain their present competitive advantage, while working to extend this to other markets, must embed processes that will increase their stocks of crucial attributes that employees gift to organizations. Only through investments in these various assets, including education and training, experience and expertise, capacity for creativity and ingenuity, and the ability to work in groups, be flexible, and assume leadership roles together with a willingness to embrace a growing range of soft skills, can enterprises be more assured that they will continue to be successful in the marketplace. Higher levels of employee health and well-being constitute a desirable addition to this list. In addition, it is equally important that an appropriate enabling organizational culture prevails, promoting the pursuit of excellence in every aspect of working life.

More recently the value creation and delivery literature has seen the addition of a third dimension, that of value capture. Unlike value creation and value delivery, both of which have a defining customer focus, as above, value capture incorporates the shareholder within the process—successful value creation and delivery are the prerequisites of successful value capture. In this regard value capture is by no means a new phenomenon since throughout its existence, capitalism has been characterized as the relentless pursuit of profitability, traditionally portrayed as the legitimate appropriation of the surplus value created by employees as the reward for risk-taking by the legal owners of enterprises. The value creation triptych entails something more than a reframing of older, possibly discredited terminology, however. The defining importance of the customer is highly significant and is matched by the acceptance that the value that must be successfully created and delivered to customers emanates from the endeavors of employees. As a result, shareholders (owners) are no longer to be understood as the principal participants in the value creation, delivery, and capture process, the position they have held in mainstream economic theory for many generations.

5 Engaging the Health and Well-Being Challenge

The importance that contemporary strategic management theory affords employees is at odds with the well-founded observation that in the UK employers are currently falling short of promoting the highest levels of work health and well-being. This situation seems unlikely to be about to change in the foreseeable future. It is probable that many employers will claim that some of the causes of current health and well-being challenges are easier to identify than to address and that while rapid change may be painful and in some part dysfunctional, in the long term, there are benefits to be had for everyone. In the case of the UK's public services sector, the continued pursuit of financial austerity is portrayed as being unavoidable by the governing party, while its principal opponents are quietly reliant on a sea change in public attitudes toward significantly higher levels of taxation as the solution. A more unvarnished assessment of the prevailing situation is that UK employers in general seem prepared to bear the costs of compromised work health and well-being because these may be less than the expenditures that would be entailed in seeking to address the problem. In addition, their assessment might also be that such actions as may be required could undermine the prevailing social organization of work that has benefited them for so long.

The evidence presented by the CIPD suggests that many employers are not prepared to invest further funds in attempts to address the present level of sickness absence or attempt to prevent its continuation. In 2018 they report that only one in five respondents to their survey claims currently have a stand-alone well-being strategy as part of their wider organizational strategy. This is an improvement since 2016 when only 10% responded in this way, with a further 25% claiming that such a plan or program forms an element of a wider people strategy. At the same time, however, while in 2016 only 8% of respondents were prepared to admit to not "currently doing anything to improve employee health and well-being," for 2018 the figure had risen to 20%. The single largest response in 2016 was that provision was essentially ad hoc, according to need and in the absence of a formal strategy or plan, suggesting an upward movement for 2018 and beyond.

The nature of actual interventions varies considerably. In 2016 under the designation "health promotion," 13 provisions are listed in the CIPD report as attracting support in double digits, the most popular being advice on healthy eating (34%) reinforced by healthy canteen options (24%) and the provision of free fresh fruit (22%). Subsidized gym membership (30%) is the second most popular provision, again reinforced by walking initiatives (15%) and in-house gyms (11%). For those who might overdo exercise, access to physiotherapy (22%) exists together with massage provision (12%). The next most popular provision (29%) is health screening, with smoking cessation also reported as a major initiative (25%). Well-being days (21%), "mindfulness" (20%), and relaxation or exercise classes (12%) might be adjudged relatively more progressive initiatives skewed at unwellness rather than physical ill health. These findings document a welcome, albeit modest continuation in employee health and well-being concern—with 46% of respondents reporting an increase in their focus on such issues and only 3% a decrease.

In this section of their 2016 report, the CIPD also repeats the earlier observation that the dominant orientation in relation to employee health and well-being is reactive with almost 60% of respondents taking the view that their organizations are "much more reactive than proactive regarding well-being" (p. 41). Irrespective of whether individual provisions are regarded as being either proactive or reactive, *it is difficult to recognize most of them as providing a serious response to the principal causes of stress-related absence and mental health conditions as these are identified earlier in the report.* While the majority of employees would probably benefit from eating more healthily, including more fruit, as they would taking more exercise and if necessary more massages and physiotherapy, it seems improbable that such interventions will begin to make the shortcomings of management practice, across a range of issues, more tolerable. Likewise, the provision of assistance for smoking cessation or reducing alcohol and substance abuse seems an inadequate response, regardless of their widely known general health benefits. The observation that organizations continue to proudly advertise such interventions perhaps signifies a desperate wish to cling on to the belief that lifestyle factors remain a serious part of the sickness absence phenomenon. Alternatively, it may be that their status as relatively low-cost options probably consolidates their appeal.

Although well-being days, mindfulness sessions, and relaxation classes reflect a welcome broadening of the portfolio of interventions and ostensibly relate more to well-being issues, their substance suggests them to be largely accommodative in nature. At the risk of being regarded as overly cynical, taking a yoga class, pursuing aromatherapy, or relaxing in candle-filled spaces might be the contemporary equivalent of smoking a cigarette, having a glass of wine, or using soft drugs. For many people the temptation these days is to combine the traditional and the modern approaches in the pursuit of stress relief, in an attempt to make life in general, and for too many people the workplace, tolerable if not better. The gulf between the problem of persistent workplace sickness absence, presenteeism, and leaveism in the UK as a consequence of mental unwellness or physical ill health and in large part the result of widely recognized and well-understood causal factors and the current stock of generally jejune responses to them is therefore immense and probably growing. As noted in the previous section, it is also greatly at odds with the importance (value) attributed to human capital and its contribution to contemporary value creation, delivery, and capture.

6 By Way of Corroboration (Unfortunately)

As an element of her doctoral studies, one of the authors secured a modest number of interviews with senior managers in UK organizations with responsibility for the promotion of employee health and well-being. The majority of interviewees were from the HR function together with occupational medicine specialists and a couple of well-being promotion specialists. Most were highly enthusiastic about promoting health and well-being, and several had long experience in the area, perhaps casting some doubt on the representativeness of their views. Given the problems encountered in securing these interviews, there is a strong argument for regarding the following overview of their responses as constituting the leading edge of health and well-being promotion in UK organizations at this time (Monk, Murray, & Roslender, 2018 provide a more detailed review of the interview responses).

There was little disagreement among the interviewees that it was the organization's responsibility to do as much as it could to ensure that employees' health and well-being levels were as good as they might be. Although it was acknowledged that employees themselves also have a role to play in this process, there was little to suggest that their respective employees behaved irresponsibly. Securing buy-in from line managers and supervisors was suggested to be more of a problem in this regard, necessitating the existence of effective communication of the issues and the availability of support to ensure that managers and supervisors were conscious of the expectations the organization had of them. Continuous reinforcement of the health and well-being message was viewed to be a given for success. As suggested in the previous section, the substance of actual interventions in support of enhanced employee health and well-being was disappointingly modest. The absence of a dedicated well-being strategy in some organizations was acknowledged, together with interventions that were necessary to comply with factory legislation or employment obligations. Several more progressive interventions were described. In one organization the decision had been taken to secure the services of an ex-medical director of a football club in an attempt to better engage men's health and well-being concerns. Another organization have sought to establish a well-being calendar with different themes or foci every month. Experiments with establishing in-house support networks were also identified, extending beyond help with smoking cessation, embracing exercise, or dealing with chronic medical conditions, to support with mental health issues or gender issues.

All the interviewees appreciated that however modest specific interventions might be, they largely proved successful. Equally, unless initiated independently by employees themselves, they necessarily entailed the investment of financial resources by the organization, resources that were constantly in short supply. As a result, it was always necessary to "make the business case" for the retention of any existing provision or extension of interventions. This is nothing new to the HR profession, whose discretionary expenditure on staff development initiatives has regularly been a target when budgetary restraint is perceived to be necessary, alongside marketing expenditure and research and development expenditure. The HR profession is no longer incapable of making such business cases and in recent times has been able to invoke a number of considerations in this direction. Absenteeism costs money directly through the loss of the services of individual employees. Indirectly there are costs associated with employing cover for such absences, training them, potential losses in quality of value proposition, etc. Presenteeism is no longer a hidden cost—managers can see that people are unfit to work and that their output is diminished. Compromised health and well-being are now understood to effect employee retention—who would wish to continue to work for an organization that makes you unwell if alternative employments are available? Likewise, the potential degradation of the employer brand and its recruitment implications or unwillingness on the part of some customers to continue their relationship with poor employers.

Making the case and having the case accepted are two different matters. A number of the interviewees highlighted a perceived lack of convincing evidence as the major stumbling block to securing the necessary resources to promote employee health and well-being. Crucial to the situation is the awe with which top management views the return on investment (ROI) metric. One interviewee referred to it as "the Holy Grail," while another observed that "businesses are run by business men, who are run by the bottom line." Even one of the interviewees appeared to have swallowed this narrative, talking about never having seen evidence that spending £1000 returns £1001. There is evidence out there if one is prepared to look for it. Hesketh and Cooper (2018) cite BUPA's medical director, Steve Luttrell's observation that every pound invested in well-being returns three (p. 23). This mirrors the estimate in Berry, Mirabito, and Baun (2010) that a dollar invested in this way yields a benefit of $2.71. The key observation is that the default position of many top management in the UK is to assert that this and similar evidence is simply not convincing enough, probably because they don't want it to be.

A number of additional issues that served as obstacles to more extensive health and well-being activity in the UK organizations were identified during interviews. The level of commitment evidenced by the present UK government was regarded as being limited, thereby providing a measure of justification for employers who wished to argue that interventions of this sort might not be regarded as a major priority at this time. This would seem to cohere with the limited attention work health and well-being issues currently attract in the public narrative. Reference was also made to a general aversion to being told what is good for people, with over-consumption of alcohol a case in point, or initiatives that might be labeled evidence of a "nanny state." The latter was a powerful component of the political rhetoric of successive Conservative administrations between 1979 and 1997. A couple of interviewees observed that even when it had been possible to successfully lobby someone within top management about the benefits of pursuing greater efforts on employee health and well-being, there was no certainty that he/she would continue to act a champion for them over time or in the event of securing advancement within an organization. Last but by no means least, arguments about the relatively limited influence that the HR function has with UK organizations as compared with the USA, Australia, or Scandinavian countries were rehearsed by several practitioners. In the UK at least, the HR function is perceived to be principally a staff function with little influence over the activities of line management.

7 What Does the Future Hold?

The scenario presented by CIPD in its most recent reports is also borne out by what many UK employees experience in their workplaces on a daily basis—excessive workloads, staff absences, failing managements, persistent reports of job cuts (currently most prevalent in the retail sector), the uncertainties of Brexit, etc. Ironically the leaveism phenomenon is not confined to those employees who feel unable to cope with their work demands within traditional timeframes. Many who might happily take laptops and iPads on vacation with them are only making the situation worse for their colleagues, and in some cases for themselves in the longer term, should they succumb to burnout. While it might be seen as an overexaggeration of the prevailing situation in many UK organizations, there is good reason to conclude that a state of denial complemented by self-deception exists. Borrowing a currently vogue notion, those who seek to reveal a different reality (as in this chapter) are open to the accusation of being the purveyors of fake news who would rather focus on the negatives rather than the positives and largely for the own ends.

To conclude, it is valuable to briefly engage with a pair of ideas that have some currency, one of which like-minded readers will take encouragement from, as opposed to the other one, which portends a further deterioration of the workplace experience. The promise of a reduced working week is not new, having attracted significant attention as part of the leisure society debate in the 1970s (Gilchrist & Wheaton, 2008). The enabling technologies identified 40 years ago have been eclipsed by the development of information technologies with the capacity to revolutionize the workplace as we know it. Five days' work can in many cases readily be accomplished in four, without any impact on the quality of work performed or the remuneration of employees, while further employment opportunities funded by the resultant cost reductions will impact on current heavy workloads and the debilitating long-hours culture that exists in the UK. Unfortunately, the (self-evident) business case against such a utopia is already well-established in the prevailing narrative of employment. It has recently been reinforced by a more worrying recipe for the future, the inculcation of greater employee resilience in the face of a generally harsher workplace experience in the face of continuing financial pressures in both the private and public sectors (Hesketh & Cooper, 2018). The objective of resilience training is to equip employees with the skills and mindset that will allow them to withstand the various negativities that they experience in the workplace. Whether such training is intended to regularize the worst forms of bullying, whether by management or colleagues is an interesting question. What is certainly worrying is the observation that the promotion of greater employee resilience has the consequence of individualizing the problem, of shifting responsibility for coping with workplace negativities onto employees, the very opposite of affirming the dignity of those who continue to be the origin of all value creation and delivery.

In the light of the latter observations, any undermining of the health and well-being of employees should be viewed as an unacceptable condition that requires to be addressed as a matter of considerable urgency. Throughout this chapter we have argued that the accommodative nature of the interventions evident in relation to the

UK's continuing sickness absence problem is insufficient in either extent or intent. A much more comprehensive set of initiatives designed to enact a new narrative of business (Freeman & Ginena, 2015; Retolaza, Aguado, & Alcaniz, 2019) is now necessary, a compelling story in which the social responsibilities of the corporation, including promoting the health and well-being of every employee, are always at the forefront of the minds of principals and agents alike.

References

Aguado, R., Alcaniz, L., & Retolaza, J. L. (2015). A new role for the firm incorporating sustainability and human dignity: Conceptualization and measurement. *Human Systems Management, 34*, 43–56.

Barney, J. (1991). Firm resources and sustained competitive advantage. *Journal of Management, 17*(1), 99–120.

Berry, L. L., Mirabito, A. M., & Baun, W. (2010). What's the hard return on employee wellness programs? *Harvard Business Review, 88*(12), 104–112.

Black, C. (2008). *Working for a healthier tomorrow: Work and health in Britain*. London: The Stationery Office.

Chandola, T. (2010). *Stress at work*. London: British Academy Policy Centre.

CIPD. (2016). *Absence management survey*. London: Chartered Institute of Personnel and Development/Simplyhealth.

CIPD. (2018). *Health and well-being at work*. London: Chartered Institute of Personnel and Development/Simplyhealth.

Edvinsson, L. (1997). Developing intellectual capital at Skandia. *Long Range Planning, 30*(3), 266–273.

Edvinsson, L., & Malone, M. S. (1997). *Intellectual capital: Recognizing your company's true value*. New York: Harper Collins.

Freeman, R. E., & Ginena, K. (2015). Rethinking the purpose of the corporation: Challenges from stakeholder theory. *Notizie di Politeia, 31*(117), 9–18.

Gilchrist, P., & Wheaton, B. (2008). *Whatever happened to the leisure society? Theory, debate and policy*. Eastbourne: Leisure Studies Association.

Guthrie, J., Dumay, J., Ricceri, F., & Nielsen, C. (Eds.). (2017). *The Routledge companion to intellectual capital*. London: Routledge.

Hemp, P. (2004). Presenteeism: At work but out of it. *Harvard Business Review, 82*(5), 1–9.

Hesketh, I., Cooper, C., & Ivy, J. (2014). Leaveism and public sector reform: Will the practice continue? *Journal of Organizational Effectiveness: People and Performance, 1*(2), 205–212.

Hesketh, I., Cooper, C., & Ivy, J. (2015). Leaveism and work-life integration: The thinning blue line. *Policing, 9*(2), 183–194.

Hesketh, I., & Cooper, C. L. (2014). Leavism at work. *Occupational Medicine, 64*(3), 146–147.

Hesketh, I., & Cooper, C. L. (2018). *Managing health and wellbeing in the public sector: A guide to best practice*. Abingdon: Routledge.

IIRC. (2013). *The International<IR> Framework*. International Integrated Reporting Council. www.theiirc.org

Johns, G. (2010). Presenteeism in the workplace: A review and research agenda. *Journal of Organizational Behavior, 31*, 519–542.

Monk, E., Murray, N., & Roslender, R. (2018). Where there's a will there (may be) wellbeing: Exploring the promotion of employee health and wellbeing in UK organizations. *Proceedings of the thirty-second British Academy of Management conference*, University of the West of England, Bristol.

Nielsen, C., & Roslender, R. (2015). Enhancing financial reporting: The contribution of business models. *British Accounting Review, 47*(3), 262–274.

Peters, T. J., & Waterman, R. H. (1982). *In search of excellence: Lessons for America's best-run companies*. New York: Harper and Row.

Porter, M. E. (1980). *Competitive strategy: Techniques for analysing industries and competitors*. New York: The Free Press.

Porter, M. E. (1985). *Competitive advantage: Creating and sustaining superior performance*. New York: The Free Press.

Retolaza, J. L., Aguado, R., & Alcaniz, L. (2019). Stakeholder theory through the lenses of Catholic social thought. *Journal of Business Ethics, 157*(4), 969–980.

Roslender, R., & Fincham, R. (2001). Thinking critically about intellectual capital accounting. *Accounting, Accountability and Auditing Journal, 14*(4), 383–398.

Roslender, R., & Monk, E. (2017). Accounting for people. In J. Guthrie et al. (Eds.), *The Routledge companion to critical accounting*. London: Routledge.

Roslender, R., & Nielsen, C. (2018). *"Accounting through the business model: Recognising the centrality of the customer", mimeo*. University of Dundee School of Business.

Roslender, R., & Stevenson, J. (2009). AccountingforPeople: A real step forward or more a case of wishing and hoping? *Critical Perspectives on Accounting, 20*(7), 855–869.

Rumelt, R. P. (1991). How much does industry matter? *Strategic Management Journal, 12*(3), 167–185.

Schaufeli, W., & Bakker, A. B. (2004). Job demands, job resources and their relationship with burnout and engagement: A multi-sample study. *Journal of Organizational Behavior, 25*, 293–315.

Wernerfelt, B. (1984). A resource-based view of the firm. *Strategic Management Journal, 5*(2), 171–180.

Humanistic Management in the Corporation: From Self-Interest to Dignity and Well-being

Ricardo Aguado and José Luis Retolaza

1 Introduction

Society as a whole and its individual stakeholders are asking corporations a change in the way they approach business, economic activity, and human beings (Dierksmeier, 2011). This demand is felt strongly in countries where the impact of the 2008–2014 economic crisis has been deeper and long lasting (Aguado, Alcaniz, Retolaza, & Albareda, 2016). At the academic level, authors from different backgrounds have made a call in order to align the interests of corporations and social well-being (Melé & Schlag, 2015). In some cases, this call tries to reconcile profit with the generation of value for stakeholders and the environmental responsibility (Porter & Kramer, 2011). In other cases, authors proposed firms to engage in community development activities (Donaldson, 2017). In this chapter, we will show how it is possible for corporations to align the interest of stakeholders and society as a whole with the aims and objectives of the corporation. Following this path, corporations could make a positive contribution to social well-being and to the dignity of the individuals engaged in their economic activities.

In spite of those proposals of change, society as a whole is dissatisfied when asked about the role of corporations in society, at least in developed economies. The last data available from the Edelman Trust Barometer (2018) points out that, in the main countries of the European Union, only 45% of the population trusts corporations (data calculated for Ireland, Poland, UK, France, Germany, Spain, Italy, and Sweden). In comparison, data for the United States shows a slightly higher percentage: 48% of the population trusts corporations. However, this number is 10 points below than in 2017, which shows a negative trend.

On the other hand, a majority of citizens agrees on the perception that corporations are not making an efficient contribution to the creation of value for the whole society

R. Aguado (✉) · J. L. Retolaza
University of Deusto, Deusto Business School, Bilbao, Spain
e-mail: ricardo.aguado@deusto.es; joseluis.retolaza@deusto.es

© Springer Nature Switzerland AG 2020
R. Aguado, A. Eizaguirre (eds.), *Virtuous Cycles in Humanistic Management*,
Contributions to Management Science,
https://doi.org/10.1007/978-3-030-29426-7_9

(Edelman Trust Barometer, 2018). This lack of alignment between society and corporations is creating a gap between economic and social agents, which may erode corporations´ legitimacy to operate at the social level (Porter & Kramer, 2011). In fact, and again following the Edelman Trust Barometer, 2018, up to 56% of the population agrees on the following statement: "companies that only think about themselves and their profits are bound to fail" (Edelman Trust Barometer, 2018, p. 38).

According to Pirson (2014), the growing mistrust between corporations and individuals lies in the fact that the objectives of society and those of corporations differ. In many corporations, there is a preeminence of the interests of shareholders over any other stakeholder of the firm (Aguado, Alcaniz, & Retolaza, 2015). At the same time, usually the remuneration of managers is linked to the value created and delivered to shareholders, overlooking rest of the stakeholders (Retolaza, San-Jose, & Ruíz-Roqueñi, 2016). This kind of management disconnects the performance of corporations (measured mainly in financial terms) from the needs and demands of society (Donaldson, 2017), increasing the aforementioned gap between firms and society (Naughton, 2015).

The main objective of this chapter is to propose an understanding of the person and the corporation which allows an alignment between the aim of corporations, individual development (or flourishing), and social well-being. In order to fulfill this objective, in Sect. 2 we will analyze the actual conception of the person and the role of corporations according to the shareholder theory. In addition, we will highlight the shortcomings of this approach and will propose a complementary one based on the stakeholder theory (Freeman, 1984) and a humanistic perspective of economic activity (Melé, 2003). In Sect. 3, we will develop this humanistic model and the ways in which it can make a positive contribution toward the integral development of employees. Finally, we will highlight the main conclusions of the chapter, recognize its limitations, and propose new paths of inquiry in this line of research.

2 From Shareholder Theory to Humanistic Management

In this section, we will present, first, the role of corporations and the conception of the person as stated in shareholder theory. In short, we will analyze the gaps that this understanding of economic activity may reinforce between the interests of society and the objectives of corporations. Second, we will present a humanistic approach to economic activity, as a way to reconcile the expectations of society and the objectives of corporations.

2.1 Shareholder Theory: Achievements and Limitations

The dominant economic paradigm that has been applied to the management of organizations for the last 200 years can be labelled as shareholder theory (Aguado, Retolaza, & Alcaniz, 2017). The origins of this approach can be found in the seminal work of Adam Smith in the last part of the eighteenth century (Smith, 1776). Although in previous works Smith introduced the idea that the well-being of an individual is linked with the well-being of others (Smith, 1759), when he addressed in particular the aim of economic activity, he highlighted the interest of the owner of the business and did not introduce any principle about dignity or morality. The monetization of this interest can be understood as the profit of the modern corporation. At the same time, Smith was able to link, in a logical way, the maximization of this profit with social well-being. In order to maximize profit, a corporation should address the needs of consumers in a way in which their utility is also maximized. These ideas constitute the central axioms of shareholder theory (Frank, 2005). Thus, leading management scholars defend that the objective of the firm is to maximize its profits, because that is the way corporations have to improve social conditions (Friedman, 2007; Jensen, 2002).

If we analyze socio-economic data for the last century globally, the level of *per capita* wealth (measured in terms of real GDP per person) has increased at an exponential rate (OECD, 2014). This fact can be seen, at least in part, as the result of applying Smith's ideas to economic activity: efficiency and self-interest have been compatible with increasing material well-being (Kanbur & Spence, 2010).

However, this understanding of economic activity has been regarded as incomplete by many researchers (Baviera, English, & Guillén, 2016; Freeman, Harrison, Wicks, Parmar, & De Colle, 2010). These academics have highlighted certain characteristics of the shareholder theory that undermine social well-being and individual development. First, the basic assumption that this model does about the behavior of economic agents is that the rational agent (a person or a corporation) is a utility (or profit) maximizer. This behavior excludes morality from economic decision-making (Naughton, 2015), as well as any other motivation for economic agents not related to self-interest (Dierksmeier, 2011). Second, the utility maximization approach does not consider directly issues regarding social and environmental sustainability, which have become critical aspects of the corporation regarding its stakeholders (Wheeler & Elkington, 2001). Finally, the shareholder model tends to ignore the interests of stakeholders, who are not shareholders directly. This situation can create stakeholder disengagement (Pirson, 2014), which is not good for stakeholders of the corporation (Alford, 2010), and it does not recognize employees' professionalism as a source of personal development through service to others in the workplace (Retolaza et al., 2016). Shortcomings such as this are creating mistrust on corporations for an increasing part of the population (Edelman Trust Barometer, 2018). In order to face this situation, academics of the shareholder theory, such as Porter and Kramer (2011), demand a change in the conduct of corporations, so that the interests of both society and corporations are aligned. Concepts such as shared value and beneficiation are trying to capture the need of linking social well-being with the objectives of the firm (Retolaza et al., 2016).

2.2   Humanistic Management: Dignity and Social Well-being

The limitations of shareholder theory (expressed in the previous section) have created a growing appeal for a deep transformation of this theory in order to promote higher levels of justice and equality (Garriga & Melé, 2004).

Recent developments of the role of the firm highlight not only the importance of shareholders and profit but also the social and environmental responsibility of the firm (Kostera & Pirson, 2017). In this line, all stakeholders (shareholders, customers, suppliers, employees, public administrations) are relevant for firms (Freeman et al., 2010). In fact, many academicians have started to use the stakeholder approach in order to widen the objective of the firm and incorporate not only financial but also social and environmental issues (Freeman, 1994). Following this approach, the objective of the firm is not limited to only one stakeholder (shareholders). Interests of employees, customers, and local communities, for example, are also taken into account because these social and economic actors are engaged in the creation of value for the firm. In fact, according to this approach, the firm is accountable to these groups. This means that the objectives of the firm and objectives of its stakeholders are correlated (Aguado et al., 2015). In this way, the gap between the interests of society and the interests of corporations tend to diminish, because the later encompasses, to a certain degree, the former.

Later development of stakeholder theory highlights the importance of the purpose of the firm, and then confronts it with the expectations of the rest of social and economic actors (Hollensbe, Wookey, Loughlin, & George, 2014). This purpose is linked to the contribution that a given corporation would like to make to its members and society (stakeholders) (Ellsworth, 2002), and in many cases, it can be a source of motivation, identity, and employee engagement (Deloitte, 2014). At the same time, an inspiring and shared purpose among all stakeholders of the corporation can be helpful in the identification of shared values, innovation opportunities, and strategic decision-making (Retolaza et al., 2016).

This new discourse about the role of businesses in society has been synthetized by Freeman and Ginena (2015) using six basic principles. The first one states that firms create value for their stakeholders: customers, suppliers, employees, communities, and shareholders. The second principle explains that businesses are purpose driven. The creation of value is developed around a central purpose that is shared by all stakeholders. This purpose binds stakeholders and can be a source of inspiration for all of them. The third principle underlines the interconnections between stakeholders. The performance of the firm needs the contribution of all stakeholders, and the potential positive results will have an impact in all of them. In this line, the fourth principle states that managers should avoid tradeoffs between stakeholders, trying to harmonize the common interest of all stakeholders over time. This common interest can be built around a shared purpose for the entire organization. However, conflicts may arise among stakeholders. The fifth principle proposes conflict as a source of value creation. Often, in order to overcome those conflicts, corporations will have to find new solutions and innovative answers that may enhance the value generated for all stakeholders. The sixth principle revisits the conception of human being as an asset or utility maximizer and proposes that persons are able to engage in cooperative efforts with others in order to achieve common goals. All these principles taken together constitute the so-called "new story of business," proposed by Freeman and Ginena (2015) to develop leading, competitive, and socially engaging corporations in the twenty-first century.

As discussed, the new story of business principle presents the conception of human resource as something that goes beyond the notion of *homo economicus*. It describes a person as a living entity who can cooperate in the pursuit of a common objective and, at the same time, is able to identify and look for his or her own interest. In this case, corporations can be viewed as entities that generate value (and profit) for their stakeholders while providing a positive service to society (Alford, 2006). This shift in the understanding of the human being is of great importance for the internal functioning of the firm and its role in society. Some academics (Melé & Schlag, 2015) have pointed out that many corporations failed in developing an internal ethical culture to be able to connect business to the common good of society, which has eroded the confidence of the general public on corporations, as shown by the Edelman barometer. In this approach, firms not only develop individual goals and interests but also a common purpose that is shared by all stakeholders. Each stakeholder may have a particular goal (the individual interest) that should be promoted through the common objective of the firm, in accordance with social well-being (Alford, 2010). Businesses, then, are perceived not only as a nexus of contracts but as a community of people. Moreover, the objective of the corporation is not reduced only to profits but also encompasses the development of the common good of all stakeholders, in connection with creation of value for the larger society (Naughton, 2015). This connection with society can happen in three ways: through the delivery of goods (high-quality products), good work (caring about employees), and wealth (sustainable value creation process) (Goodpaster, Maines, Naughton, & Shapiro, 2018).

The kind of management that proposes fulfillment of the common good and social well-being as the objectives of the corporation has been labeled as "humanistic management" (Melé & Dierskmeier, 2012). One of the main characteristics of humanistic management is to prioritize the development of the human resource in all dimensions (flourishing) and social well-being as fundamental management orientations (Melé, 2003). At the same time, humanistic management protects the dignity and freedom of every individual and understands corporations as places where both dignity and freedom are enhanced and service the common good of society (Kostera & Pirson, 2017).

Both stakeholder theory and humanistic management share meaningful principles which guide practical decision-making of managers (Freeman et al., 2010; Melé & Schlag, 2015). In both cases, there is a need to take into account the interests of all stakeholders of the firm, not just the shareholders. At the same time, at least in the new story of business developed by Freeman and Ginena (2015), there is a clear intention of aligning the common interests of stakeholders with social well-being and environmental responsibility. This common approach to management principles allows the possibility of cooperation in order to achieve common goals (Aguado et al., 2015).

However, humanistic management (HM) proposals go further than the inclusion of shareholders' interests. In fact, humanistic management focuses o n he ideas of human dignity and social well-being as guiding principles for both management and corporations. HM proposes the integral development of the person and the alignment of his personal goals with that of the common good of stakeholders of the firm and society (Dierksmeier, 2011).

In application of the aforementioned objective, in the following section, we will develop a proposal to enhance the overall development of employees in the workplace, based on HM principles.

3 Toward Integral Human Development in the Firm: The Case for Employees

In the previous sections, we discussed the idea of protecting and fostering dignity in economic activity. Inside corporations, employees are the ones that interact with other stakeholders and social participants that are engaged in the economic activity of those corporations. In this section, we will analyze how corporations can make a positive contribution in the integral development of its employees, enhancing their dignity and introducing an ethical perspective in the management of employees within organizations.

In general, both practitioners and academics follow either a motivational approach or a control approach when they propose ethical perspective in the management of employees. In the control approach, standards are set that minimize the situations in which a corporation may not respect human dignity. However, this approach is not applicable if the objective is the integral development of employees in the workplace (Aguado et al., 2015).

In line with the suggestions that Amartya Sen (1997) presented to governments and international organizations, we propose a model that aligns the objective of the firm with the development of the employees . Accordingly, we propose a motivational approach in order to introduce ethical perspective in the management of employees.

At the microeconomic level, in day-to-day functioning of the corporation, managers can contribute to the human development of their working teams, by enhancing the human quality of the organization. This happens when ethical motives in the workplace are introduced in the management system. In this way, it is easier for employees to develop a sense of meaning and identify themselves with the objective of the corporation, being more effective in their responsibilities (Fagley & Adler, 2012).

However, the main classical taxonomies on employee motivation (the ones proposed by Maslow, McClelland, Alderfer, and Herzberg) contain "a limited implicit ethical assumption, namely, that human behavior is essentially amoral" (Guillén, Ferrero, & Hoffman, 2015). This is so because all those theories state that human behavior is based on self-interest and do not consider other interests. In fact, these classical taxonomies consider motivation which is related to individual need to receive support, or relatedness, or achievement or satisfaction, but always from the individual perspective. Maslow, in his widely used theory of motivation (Maslow, 1943), proposes a hierarchical description of needs. From basic or lower needs (security, survival), the model shifts toward higher needs (esteem-building, self-actualization, or self-improvement). Some years later, McClelland identified three types of needs (achievement, power, and affiliation) that correlated motivations of accountability, status, and belonging (McClelland, 1962). The Three Needs Theory (existence, growth, and relatedness, or EGR) proposed by Alderfer (1969) agrees with the theory of McClelland in avoiding the hierarchical order. In these two cases, the aforementioned needs could be accomplished simultaneously. Herzberg (1968) distinguished between extrinsic and intrinsic factors of motivation. Extrinsic factors motivate the individual because the person will receive something external (recognition, relatedness, or power and security). On the other hand, intrinsic motivations offer internal reward to the individual (self-actualization, growth, or achievement). All these four classical taxonomies are focused on the individual self-interest and do not consider ethical aspects or social issues as sources of motivation for the person or employee.

However, other authors consider that human behavior and motivation cannot be reduced to an exclusive search of self-interest. Other issues, such as social concerns, service to others, and cooperation can also be drivers for human behavior (Folger & Salvador, 2008; Ghoshal, 2005; Grant, 2012). The consideration of ethical dimension of motivation is concurrent with the personalist approach of the human being: a person that is able to look for his/her own interest and, at the same time, is able to cooperate and seek for the good of the community in which he/she lives and works (Alford, 2006; Retolaza et al., 2016).

Following this point of view, we propose that, along with self-centered motivations (recognized in the classical taxonomies), moral goals and benevolence should be also considered as a conforming part of any motivational framework in the workplace.

In fact, different authors consider that, beyond rational self-interest, ethical, and pro-social considerations are important in motivating employees in the workplace (Grant, 2012). Following this approach, Aquino and Reed (2002) have compiled several studies which conclude that many employees define themselves as giving and caring individuals, having a pro-social identity. Furthermore, recent research in experimental economics and psychology underlines the fact that people behave in a far less selfish way than the *homo economicus* model assumes (Benkler, 2011). In this line, we propose a kind of motivation that goes beyond self-interest and seeks the good of the others. In contrast with intrinsic and extrinsic motivation, there is a transitive motivation (Melé, 2003), where the focus shifts from self-perspective to other's perspective.

In addition to self-interest (intrinsic or extrinsic) and transitive motivations, a growing number of authors suggest the importance of a different kind of motivation rooted in spirituality (Argandona, 2011; Fagley & Adler, 2012). Other authors, like

Karakas (2010), have described the upcoming of a new paradigm in management called "the spirituality movement." According to this approach, managers will shift their focus from profits to quality of life, from self-interest to social responsibility concerns, and from a materialistic to a spiritual orientation.

However, there is not a clear consensus about the meaning of spirituality at work. The search for meaning, purpose, and a sense of community are highlighted by many authors as common characteristics of the spiritual dimension at work (Fagley & Adler, 2012; Karakas, 2010). For many employees, the spiritual driver is activated when the objective of the corporation is aligned with the deepest values by which those employees live.

In our view, four kinds of motivations that have been highlighted in this section should be taken into account by corporations in order to develop overall dimension of its employees (self-centered, transitive, and spiritual). At the same time, the design of incentive and compensation systems should consider the development of the afore-mentioned dimensions, in order to create a healthy organization for employees.

An example of the different kinds of motivations and their connectedness can illustrate the importance of cultivating all of them in order to make a positive contribution to the integral development of employees, the alignment of social and corporate objectives, and the motivation of employees at work. We will use in our example the case of the director of economics department in a business school. This person, because of being a person, is able to develop self-interested and collaborative behavior. In some cases, self-interested drivers could act as motivational forces. In this case, acquire a higher level of knowledge and being able to take autonomous decisions (intrinsic motives), or receiving social consideration and recognition, as well as a safe position in the organization (extrinsic motives) can work as forms of self-interested motivation. In order to cultivate all dimensions of a person, the business school should consider the development of transitive and spiritual motivation. This could be achieved through the development of a leadership based in the service of others (servant leadership), in which the director would incorporate as an objective the growth and development of every member of the department. Additionally, the director can try to align the objectives of the department with social interests, by aligning the performance of the department with social well-being.

As it is described in this example, the integration of intrinsic, extrinsic, and transitive motivations at the workplace can produce positive outcomes not only at the individual level but also at the corporation level (affecting other stakeholders of the corporation), and also at the social level, aligning social well-being with the objectives of the corporation. This example can be applicable to any organization divided into functional departments, and it helps in the understanding how integrating a wider perspective on motivation can provide a fruitful path to develop the different dimensions of a person at work.

4 Conclusions

Civil societies expectations about corporations in developed economies are changing. According to recent studies, citizens do not trust corporations and are demanding them to adjust their operations and objectives to match social well-being. The social sustainability of corporations in the developed world is under stress.

In order to align the objectives of corporations with social well-being, we propose a shift in the understanding of the individual as an economic agent. While in the neoclassical tradition, the individual economic agent (consumer or firm) is thought to be a maximizing agent (trying to achieve the maximum level of profit or utility), and in the humanistic management approach, individuals are considered as humans who are able to cooperate and/or follow their own self-interest.

According to understanding of the human approach, we propose a motivational policy within corporations which could fulfill both self-interest and pro-social and service-oriented behavior. In short, we propose a kind of motivation that is able to foster not only personal utility maximization behavior but also foster the moral and spiritual dimensions of employees at workplace. In doing so, corporations could develop a healthier work atmosphere, reward moral and transitive conducts of employees, and align their mission and objectives, which is increasingly demanded by civil society worldwide.

The limitations of this chapter are twofold. First, it would be necessary to develop an accurate motivational plan for a given corporation in order to develop intrinsic, extrinsic, and transitive motivations. The implementation of such a plan could be the base to measure if employees are able to develop not only their self-interested behavior but also other dimensions, such as the spiritual and service-oriented ones. This study could be replicated in different organizations belonging to different sectors to assess its impacts on employees, profits, and alignment between social and organizational objectives. In the second place, a proper tool to measure the impact of this kind of motivational plan is lacking. Although there are many tools to assess the level of success of self-oriented motivational policies, there is a need to develop accurate tools to measure the impact of spiritual, ethical, and pro-social behavior of employees at the workplace.

Future lines of research could tackle these two limitations. On one hand, the implementation of empirical studies in corporations and organization in general could be helpful in understanding how employees respond to opportunities to develop not only self-interested behavior but also ethical and pro-social actions in the workplace. On the other hand, the development of tools to measure the impact of transitive motivations in the well-being of employees, results of the corporation, satisfaction of stakeholders, and alignment with social needs and interests could complement the previous line of research. At the same time, it could be helpful in the development of practices in the workplace which foster human development, including the moral, spiritual, and service-oriented dimensions that are rooted in every human being.

References

Aguado, R., Alcaniz, L., & Retolaza, J. L. (2015). A new role for the firm incorporating sustainability and human dignity. Conceptualization and measurement. *Human Systems Management, 34*(1), 43–56.

Aguado, R., Alcaniz, L., Retolaza, J. L., & Albareda, L. (2016). Jesuit business education model: In search of a new role for the firm based on sustainability and dignity. *Journal of Technology Management & Innovation, 11*(1), 12–18.

Aguado, R., Retolaza, J. L., & Alcaniz, L. (2017). Dignity at the level of the firm: Beyond the stakeholder approach. In M. Kostera & M. Pirson (Eds.), *Dignity and the organization* (pp. 81–98). London: Palgrave Macmillan.

Alderfer, C. P. (1969). An empirical test of a new theory of human needs. *Organizational Behavior and Human Performance, 4*, 142–175.

Alford, H. (2006). *Stakeholder theory. The good company: Catholic social thought and corporate social responsibility in dialogue*. Pontifical University of St Thomas, Rome. Plenary Session, Saturday October 7. Accessed July 21, 2018, from http://www.oikonomia.it/images/immagini_X_Articoli/2007/2007_giugno/pdf/05_studi_Helen%20alford.pdf

Alford, H. (2010). The personal wisdom of personalism. *Journal of Management Development, 29*(8), 697–705.

Aquino, K., & Reed, A. (2002). The self-importance of moral identity. *Journal of Personality and Social Psychology, 83*, 1423–1440.

Argandona, A. (2011). Beyond contracts. Love in firms. *Journal of Business Ethics, 99*, 77–85.

Baviera, T., English, W., & Guillén, M. (2016). The logic of the gift: Inspiring behaviour in organizations beyond the limits of duty and exchange. *Business Ethics Quarterly, 26*(2), 159–180.

Benkler, Y. (2011, July/August). The unselfish gene. *Harvard Business Review, 89*(7–8), 67–75.

Deloitte. (2014). *The 2014 global report*. Accessed September 3, 2018, from https://www2.deloitte.com/gz/en/pages/about-deloitte/topics/global-report-2014.html

Dierksmeier, C. (2011). *Reorienting management education: From the Homo economicus to human dignity*. Humanistic Management Network, research paper series no. 13-05. Accessed July 2, 2018, from SSRN: https://ssrn.com/abstract=1766183 or https://doi.org/10.2139/ssrn.1766183

Donaldson, T. (2017). Donaldsonian themes: A commentary. *Business Ethics Quarterly, 27*(1), 125–142.

Edelman Trust Barometer. (2018). Accessed July 2, 2018, from http://cms.edelman.com/sites/default/files/2018-02/2018_Edelman_Trust_Barometer_Global_Report_FEB.pdf

Ellsworth, R. (2002). *Leading with purpose. The new corporate realities*. Stanford: Stanford University Press.

Fagley, N. S., & Adler, M. G. (2012). Appreciation: A spiritual path to find value and meaning in the workplace. *Journal of Management, Spirituality, and Religion, 9*(2), 167–187.

Folger, R., & Salvador, R. (2008). Is management theory too "Self-ish"? *Journal of Management, 34*(6), 1127–1151.

Frank, R. (2005). *Microeconomics and behavior*. New York: McGraw-Hill.

Freeman, R. E. (1984). *Strategic management: A stakeholder approach*. Boston, MA: Pitman.

Freeman, E. (1994). The politics of stakeholder theory: Some future directions. *Business Ethics Quarterly, 4*(4), 409–421.

Freeman, E., & Ginena, K. (2015). Rethinking the purpose of the corporation. *Notizie di Politeia, 31*(117), 9–18.

Freeman, R. E., Harrison, J. S., Wicks, A. C., Parmar, B. L., & De Colle, S. (2010). *Stakeholder theory: The state of the art*. New York, NY: Cambridge University Press.

Friedman, M. (2007). The social responsibility of business is to increase its profits. In W. C. Zimmerli, M. Holzinger, & K. Richter (Eds.), *Corporate ethics and corporate governance* (pp. 173–178). Berlin: Springer.

Garriga, E., & Melé, D. (2004). Corporate social responsibility theories: Mapping the territory. *Journal of Business Ethics, 53*(1), 51–71.

Ghoshal, S. (2005). Bad management theories are destroying good management practices. *Academy of Management Learning & Education, 4*(1), 75–91.

Goodpaster, K. E., Maines, T. D., Naughton, M., & Shapiro, B. (2018). Using UNPRME to teach, research, and enact business ethics: Insights from the Catholic identity matrix for business schools. *Journal of Business Ethics, 147*(4), 761–777.

Grant, A. M. (2012). Leading with meaning: Beneficiary contact, prosocial impact, and the performance effects of transformational leadership. *Academy of Management Journal, 55*(2), 458–476.

Guillén, M., Ferrero, I., & Hoffman, M. (2015). The neglected ethical and spiritual motivations in the workplace. *Journal of Business Ethics, 128*, 803–816.

Herzberg, F. (1968). One more time: How do you motivate employees? *Harvard Business Review, 46*, 53–62.

Hollensbe, E., Wookey, C., Loughlin, H., & George, C. (2014). From the editors. Organizations with purpose. *Academy of Management Journal, 57*(5), 1227–1234.

Jensen, M. C. (2002). Value maximization, stakeholder theory, and the corporate objective function. *Business Ethics Quarterly, 12*(2), 235–256.

Kanbur, R., & Spence, M. (2010). *Equity and growth in a globalizing world*. Washington, DC: World Bank. Accessed July 5, 2018, from https://openknowledge.worldbank.org/handle/10986/2458

Karakas, F. (2010). Spirituality and performance in organizations: A literature review. *Journal of Business Ethics, 94*, 89–106.

Kostera, M., & Pirson, M. (2017). *Dignity and the organization. Humanism in business series*. London: Palgrave Macmillan.

Maslow, A. (1943). *Motivation and personality*. New York: Harper & Row.

McClelland, D. C. (1962). Business, drive and national achievement. *Harvard Business Review, 40*, 99–112.

Melé, D. (2003). The challenge of humanistic management. *Journal of Business Ethics, 44*(1), 77–88.

Melé, D., & Dierskmeier, C. (2012). *Values and humanistic management in the encyclical 'Caritas in Veritate'*. London: Palgrave Macmillan.

Melé, D., & Schlag, M. (Eds.). (2015). *Humanism in economics and business. Perspectives of the Catholic social tradition*. New York: Springer.

Naughton, M. (2015). Thinking institutionally about business: Seeing its nature as a community of persons and its purpose as the common good. In D. Melé & M. Schlag (Eds.), *Humanism in economics and business. Perspectives of the Catholic social tradition* (pp. 179–199). New York: Springer.

OECD. (2014). *Better life index 2014: Definitions and metadata*. Paris: OECD.

Pirson, M. (2014). Reconnecting management theory and social welfare: A humanistic perspective. *Academy of Management proceedings, annual conference of the Academy of Management 2014*.

Porter, M. E., & Kramer, M. R. (2011). Creating shared value: How to reinvent capitalism and unleash a wave of innovation and growth. *Harvard Business Review, 89*(1–2), 62–77.

Retolaza, J. L., San-Jose, L., & Ruíz-Roqueñi, M. (2016). *Social accounting for sustainability: Monetizing the social value*. Berlin: Springer.

Sen, A. K. (1997). *On ethics and economics*. New York: Basil Blackwell.

Smith, A. (1759). *The theory of moral sentiments*. London: A. Millar.

Smith, A. (1776). *An inquiry into the nature and causes of the wealth of nations*. London: Strahan and Cadell.

Wheeler, A., & Elkington, J. (2001). The end of the corporate environmental report? Or the advent of cybernetic sustainability reporting and communication. *Business Strategy and the Environment, 10*(Jan/Feb), 1–14.

Civil Economy and Population Aging: A Prospective Framework for a Global Phenomenon

Iñigo Calvo-Sotomayor and Massimo Cermelli

1 Introduction

The aim of this chapter is to introduce a new framework of analysis that tries to humanize economics identifying the philosophical roots of the limits of our socio-economic system in the reductionist views of human beings, corporations, and value. We believe that humanizing economics is relevant to better understand phenomenon such as population aging, transforming it in an opportunity for our society rather than a problem.

Because of this, we are going to introduce the Civil Economy paradigm whose goal is to address the limits of the current economic thought (and especially the suboptimal outcome it creates in terms of richness of the meaning of life) by proposing a change of paradigm for understanding population aging.

Population aging is already a global phenomenon and will accelerate in the next decades. This field of study is considered relevant since it is a new and unprecedented phenomenon in the history of mankind (Bloom, Canning, & Fink, 2010), as well as being one of the most influential forces during this century (Hayward & Zhang, 2001; United Nations, 2015).

A better understanding of population aging—and its possible socioeconomic effects—is of interest to policy makers, companies, public administrations, the third sector, and civil society, given that the demographic structure of a society has a direct impact on social, economic, and political issues (Guijarro & Peláez, 2008, p. 2). Furthermore, nowadays it seems that there is not enough knowledge about the processes of demographic aging and the existing knowledge about its effects is scarce and full of myths (Börsch-Supan, 2013b, p. 407; Rowe, 2009). This reinforces the need to carry out more research in this field and to continue to look into its causes, as

I. Calvo-Sotomayor (✉) · M. Cermelli
Deusto Business School, University of Deusto, Bilbao, Spain
e-mail: inigo.calvo@deusto.es; massimo.cermelli@deusto.es

© Springer Nature Switzerland AG 2020   163
R. Aguado, A. Eizaguirre (eds.), *Virtuous Cycles in Humanistic Management*,
Contributions to Management Science,
https://doi.org/10.1007/978-3-030-29426-7_10

well as in its socioeconomic consequences. In addition, more research in the field of population aging would produce new metrics, tools, and theoretical frameworks which would facilitate further study.

Consequently, the objective of this chapter is to consider the Civil Economy perspective as a framework to take into consideration the re-emergence of theoretical approaches to aging, as it can arise as a useful lens to understand and explain this phenomenon. As far as the authors know, the present text is the first approximation to demonstrate the use of the Civil Economy paradigm as a prospective framework for population aging analysis.

The Civil Economy took root in the second half of the eighteenth century (1750–1780) thanks to the renowned author Antonio Genovesi (1765) who, starting from a theological formation, dedicated the last years of his life almost exclusively to the economic, ethical, and anthropological field, making his teachings a true magisterium recognized throughout enlightened Europe. The Civil Economy emerged in those decades as an open and inclusive space for critical approach to economic issues, and to debate about the capitalist system.

As will be discussed with regard to the understanding of population aging, the Civil Economy paradigm is a relational and social economy that has a cooperative approach to the market capable of overcoming the dichotomy of weak (unintentional) market cooperation and strong (intentional) business cooperation. Similarly, the Civil Economy approach attempts to bridge the gap created between the market and democracy. In this sense, the population aging phenomenon may represent an economic and social resource rather than be a mere financial problem.

2   The Civil Economy

2.1   The Civil Economy Framework

The Civil Economy is a paradigm that has its roots in the classic tradition of moral philosophy, the so-called Aristotelian-Thomistic approach. This paradigm was developed in the Italian school of thought in the eighteenth century, which, in parallel to the development of the neoclassical vision, was pursuing a broader perspective where economic activity and material achievement were seen not as an end in themselves but as a tool to pursue public happiness (Becchetti, Bruni, & Zamagni, 2015).

This tradition is based on the contribution of Antonio Genovesi (1765), a Neapolitan philosopher and economist who lived around the same time as Adam Smith. The main idea of Genovesi and the Italian school was that the concept of individual happiness was related to the capacity of fostering happiness of others as essential to one's own happiness (they call this "generativity" or "civic fertility"). Genovesi considered civil life as the place where happiness may be fully realized and men are free to practice their natural sociability. The Neapolitan philosopher and economist followed the Aristotelian-Thomistic approach when he argued that "every person has a natural and inherent obligation to study how to procure her happiness;

but the political body is made of persons; therefore, the entire political body and each of its members has an obligation to do what is on their part, i.e. all that they know and can for the sake of common prosperity, as long as that which is done does not offend the rights of the other civil bodies" (Genovesi, 1765, p. 29).

Genovesi focused on the relational and interpersonal nature of human beings (beyond anthropological reductionism) that through trust, reciprocity, and equity could build those moral societal channels of communication that could create public happiness. In this way, while Adam Smith was emphasizing the invisible hand of the market, Genovesi was stressing the fundamental role of the visible fabric of human virtues as crucial for the functioning of the economic system (Bruni, 2006).

What is really relevant in the Neapolitan school of Civil Economy is the idea that human beings go beyond the "animal" sociality developing reciprocity, friendship, mutual assistance, or fraternity. Reciprocity is something rooted in human nature but, at the same time, is something more than relationality or sociability because it implies the reciprocal right to be assisted and consequently the reciprocal obligation to assist others in need (Becchetti & Cermelli, 2018).

Reciprocity is not the same thing as the power of persuasion, which for Adam Smith constitutes the typical characteristics of human sociality. While Smith was emphasizing the invisible hand of the market, Genovesi was stressing the fundamental role of the visible fabric of human virtues as crucial for the functioning of the economic system. Market is a matter of fides, i.e., trust and confidence are at the heart of commerce; this concept is quite similar to what modern theorists call today "social capital." Furthermore, cultivating public trust is the precondition for any possible discourse concerning civil and economic development (Judt, 2012), and the only way to do this is enhancing authentic reciprocity.

In the Civil Economy paradigm, individuals are sense seekers rather than utility maximizers; companies socially, environmentally, and responsibly create value for stakeholders, and they are not profit maximizers, and, finally, GDP is not a sufficient statistic to measure well-being, while the stock of spiritual, relational, economic, and environmental goods is the root of well-living. Because of this, one key point of the Civil Economy consists in overtaking three reductionisms assumed today as normal: the anthropological reductionism, the corporate reductionism, and the value reductionism.

In this sense the Civil Economy paradigm supports the concept of humanistic management from its origin substituting the political economy's idea that individuals and corporations should just pursue their own self-interest without any interest or drive for social goals. The key point for humanizing economics and management from the Civil Economy point of view is replacing the three reductionisms.

2.2   The Three Reductionisms

This epigraph analyzes in more detail the three reductionisms, relative to the concepts of person, company, and value. As far as anthropological reductionism is concerned, there are two aspects in the dominant economic anthropology which are especially relevant. The first of them states that human beings are capable of ordering their priorities in a way that helps them to set and define clear objectives and how to act strategically in order to achieve them. It is important to take into account that this pattern works under restrictions of time, technology, and money. The second one is based on the belief that the objective or utility function of the *homo economicus* is aimed at achieving happiness which is understood to be proportional to the material goods acquired (Bruni, 2006).

A fundamental limit of reductionism in the definition of the objectives of the *homo economicus* is in paying no attention to the importance of relational goods in achieving happiness. Empirical studies clearly show that relational goods have a decisive importance for the purposes of our satisfaction in life. Relational goods are interpersonal interactions that produce beneficial effects in our life satisfaction. They are generated every time than two or more people with common ideas or experiences participate in a common activity (Becchetti & Cermelli, 2014, 2018; Gui, 2005).

Scientific empirical literature has widely documented that the *homo economicus* paradigm does not take into account relational goods. In other words, the *homo economicus* is unhappy, minority, and socially harmful. Different studies (Becchetti, Gianfreda, & Pace, 2012; Johnson & Mislin, 2011) also confirm that purely self-regarding rationality of *homo economicus* is an inferior form of rationality producing suboptimal results for oneself and for the rest of the society. Individuals going beyond anthropological reductionism mix self-interest and other preferences, satisfy better their sense of purpose and their generativity and, if they overcome the "lack of confidence trap" and are able to trigger reciprocity in social dilemmas, they create cooperative networks that produce super additivity. This point underlines the need to reintroduce the concept of reciprocity beyond social relations to substitute the anthropological reductionism.

The second reductionism that has progressively contaminated the construction of the economic theory is that profit maximization constitutes the optimal management strategy for a company and its normal modus operandi. This idea still appears in the majority of the economic text books and economic models.

In order to clarify this reductionism, it is necessary to understand that corporations are organizations which have a relevant impact on the welfare of different categories of interest (stakeholders). The neoclassical view ignores the fact that large parts of productive organizations depart from this goal (i.e., consumer, worker and social cooperatives, work reintegration cooperatives, nonprofit maximizing microfinance institutions, cooperative and community banks, and in general all for-profit organizations that adopt social and environmental responsibility practices or develop corporate welfare policies). The strongest point of attack on corporate reductionism is its inefficiency also in terms of corporate self-interest. The goal of the maximization of shareholder wealth implies that the interest of one stakeholder (the shareholder) comes before that of all other stakeholders (workers, consumers, suppliers, local communities). In this respect profit maximization, by definition, creates an additional source of corporate risk represented by the likelihood of conflicts with other stakeholders. A further profit maximization paradox that clearly demonstrates that the reductionist view produces gaps between private and social optimum is that of banks maximizing shareholders' wealth. If they do so, they will never find it optimal to lend to small-sized borrowers, given that per unit fixed screening and monitoring costs are too high with respect to interest payment revenues on small loans. This is why we need to refocus our attention toward a multi-stakeholder vision of companies in order to overcome the corporate reductionism (Chang, 2012; Freeman, 1984, 1994).

Finally, the third reductionism concerns the definition of what is value for a society. The implicit point of the reductionist view of the economy is that the pursuit of economic growth automatically implies higher level of well-being. As a consequence, GDP is also a synthetic sufficient measure of community well-being (Becchetti & Cermelli, 2018).

The choice of specific indicators for measuring the community well-being determines the direction towards which the society will move. For example, in 1933 Franklin Delano Roosevelt asserted that people recognize that human well-being is not achieved only through materialism and luxury but that it grows thanks to integrity, altruism, a sense of responsibility, and justice. The Sen-Stiglitz Commission, promoted by the ex-French President Sarkozy, also underlined the importance of measuring the wealth of nations beyond the parameters of GDP. This commission stressed that not even economic well-being can be expressed by GDP, but rather with the disposable income in the pockets of families, after paying for essential public goods and services, such as health and education. In this sense, we need to redirect the way in which we measure well-being thinking in terms of social development rather than economic growth.

2.3   The Civil Economy Paradigm: From a Two-Hand to a Four-Hand Approach

The mainstream political economy paradigm is two-handed. The invisible hand of the market reconciles (via competitive pressure) the self-interested profit maximizing appetites of producers with low and affordable prices of goods and services that improve consumer surplus. The limit of this approach is that it is too demanding toward the *deus ex machina* of the second institutional hand (which is also required for the proper functioning of the first hand).

The Civil Economy paradigm is that the two-hand system (markets-institutions) often fails to achieve the proposed goals since institutional failures are as common as market failures. The Civil Economy proposes an alternative four-hand system where the two hands of markets and institutions are not eliminated but complemented by the work of a third hand (active citizenship) and a fourth hand (socially responsible productive organizations) (Becchetti & Cermelli, 2018). In this way we can replace the anthropological, corporate, and value reductionism reinforcing the holistic view of our societies and generating added value that is more equally divided among shareholders and that cares about the social and environmental impact of their actions.

Solutions to the problems we are facing (inequality, environmental sustainability, poverty of sense of life) cannot be generated by a system where only two hands (the invisible hand of the market and the visible hand of institutions) are at work. In order to be effective, these two traditional hands need a strong support from the third hand of active citizenship and from the fourth hand of sustainable productive organizations. The two qualifying points of civil economics (going beyond individual, corporate, and value reductionism and moving from a two-hand to a four-hand political economy approach) are strictly connected with each other since the third hand (active citizenship) implies the rejection of anthropological reductionism and the fourth hand (responsible companies) the rejection of corporate reductionism.

The four-hand approach is gaining momentum through the UN Sustainable Development Goals, but in general, this framework is extremely useful for our approach to the phenomenon of population aging because it implies the two additional hands of active citizenship (beyond anthropological reductionism) and responsible firms (beyond corporate reductionism) adding up to the market and state in bridging the gap between individual and social optimum.

3 Theoretical Frameworks of Aging (and a Possible Connection with the Civil Economy Paradigm)

This section presents the recent evolution of the theoretical frameworks of aging and its main challenges, as well as the need to find new lenses to keep researching about this global phenomenon. Humanistic approaches can be useful to better understand the socioeconomic consequences of population aging. In this sense, the Civil Economy paradigm arises as a possible prospective framework to study demographic aging.

3.1 The Importance of Theory: Description, Explanation, and Understanding

The advance of science generates a knowledge accumulation that provokes, through the appropriate theoretical frameworks, explanations that in turn generate greater accumulated knowledge (Bengston & Settersten, 2016). This cycle emphasizes the importance of developing theoretical frameworks acting as different lenses that allow describing, explaining, and understanding data, variables, relationships, and experiences. These authors also defend that theory serves a triple purpose: to integrate knowledge, to carry out predictions, and to intervene in order to improve human condition. This idea is also supported by Hagestad and Dannefer (2001) within the field of study of demographic aging, which defends the value of applying a theoretical framework of analysis that implies explanation.

In the field of theoretical frameworks of aging, it is interesting to highlight what Birren and Bengston (1988) warned three decades ago: that demographic analysis practiced a "barefoot empiricism" during the second half of the twentieth century. According to these authors, demographic research, in general, and population aging, in particular, presented rich data but poor theoretical analysis. The emergence, evolution, and adoption of theoretical frameworks in the field of aging are due in part to the effort made by these authors to promote them. In summary, the theoretical framework and theorization have been, and continue to be, the cornerstone of scientific research and the gateway to an improved understanding of the variables and phenomena that are objects of study, as well as being totally necessary to achieve a systematic development of knowledge (Bengston & Settersten, 2016, p. 2).

3.2   Theoretical Frameworks of Aging Re-emergence and Challenges

The interest in different theories that can be used to understand the aging phenomenon has re-emerged in the last three decades. An example of this trend is the book *Emergent Theories of Aging* (James E. Birren & Bengston, 1988), a work later complemented with the publication of *Handbook of Theories of Aging* (Bengston & Settersten, 2016; Bengston, Silverstein, Putney, & Gans, 2009; Gans, Putney, Bengston, & Silverstein, 2009). These publications examine the field of theoretical and conceptual frameworks of the aging phenomenon. Besides, they provide one of the most relevant and best structured efforts to classify and expose the different theories, concepts, and advances in what the authors call the "multifaceted puzzle of aging" (Bengston et al., 2009, p. 734). The objective of the present chapter is not only to defend the possibility of the Civil Economy perspective joining this re-emergence trend of theoretical approaches to aging but also to present it as a prospective framework of analysis to understand and explain population aging.

If the evolution in the aforementioned works on theoretical frameworks of aging is analyzed, it can be observed that research in the fields of aging and gerontology is growing due to its relevance, but it still presents important challenges:

- The search for interdisciplinarity and/or multidisciplinarity
- Overcoming "level myopia" (or the obsession with issues at a micro level)
- The search for a unified theory

These challenges are present in theories of aging literature, and the approach of the Civil Economy paradigm can provide an interesting framework to approach them. In the following pages, these three major challenges are exposed and analyzed.

3.2.1   The Search for Interdisciplinarity and/or Multidisciplinarity

Interdisciplinarity has an increasing relevance in the theoretical frameworks of aging field. Bengston et al. (2009, p. 6) open the first chapter of the second edition of *Handbook of Theories of Aging* pointing out that the most important fact that had occurred since the publication of the previous edition, a decade before, was the appearance of the interdisciplinary approach when dealing with aging issues.

The authors, in fact, qualify this burst on the aging stage as the most relevant trend in the theoretical frameworks of this field and highlight the emergence of the biodemography of aging or the biopsychosocial understanding of healthy aging as an example. Bengston et al. (2009, p. 734) also point this out in the closing chapter of the aforementioned book, emphasizing that using a "unidisciplinary" point of view to understand the phenomenon of aging is not recommended, given that it would be like using blinders instead of powerful lenses. They also stress the fact that many authors defend "cross-pollination" and the use of different perspectives, theories, and knowledge to understand aging. In this sense, the Civil Economy framework can be useful to respond to this challenge because its approach defends a broad conception of the economy and moves away from the neoclassical approach, which is considered suboptimal in terms of life flourishing, generativity, and life sense. The Civil Economy paradigm seeks to transcend the reductionist vision of neoclassical paradigm on individuals, corporations, and well-being, to focus on "human flourishing" (Becchetti & Cermelli, 2018), a key input for a broad, positive, and non-reductionist population aging research.

Finally, it is interesting to highlight that Bengston and Settersten (2016) open the book *Handbook of Theories of Aging* defending the collaboration between different disciplines, as an important issue of the theoretical approaches to aging.

3.2.2   Avoiding "Level Myopia"

Another challenge facing theories of aging is what Hagestad and Dannefer (2001, p. 11) call "level myopia," or how sometimes the excessive micro-focus adopted by different aging theoretical frameworks limits their explanatory capacity. These authors affirm that an excessive focus on individuals, and a neglect of the macro level, can lead to a loss of understanding of broad social aspects.

This concern is shared by Gans et al. (2009, pp. 732, 736), who affirm that one of the main issues when developing aging theoretical approaches is to accomplish a connection between individuals and their contexts. An idea that they reinforce when affirming that demographic aging must be understood taking into account the environments in which individuals are "embedded" or, to put it in other words, understanding the phenomenon transiting "from cells to societal level". And it is precisely this last phrase which Bengston and Settersten (2016, p. 5) use to warn that theoretical approaches should be able to describe, explain, and understand the aging phenomenon at the micro level and at the macro level. For his part, Rowe (2015,

p. 8) also points out that one needs to understand not only the societal level but also the individual level in aging research, in order to preserve the intergenerational pact, a basic ingredient for social cohesion. This tension between levels while approaching different theoretical approaches can also be conceptualized as a tension between structure and agency (Bass, 2009), so theoretical frameworks should be built and developed integrating both aspects: the micro level and the macro level.

The Civil Economy perspective can help to overcome this challenge since it tries to refute the political economy "two-hand" approach that defends a system composed of the invisible hand of the market and the visible hand of the institutions. The Civil Economy framework evolves toward a "four-hand" system, where the role of the state and the role of the market would be complemented with an active citizenship (third hand) and socially responsible productive organizations (fourth hand) (Becchetti & Cermelli, 2018, p. 4). This broad understanding of how society works includes both the macro level (state and the market) and the micro level (the civil society and organizations), a useful approach to avoid falling in the "level myopia" trap.

3.2.3   The Search of a "Great Theory" in Different Areas of Aging

During the historical development of aging theories in the mid-twentieth century, there were attempts to build a "grand theory" from the biological and from the psychological point of view (Bengston & Settersten, 2016, p. 4). These efforts declined in the second half of that century, given that an era rich in data but poor in theoretical frameworks began. The trend was coined as "barefoot empiricism" due to its lack of theoretical rigor, as it has been previously mentioned. Despite that, in recent years, there has been a progression in the search for theories that agglutinate different theories existing in the field of aging.

Following this line of thought, Bass (2009) proposes an integrated gerontology theory, a field on the rise within aging studies that tries to address the aforementioned challenges in relation to "level myopia" and the necessary connection between the micro and macro level. On their part, Gavrilov and Gavrilova (2016) analyze the biodemography of aging and longevity theoretical perspectives to propose the search for a general biodemographic theory of aging, with the aim of combining different theories within this field. These efforts show how, after decades of "barefoot empiricism," during the last lustrums not only different and interesting approaches and theoretical lines in different fields (e.g., biological, psychological, biodemographic, etc.) have proliferated, but also research has started to look for unifying theoretical frameworks.

Although the use of the Civil Economy paradigm as a theoretical framework for analyzing population aging can be useful to respond to the first two aforementioned challenges (seeking interdisciplinarity and avoiding "level myopia"), it seems less appropriate to look for a "grand theory" of population aging in the field of economic research. In any case, this question may be open to debate and arises as a future research path.

3.3   Disciplines and Theories of Aging

Aging is a broad and multifaceted field of study, and the different existing theories of aging can be classified into five major areas: the biological, the psychological, the social science, the intervention and public policy, and the so-called interdisciplinary and multidisciplinary theories of aging, which combine two or more fields of knowledge to address this complex topic (Bengston & Settersten, 2016; Bengston et al., 2009). These five large areas of theories of aging are exposed and explained in the next pages, with the aim of finding in which group a possible "Civil Economy of population aging" might fit:

(a) Biological Theories of Aging
During the last decades, biological theories of aging have been maturing; some examples of them are evolutionary theories, those related to genetics (such as antagonistic pleiotropy), hypotheses about aging and fecundity of different species, or the study of the aging of invertebrate beings such as worms and flies (Kennedy, 2016). This branch of aging theories attempts to analyze how and why the aging process occurs through a biological approach.

(b) Psychological Theories of Aging
The psychological theories of aging, of which one of the founding fathers is James E. Birren (1988), look at how social relations, personality, cognitive capacity, or emotion regulation—among other issues—vary and are influenced by aging and human senescence (Smith, 2016).

(c) Social Science Theories of Aging
This group of theories emphasizes that aging is a social process and that the concept of age is present in all societies (Settersten, 2016). They also defend the dynamic aspects of the aging process, through relevant theories in this field such as life course perspective, feminist, or critical gerontology approaches. The theoretical lines on the rise in this area are, among others, those analyzing the relationship between aging and inequality or social relations. The social science theories of aging are broad and overcome the aforementioned "level myopia" given that they focus on the individual level as well as on the societal level.

(d) Society and Public Policies Theories of Aging
The fourth group is composed of those theories oriented to the objective of explaining the complex interrelation between social processes at the macro level, the formulation of public policies, and the well-being of the elderly (Bengston et al., 2009, p. 18). Among them it can highlight the political economy of aging (Kail, Quadagno, & Keene, 2009; Walker & Foster, 2014), the impact of globalization on critical gerontology (Phillipson, 2009), or those related to demographic aging and well-being (Thorslund & Silverstein, 2009).

(e) Interdisciplinary and Multidisciplinary Theories of Aging
The fifth and last group refers to those theories that adopt an interdisciplinary or multidisciplinary perspective. Regardless of the differences between these two

perspectives, the main objective of the theories behind them is crossing the disciplinary boundaries to combine and/or connect different fields of knowledge. In this sense, Bengston et al. (2009, p. 17) argue that social sciences have historically benefited less from the tendency towards mixing and connecting disciplines.

Taking into account the five different areas exposed, a possible theoretical framework called "Civil Economy of demographic aging" could fit within the group of "society and public policies theories of aging," given that it would widen the political economy of aging approach that focuses on analyzing sociopolitical aspects and the economic processes linked to the production and distribution of scarce resources, as well as the role of the state and the market (Kail et al., 2009, p. 555). Accordingly, the "Civil Economy of aging" framework would take into account a less reductionist and more holistic view on the aging phenomenon, by including civil society and socially responsible productive organizations.

4 Conclusions: The Civil Economy Paradigm as a Prospective Framework for Population Aging Research

The main objective of this chapter is to expose the Civil Economy framework and a useful tool to humanize economics taking into consideration the philosophical roots of the limits of our socioeconomic system. Furthermore, we also think that humanizing economics is relevant to better understand the global phenomenon of population aging. Because of that, the chapter proposes the Civil Economy approach as a theoretical framework to analyze the complex and multifaceted phenomenon of population aging, a global trend that will accelerate during the present century. This effort lies in the fact that the interest in the different theories that are used—or can be used—to understand the aging phenomenon has re-emerged in the last three decades. Moreover, as far as the authors know, this is the first proposal to expose and explore this possibility.

The Civil Economy paradigm appeared in the eighteenth century (1750–1780) thanks to the works done by the Neapolitan philosopher Antonio Genovesi. This approach defends not only a relational and social economy but also a cooperative approach to the market, and it tries to overcome the dichotomy of weak market cooperation (unintentional) and strong business cooperation (intentional). In this sense, it aims to bridge the gap between the market and democracy.

A keystone for the Neapolitan school of Civil Economy is the belief that human beings go beyond the "animal" sociability developing friendship, reciprocity, fraternity, and mutual assistance. Furthermore, the Civil Economy paradigm defends that individuals are sense searchers more than utility maximizers and that companies are not profit maximizers and create value for stakeholders in a social, environmental, and responsible way. Finally, GDP is seen as an insufficient measure for well-being, and the stock of spiritual, relational, economic, and environmental goods is a better way to grasp the root of well-living. As a result of this, the Civil Economy approach tries to overtake the three aforementioned reductionisms: the anthropological reductionism, the corporate reductionism, and the value reductionism.

Additionally, the Civil Economy paradigm asserts that the two-hand system (the invisible hand of the market and the visible hand of the institutions), defended by the political economy approach, often fails since institutional failures are as common as market failures. In this sense, the Civil Economy approach proposes a four-hand system where the first two hands (markets and institutions) are complemented by a third (active citizenship) and a fourth hand (socially responsible productive organizations) in order to overtake the anthropological, corporate, and value reductionism and reinforce a holistic view for understanding the economy.

Taking into account what is Civil Economy and from where it arises, it is important to highlight that back in the 1980s, it was noticed that demographic analysis suffered from a "barefoot empiricism." In other words, it presented a large amount of data and quantitative analysis but poor theoretical frameworks to understand them. Therefore, in the last decades, a movement has emerged to propose and advance in the construction of different theoretical frameworks to analyze demography, in general, and population aging in particular.

After reviewing the scientific literature regarding theoretical frameworks of aging, it can be said that there are three important challenges in relation to them. First, a deeper interdisciplinarity is needed in the study of aging. This fact is justified by the idea that such a multifaceted phenomenon can only be understood if it is observed from a broad view. Second, the analysis of aging must overcome what has been called "level myopia," or the excessive focus on the micro level and individuals, without taking into account the repercussions at the macro or aggregate level. The analysis of only one of these levels, without taking into account the other, makes theories and findings regarding population aging poor in explanatory power. The third and last challenge to highlight is the attempt to find a "big theory" for different areas of aging. This effort arises because in recent times not only have different theoretical lines emerged in different fields of analysis (e.g., biological, psychological, biodemographic, etc.), but research is also looking for theories to unify them.

The Civil Economy can be useful to respond to the first two challenges of the three exposed, that is to say, to the needed interdisciplinarity approach, and to overcome the "level myopia." The framework of the Civil Economy can respond to the first challenge given that it provides a plural perspective. It overcomes the three reductionisms discussed and takes into account not only economic but also social and welfare aspects, so it goes beyond the economic field, to access broader aspects linked to a humanistic conception. Moreover, given that the Civil Economy school of thought goes beyond the "two-hand" approach (markets and institutions), and adopts a "four-hand" approach, which encompasses both institutions and markets (macro level) and active citizenship and productive and sustainable organizations (micro level), it is considered as an interesting theoretical framework to overcome the aforementioned "level myopia."

Taking into account these ideas, it has been shown throughout the text that different theories of population aging can be structured around five major groups, namely:

(a) Biological theories of aging.
(b) Psychological theories of aging.
(c) Social science theories of aging.
(d) Society and public policies theories of aging.
(e) Interdisciplinary and multidisciplinary theories of aging.

Among society and public policies theories of aging, it can be found the "political economy of demographic aging" focused on exposing and studying both the socio-political aspects and the economic processes linked to the production and distribution of scarce resources, with special emphasis on the role of the state and the market. Based on all of the above, the present text proposes to overcome this framework, and to start adopting a "Civil Economy of aging" approach, which presents a broader and less reductionist view, by including the civil society and sustainable and productive organizations.

The goal of the Civil Economy perspective is that of addressing the limits of the current economic thought (and especially the suboptimal outcome it creates in terms of richness of sense of life) by proposing a change of paradigm (Bruni & Sugden, 2007; Bruni & Zamagni, 2004, 2015). Because of this, it could represent an interesting framework for analyzing the aging effect on our societies and economies focusing our attention in direction on higher generativity and participation above all supporting the idea, for example, that life expectancy is positively associated with productivity (Franklin, 2018).

On basis of the above, we think that economic research should start using new points of view to analyze the population aging phenomenon. Moreover, further research on the positive aspects of aging should be made to start using new frameworks, as the Civil Economy of aging, as well as keep studying its various effects from a non-aprioristic approach. These efforts are to make population aging not only a "pleasant macroeconomic experience" (Börsch-Supan, 2013a, p. 406) but also a kind social transformation where the "four hands" of the Civil Economy help us to better understand the fascinating phenomenon of demographic aging.

References

Bass, S. A. (2009). Toward an integrative theory of social gerontology. In V. L. Bengtson, M. Silverstein, N. M. Putney, & D. Gans (Eds.), *Handbook of theories of aging* (2nd ed., pp. 347–374). New York: Springer.

Becchetti, L., Bruni, L., & Zamagni, S. (2015). Human values, civil economy, and subjective well-being. In J. Helliwell, R. Layard, & J. Sachs (Eds.), *World happiness report*. New York: Sustainable Development Solutions Network.

Becchetti, L., & Cermelli, M. (2014). Reduccionismos económicos y "Voto con la cartera". *Revista de Fomento Social, 69*(273 & 274), 121–135.

Becchetti, L., & Cermelli, M. (2018). Civil economy: Definition and strategies for sustainable well-living. *International Review of Economics, 65*(3), 329–357.

Becchetti, L., Gianfreda, G., & Pace, N. (2012). Human resource management and productivity in the "trust game corporation". *International Review of Economics, 59*(1), 3–20.

Bengston, V. L., & Settersten, R. A. J. (2016). Theories of aging: Developments within and across disciplinary boundaries. In V. Bengston & R. A. Settersten Jr. (Eds.), *Handbook of theories of aging* (3rd ed., pp. 1–8). New York: Springer.

Bengston, V. L., Silverstein, M., Putney, N. M., & Gans, D. (2009). Theories about age and aging. In V. L. Bengston, M. Silverstein, N. M. Putney, & D. Gans (Eds.), *Handbook of theories of aging* (Vol. 36, 2nd ed., pp. 3–23). New York: Springer. https://doi.org/10.5860/CHOICE.36-5149

Birren, J. E. (1988). A contribution to the theory of the psychology of aging: As a counterpart of development. In J. E. Birren & V. L. Bengtson (Eds.), *Emergent theories of aging* (pp. 153–176). New York: Springer.

Birren, J. E., & Bengston, V. L. (1988). *Emergent theories of aging.* New York: Springer.

Bloom, D. E., Canning, D., & Fink, G. (2010). Implications of population ageing for economic growth. *Oxford Review of Economic Policy, 26*(4), 583–612. https://doi.org/10.1093/oxrep/grq038

Börsch-Supan, A. (2013a). Ageing, labor markets and well-being. *Empirica, 40*(3), 397–407. https://doi.org/10.1007/s10663-013-9216-0

Börsch-Supan, A. (2013b). Myths, scientific evidence and economic policy in an aging world. *The Journal of the Economics of Ageing, 2*, 3–15. https://doi.org/10.1016/j.jeoa.2013.06.001

Bruni, L. (2006). *Civil happiness: Economics and human flourishing in historical perspective.* London: Routledge.

Bruni, L., & Sugden, R. (2007). The road not taken: How psychology was removed from economics, and how it might be brought back. *The Economic Journal, 117*(516), 146–173.

Bruni, L., & Zamagni, S. (2004). *Economia civile, efficienza, equità, felicità pubblica.* Bologna: Il Mulino.

Bruni, L., & Zamagni, S. (2015). *Ll'Economia Civile.* Bologna: Il Mulino.

Chang, H.-J. (2012). *23 Things they don't tell you about capitalism.* London: Penguin Books Ltd.

Franklin, B. (2018). *Towards a longevity dividend: Life expectancy and productivity across developed countries.* London: International Longevity Centre - UK.

Freeman, R. E. (1984). *Strategic management: A stakeholder approach.* Cambridge: Cambridge University Press.

Freeman, R. E. (1994). The politics of stakeholder theory: Some future directions. *Business Ethics Quarterly, 4*(04), 409–421. https://doi.org/10.2307/3857340

Gans, D., Putney, N. M., Bengston, V. L., & Silverstein, M. (2009). The future of theories of aging. In M. Silverstein, V. L. Bengtson, M. Putnam, N. M. Putney, & D. Gans (Eds.), *Handbook of theories of aging* (2nd ed., pp. 721–737). New York: Springer.

Gavrilov, L. A., & Gavrilova, N. S. (2016). Theoretical perspectives on biodemography of aging and longevity. In V. L. Bengtson & R. A. J. Settersten (Eds.), *Handbook of theories of aging* (pp. 643–667). New York: Springer.

Genovesi, A. (1765). *Delle lezioni di commercio, ossia d'economia civile.* Napoli: Stamperia Simoniana.

Gui, B. (2005). From transactions to encounters: The joint generation of relational goods and conventional values. In B. Gui & R. Sugden (Eds.), *Economics and social interaction: Accounting for interpersonal relations.* Cambridge: Cambridge University Press.

Guijarro, M., & Peláez, Ó. (2008). La longevidad globalizada: Un análisis de la esperanza de vida en España (1900–2050). *Scripta Nova, 12*(160), 1–26.

Hagestad, G. O., & Dannefer, D. (2001). Concepts and theories of aging. In R. H. Binstock & L. K. George (Eds.), *Handbook of aging and the social sciences* (5th ed., pp. 3–21). Burlington: Academic Press.

Hayward, M. D., & Zhang, Z. (2001). Demography of aging 1950–2050. In R. H. Binstok & L. K. George (Eds.), *Handbook of aging and the social sciences* (5th ed., pp. 69–85). Burlington: Academic Press.

Johnson, N. D., & Mislin, A. A. (2011). Trust games: A meta-analysis. *Journal of Economic Psychology, 32*(5), 865–889.

Judt, T. (2012). *Algo va mal.* Madrid: Taurus.

Kail, B. L., Quadagno, J., & Keene, J. R. (2009). The political economy perspective of aging. In M. Silverstein, V. L. Bengtson, M. Putnam, N. M. Putney, & D. Gans (Eds.), *Handbook of theories of aging* (2nd ed., pp. 555–571). New York: Springer.

Kennedy, B. K. (2016). Advances in biological theories of aging. In V. L. Bengtson, M. Silverstein, N. M. Putney, & D. Gans (Eds.), *Handbook of theories of aging* (3rd ed., pp. 107–113). New York: Springer.

Phillipson, C. (2009). Reconstructing theories of aging: The impact of globalization on critical gerontology. In V. L. Bengtson, M. Silverstein, N. M. Putney, V. L. Gans, M. DaphnaBengtson, N. Silverstein, M. Putney, & D. Gans (Eds.), *Handbook of theories of aging* (pp. 615–628). New York: Springer.

Rowe, J. W. (2009). Facts and fictions about an aging America. *Contexts, 8*(4), 16–21. https://doi. org/10.1525/ctx.2009.8.4.16

Rowe, J. W. (2015). Successful aging of societies. *Dædalus – Journal of the American Academy of Arts & Sciences, 144*(2), 5–12.

Settersten, R. A. J. (2016). Advances in social science theories of aging. In V. L. Bengtson & R. A. J. Settersten (Eds.), *Handbook of theories of aging* (3rd ed., p.301). New York: Springer.

Smith, J. (2016). Advances in psychological theories of aging. In V. L. Bengtson & R. A. J. Settersten (Eds.), *Handbook of theories of aging* (3rd ed., p.189). New York: Springer.

Thorslund, M., & Silverstein, M. (2009). Care for older adults in the welfare state: Theories, policies and realities. In M. Silverstein, V. L. Bengtson, M. Putnam, N. M. Putney, & D. Gans (Eds.), *Handbook of theories of aging* (pp. 629–639). New York: Springer.

United Nations. (2015). *World population ageing 2015.* New York: Department of Economic and Social Affairs - UN. https://doi.org/ST/ESA/SER.A/390

Walker, A., & Foster, L. (Eds.). (2014). *The political economy of ageing and later life.* Cheltenham: Edward Elgar.

Lessons to Be Learned from the Theoretical and Empirical Developments of Humanistic Management: Virtuous Cycles in Practice

Ricardo Aguado and Almudena Eizaguirre

The first aim of this book has been to show the interactions between business education at the university level and the current managerial practices at the corporate level. It seems that there is a feedback between a business education focused in profit maximization on one hand and business practices focused in shareholder value maximization, on the other hand. As we have shown in the first section of this book, it is possible to introduce in business schools a type of management education that has as inspiring principles the dignity of the human being and social well-being. We have proposed different perspectives and initiatives in order to design and implement this kind of business education, in various geographical areas, and also in different types of universities (with dissimilar missions and identities). In all the cases that are presented in the book, the shift from profit maximization toward a humanistic perspective has been possible, and welcome, by the main stakeholders of business education (students, corporations, public administrations, professors, and presidents of universities). At the same time, accreditation agencies in the field of business education tend to value in a positive way the social impact of universities, and the promotion of prosocial values inside management studies.

In our view, if business schools are able to transform its main educational paradigm and introduce humanistic principles in core subjects, this shift could have a big impact on the present and future business leaders. This transformational effect is what we have labelled as a "virtuous cycle," that starts in the academia and impacts corporations through current leaders (via postgraduate programs) and future business leaders (through undergraduate programs).

The second aim of this book is to show paths in which corporations may apply humanistic principles to their decision-making processes, and their relationships with meaningful stakeholders. This task is specially developed in sections two and three of this book. We understand these two sections as a continuation of the virtuous cycle presented in section one.

R. Aguado (✉) · A. Eizaguirre
Deusto Business School, University of Deusto, Bilbao, Spain
e-mail: ricardo.aguado@deusto.es; almudena.eizaguirre@deusto.es

© Springer Nature Switzerland AG 2020
R. Aguado, A. Eizaguirre (eds.), *Virtuous Cycles in Humanistic Management*,
Contributions to Management Science,
https://doi.org/10.1007/978-3-030-29426-7

Once we have present and future business leaders trained in the principles of humanistic management, we should be able to show those leaders that pioneering organizations are in fact implementing this kind of management, and also the necessity of adopting humanistic practices inside organizations to achieve economic, social, and environmental sustainability. In this way, it may be easier for business leaders to implement a paradigm shift in their organizations and adopt humanistic practices.

In the book, we have stressed the importance of adopting humanistic principles inside corporations in relation to two main objectives: making a positive contribution to the development of all stakeholders (not only, but also shareholders), and aligning the objective of the corporation with the well-being of society.

In our view, and according to other academics that are demanding a paradigm shift in management, these two objectives should be present in any successful organization in the twenty-first century. Talented business students are reluctant to link their professional careers to unsustainable organizations; public administrations are regulating markets and imposing fines to corporations which seek profits at the expense of the common good; customers are shifting toward sustainable options; and even international investors are demanding to corporations not only profitability but also a growing involvement in promoting social well-being, with special attention to the Sustainable Development Goals.

Organizations that embrace humanistic management will lead to this change in favor of a management culture that reconciles society and the dignity of the person with economic activity.

In this last section of the book, we can highlight certain conclusions or lessons that may guide academics and practitioners in their quest for humanistic management:

- Management education in business schools is key in order to create a new story for businesses that encompass human dignity and social well-being.
- Business schools can create this new route map for businesses both with post-graduate and with undergraduate programs.
- New research in the field of management is required in at least two fields: theoretical developments in order to make compatible microeconomic science with humanistic management, and empirical studies in order to show the possibility of implementing humanistic principles to management in a successful way.
- A standardized social accounting method is necessary in order to measure in a comparable way the contributions made by corporations to all stakeholders and to society in general. This accounting method should be compatible and complementary with the traditional financial accounting.
- It is possible to design scientific and useful academic programs in business schools that focus the attention on the creation of value for all stakeholders and not only for shareholders.

The editors of this book would like to encourage academics that share the aforementioned points to develop theoretical and empirical insights which may be useful to disseminate humanistic management among students, other academics, and practitioners. This book is a part of that common effort.